Helen Clifford.

D1635466

£8-00
ARF
9/2

# Contents

KENSINGTON PALACE

From: HRH The Duchess of Gloucester, GCVO

I am delighted to have been Patron of NADFAS since 1995 and to have seen its continued growth and development in education and volunteering within the Arts. Since its beginning in 1968 among a small group of friends to the present 382 Societies in the United Kingdom, Mainland Europe, Australia and New Zealand, the Association has given its members many enjoyable opportunities to increase their knowledge and appreciation of the Arts. At the same time, NADFAS has contributed greatly to the cultural fabric of our lives through the work of the Heritage Volunteers, Church Recorders, its Young Arts activities and the grants which it awards to develop the skills of young artists and craftsmen and women.

As we look back over the events recorded in this book, published to celebrate the fortieth anniversary of its founding, the Association can be seen to have risen to the challenges of growth and the many ways in which life has changed while remaining true to the original inspired vision of its Founder, Patricia Fay.

I wish NADFAS every success in the years ahead.

Cover photo: Corinthian order corner capital on the portico of Chiswick House London. © Steve Taylor/Alamy.

Text copyright © 2008 The National Association of Decorative and Fine Arts Societies (Registered charity number 1089743) and NADFAS Enterprises Ltd, NADFAS House, 8 Guilford Street, London WC1N 1DA. 020 7430 0730, www.nadfas.org.uk

Helen Clifford has asserted her moral rights to be identified as the author of this work.

Published in the UK by The National Association of Decorative and Fine Arts Societies/NADFAS Enterprises Ltd.

First published in 2008.

Design: Touchline Publishing Ltd
Art Editor: Fiona McCready
Reproduction: XY Digital Ltd
Printer: 1010 Printing

ISBN 9780954019112
A CIP catalogue is available for this book from the British Library.

All rights reserved
No part of this publication may be reproduced, stored in a retrieval system or transmitted, in any form or by any means, electronic, mechanical, photocopying, recording or otherwise, without the consent of the copyright owners. Application should be made in writing to the publisher. Only written permission from the publisher or the copyright holders will be accepted as evidence of such consent.

© Photography: Abingdon DFAS; Alamy Images; Arden DFAS; *Bucks Life*; The Bundanon Trust; Shelagh Collingwood; Costa Del Sol DFAS; K. Dalton; Dukeries DFAS; Egerton DFAS; Epsom DFAS; The Goldsmiths' Company; Girton College, Cambridge; English Heritage; Damien Hirst/Jay Jopling/White Cube (London); Fototeca ENIT; K. Hollands/Malvern Hills DFAS; Hamburg DFAS; *Harper's Bazaar*; Harrogate DFAS; *Kentish Gazette*; Lady Lever Art Gallery/National Museums Liverpool; Tom Miller/NPG; Tony Marshall/*Daily Telegraph*; Museum für Kunst und Gewerbe; NADFAS Archives; *NADFAS Review*; NTPL/Oliver Benn; Octopus Publishing Group Ltd/Tim Ridley/Nikki Lynes; Desmond O'Neill; Orient Express; Royal Albert Museum, Exeter; Rutland DFAS; Naomi Schillinger; Veronica Shaw; Shutterstock.com; Marks & Spencer; Mark Simpson; Sparkenhoe AS; Frieda Stanburg; Studio Vista London; Thames and Hudson London; Theatre Royal, Bury St Edmunds; Ronald Traeger/Tessa Traeger (p.11); Truro DFAS; V&A Images/Victoria and Albert Museum, London; Christoph von Virag; Walker Art Gallery/National Museums Liverpool; Cpl David Whitta/Crown Copyright/MOD/Controller of Her Majesty's Stationery Office; Ken Woolverton; Worthing Museum and Art Gallery; The W.R. Johnston Collection; The *Yorkshire Post*.

*The National Association of Decorative and Fine Arts Societies wishes to extend a special thank you to the family of Desmond O'Neill, who have very kindly allowed us to use his extensive portfolio of black and white photographs of the early days of NADFAS throughout this book.*

Every effort has been made to credit owners of the photography reproduced in this book. The publisher accepts no responsibility for errors and omissions.

# Foreword
## *Christopher Lloyd CVO, President of NADFAS*

'Large streams from little fountains flow,
Tall oaks from little acorns grow'
David Everett (1769-1813), 'Lines Written for a School Declamation'

One of the defining characteristics of our age is the desire to know more about our artistic heritage. It so happens that this desire has coincided with a dramatic increase in the number of opportunities for pursuing such an interest. As Helen Clifford so vividly demonstrates in her absorbing and often amusing book, the official foundation of NADFAS in 1968 and its subsequent development were the direct result of a particular set of interconnecting circumstances reflecting changing social and cultural patterns in this country during the 1960s – principally, the growth of affluence, the increase in leisure, and the broadening of education. The enlightened founders of NADFAS, together with their distinguished advisers and supporters in the art world, correctly identified the need for an organisation that was efficiently administered from the centre yet, most importantly, allowed for local diversity and individuality. In effect, what was created was no less than a federation for the understanding and promotion of the arts. This remarkable combination of shared aims and ambitions allied to a flexible application and a wide interpretation remains the underlying strength of NADFAS. It is hardly surprising, therefore, that this successful formula has allowed for expansion into mainland Europe and even on a global basis.

The model for the evolution of NADFAS was the Chiltern Antiques Group set up in 1965. No one, however, should be misled by the almost innocent quaintness of this name from which any number of misunderstandings might, and did often, follow. From the outset NADFAS was determined not to be narrow-minded or limited in its outlook towards the arts or the artistic heritage. This is reflected in the great variety of lecture topics, study days, links to higher education, activities for younger members, visits made throughout the United Kingdom, and more extensive travel overseas that have always filled its programmes. From the start NADFAS also wanted its enthusiasm to have a practical outlet. This has been expressed in two ways: the 'hands-on' approach of volunteers of all age-groups engaging in specific projects and the award of grants to encourage young people already committed to the arts. The growing popularity of the organisation and the widespread recognition that it has won for its various pursuits shows not only how prescient the founders were forty years ago, but also how NADFAS continues to answer specific needs and to fulfil particular expectations. Indeed, in doing this NADFAS clearly demonstrates that it possesses the necessary flexibility for becoming an even greater force in the modern art world.

A sense of the historical perspective serves to highlight the role that NADFAS now plays in society and helps to explain why the Association has quietly over the years acquired such a high reputation for its contributions to the cultural scene. There has always been a need for an awareness of the past. It first manifested itself at a very early date in the establishment of dynastic tradition and in the exploitation of political propaganda, but it emerged as an academic discipline during the late seventeenth and eighteenth centuries based initially on archaeological investigation and the formation of collections of artefacts known then as 'curiosities'. By the end of the eighteenth century the rediscovery of antiquity and the beginning of the fascination for medievalism indicated the rich potential in the appreciation of the past. The Victorians in turn had a pronounced feeling for historicism leading to numerous fanciful recreations in novels and pictures.

Such publications as *Mansions of England in the Olden Time* by Joseph Nash (4 vols, 1839-49) provided accurate depictions of buildings, often with imaginative reconstructions of historical incidents such as Henry VIII's courtship of Anne Boleyn. This was a sanitised form of history suggestive of the dressing-up box in the corner of the nursery.

These various approaches to the past can also be traced through the institutions set up to study and preserve various aspects of our heritage: the Society of Antiquaries (1707), the Society for the Protection of Ancient Buildings (1877), the National Trust (1895), the National Art Collections Fund (1903), the Council for the Protection of Rural England (1926), the Georgian Group (1937), the Victorian Society (1957), the Historic Houses Association (1973), and English Heritage (1984). Each of these organisations devises different strategies and employs different emphases, but essentially they are all actively engaged in pursuing the same end. NADFAS, therefore, fits comfortably into a well-authenticated tradition and can be said to be keeping good company. It remains fiercely independent in outlook, as indeed do all the other nominated groups, believing for example that in order to appreciate and to preserve the past it is vital to engage with the present and to anticipate the future. Even so, if each of these organisations were in an emergency ever to be mobilised as a single unit it would represent a powerfully motivated and abundantly articulate voice for the preservation of this country's heritage.

To this end it is vital that NADFAS continues on its course with an ever-increasing membership and so plays its all-important part in our national life.

*Christopher Lloyd*

# Preface
## Helen Clifford

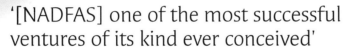

'[NADFAS] one of the most successful
ventures of its kind ever conceived'

*National Art Collection Fund Newsletter*, 1983, p.13

There have been a number of histories of NADFAS in its various forms, from Sheila Marshall's personal memoir *Development of a Dream* (1982) to the individual records of the evolution of the Church Recorders (1986), Young NADFAS (1987) and the Voluntary Conservation Corps (1988). It is perhaps because Patricia Fay, the founder of NADFAS, died so young, at the age of 46, and so unexpectedly, in 1979, that NADFAS Committee members have been so acutely aware of the need to put down on paper what actually happened.

This history combines the chronology of events that have cumulatively led up to what NADFAS is now, taking us from 1965 when Patricia Fay launched her Chiltern Antiques Group, to ideas about the future, with a thematic approach dealing with the sub-histories of the key elements that make up the multi-faceted character of NADFAS.

Most importantly this history is about people. It is these people that make NADFAS such an extraordinarily successful combination of education, entertainment and sociability. Each Society has its own history that relates to and informs the wider history of the Association.

It is a story that could not have been written without the support of you, the membership, reporting from your Societies, from countless committee members, locally, regionally, nationally and internationally, who have taken the time to send in their memories, to ransack their lofts and garages for NADFAS paperwork, and talk to founder members. It also benefits from the impressive Archive at Head Office which, over ten years ago, began to be collated, sorted and indexed – leaving a legacy that has long needed to be tapped in a systematic way. Despite the riches of these resources I suspect that most of the 90,000 membership know very little, if anything, of this past. As Hannah Gould, a founder member of Enfield DFAS (1968), recently discovered, 'the majority of our members were absolutely ignorant of the history of NADFAS'. This book aims to address this gap in knowledge. In writing it I share the sentiments of Rosemary Kimmel, archive secretary of Blackheath DFAS, when she started to write the history of her Society: 'once started it was difficult to know when to stop'.

This book aims to give a broad introduction to the foundation and development of the Association. It does not set out to be a definitive history, but rather to give a flavour of its extraordinary character and achievements, which on its 40th birthday we should be proud to celebrate. There are, of course, many figures within this story who deserve their own individual biographies. On the one hand we have been overwhelmed by the amount of material that has been sent, meaning that it has been impossible to include everything. On the other, of the many photographs and illustrations we received, we were able to reproduce relatively few due to a number of factors, including the picture quality needed for book production, copyright fees and restrictions on the publication of images of children. Within the constraints of producing an affordable good-looking book of 176 pages some very difficult decisions had to be made. The seeds of this book may, however, one day grow into a much larger volume – perhaps for the 50th anniversary.

The founders of NADFAS chose the acanthus plant as a fitting symbol for the aims and aspirations of the Association. Although our wider society has changed over the 40 years of its existence, the symbolism of the acanthus remains the same. It has inspired artists and architects through the ages. It stands for quality, longevity, and creativity. The acanthus ties us to the past and the present, and it will continue to be around long into the future – just as NADFAS plans to be.

*Helen Clifford, North Yorkshire, 2007*

Helen read History at Girton College, Cambridge, before working as an archivist. An interest in objects as historical evidence took her to the Victoria & Albert Museum/Royal College of Art postgraduate course from where she completed her Ph.D. in 1989, on a partnership of 18th-century London goldsmiths, published by Yale University Press in 2004. She was appointed a Leverhulme Research Fellow at the Ashmolean Museum, which culminated in the exhibition *A Treasured Inheritence, 600 Years of Oxford College Silver* (2004). For many years she taught at the Victoria & Albert Museum, and has curated exhibitions on historical and contemporary silver, including *Sporting Glory* (V&A, 1992) and *Twentieth-Century Silver* (Crafts Council, 1993). She has written extensively in popular and academic journals on the goldsmiths' and associated luxury trades. She is a Freeman of the Worshipful Company of Goldsmiths and a Fellow of the Society of Antiquaries. Helen is currently a Senior Research Fellow at the University of Warwick, and runs the Swaledale Museum in Reeth, where she lives with her husband, Alan Bainbridge. She became a NADFAS lecturer in 1995.

# Acknowledgements

This book would never have appeared without the enthusiastic support of Thomas Cocke. Thomas took up the idea and nurtured the ground on which it was to grow and the Trustee Board at all times gave warm endorsement to the project. Without the guidance of the Advisory Committee we would not have achieved such an ambitious range and depth of content. I am particularly indebted to Patricia Braun for introducing me to the NADFAS Archives, and Sheila Chapman who generously delved into them to answer countless questions, to check facts and share her wide knowledge of NADFAS with me with warmth and kindness. Patricia and Sheila also bravely took on the task of reading draft chapters. Susan Sellers' infectious enthusiasm for NADFAS and her commitment to its future has meant the book is as much about the present as the past. Christopher Lloyd, as our new President, threw himself into the project with verve and inspiration. Judith Quiney has with humour and patience set the framework for the evolution of the book, and has overseen its development from abstract idea to handsome finished product. Stuart South masterfully controlled the sacks of correspondence and photographs and dealt with myriad calls, co-ordinating the flow of material that came from so many different sources. Judith and Stuart were always at the end of a telephone to sort out problems and make connections. The staff at NADFAS House were generous with their time and knowledge, and I would especially like to thank Chloe Bevan and James Wilkins. Others gave up their time to read draft chapters connected with their own experience of NADFAS including Roger Allan, David Bell, Christina Briant, Rachel Fay, Angela Goedicke, Katherine Hill, Kath Hollands, Pauline Hopkins, Sylvia Horwood-Smart, Caroline Lorimer, Buff Reid, Kate Siebert, Susan Sellers, and Pat Turner. Their comments and ideas have improved the book immensely. I am also very grateful to those who allowed me to 'interview' them, including Audrey and Christopher Chavasse,

Diana Good, Eve King, Ann Parkinson and Anne White, and those with whom I have had very helpful conversations including Sir John Boyd, Peter Darty, Rachel Fay, Jennifer and Brian Garvan, John Hardy, Rosemary Lennox-Simpson, Lindley Maitland, Judith Thomas and Jeremy Warren. There are many too who helped with the research including Gri Harrison, Jane Wainwright and Margaret Webb, and many others who in big ways and small have added much to the book. I would also like to express my enormous thanks to all those Society members who took the time and trouble to respond to the call for information. Many went to immense lengths to find photographs, contact senior members, and dig out old notes. The richness and variety of the book is largely due to them. From all of these and many others I have learnt first-hand about NADFAS. Despite rigorous checking of facts and figures (often contradictory) I am sure there will be the eagle-eyed who will spot mistakes, and for these I take responsibility. I am grateful also to Liz Hamlin, Heritage Volunteers Representative for the Kent Area, whose suggestion led to the title. The manuscript has been turned into a beautiful book thanks to the team at Touchline. Glyn Wilmshurst, Danielle Green and Fiona McCready, who also work on the NADFAS Review, have produced a publication that is thoroughly 'at home' with the Association, as well as making it suitably special. There are however, as in every DFAS, those whose energy and commitment transcend the 'ordinary'. Barbara Hickman as Chairman of the Book Advisory Committee has with wise counsel, good cheer and sheer hard labour helped make this publication happen. I owe her a great debt of thanks. There are those too who stand in the wings to whom I would also like to pay tribute, all those partners, my own husband included, who live with NADFAS. Finally I would like to thank Dinah Reynolds for introducing me to NADFAS 12 years ago – little did she know where it was to lead!

# 1
# Foundations:
## *The First Five Years...*

*'Women's changing role could be the Art World's gain'*
From the National Chairman's speech, 1968

### Early Days: An Interest in the Past

NADFAS was born in the 1960s, a time of great change in culture and society. In politics, Eisenhower was replaced by John F. Kennedy who was assassinated in 1963. Beeching made his report on the British railways, leading to their systematic dismantling and the Profumo Affair broke. In the following year, 1964, Harold Wilson (1916-95) became Prime Minister, heralding a new Britain, 'forged in the white heat' of scientific and technological revolution. His social reforms affected capital punishment, homosexuality, abortion, divorce and theatre censorship, cumulatively leading to what was called a 'permissive society'. In 1969 Neil Armstrong stepped out of Apollo II to be the first man on the moon. New 'plate glass' universities were being built, like Essex and Warwick, and the Open University was launched in 1969. Mods replaced Rockers, and Jayne Mansfield, Marilyn Monroe and Diana Dors were challenged in popularity by Mia Farrow, Liza Minelli and Glenda Jackson. 1967 saw the first broadcast of *The Forsyte*

*Saga* and *The Avengers*. The miniskirt took off in the mid sixties and Twiggy became the icon of the age. Ladies with taste and money bought their jewellery at Grima and the more daring went to Biba for their clothes. A new wave of industrial-designers transformed our homes, the Morphy Richards electric toaster was dressed by Mary Quant, and fashionable dinner tables were set with silver or stainless steel cutlery designed by Gerald

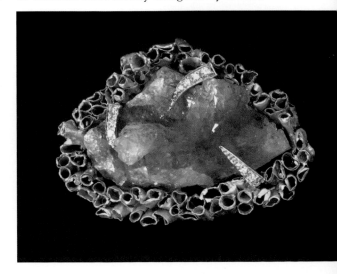

had a major impact on the birth of NADFAS. First in an age of youth culture, a broad-based appreciation of the past and its objects began to appear; and secondly, the role of women in society was shifting.

Our fascination with the fine and decorative arts of the past seems such a central part of contemporary life. Today many best-selling books and television programmes focus on the subject. However in the early 1960s, it was a very new area of interest for the general public, something we perhaps do not readily connect with the more brashly advertised youth culture that elbowed its way into our consciousness of the times. The mid 1960s were a time of change in attitude, when people were becoming more aware of the attractions of the past. Growing affluence accompanied by increased leisure time, and cheaper and easier transport, for a larger sector of the population, resulted in an unprecedented enthusiasm for antiques. In order to cope with the increasing tax burdens, a number of stately homes were also opening their doors for the first time to a curious general public, so a wider section of the populace than ever before was exposed to these treasures. As a result many:

*started to look at their own belongings, to compare them with items in the shops and then to drift into museums and galleries. There followed a desire to know more about these treasures of the past, and many sought ... to increase their knowledge.*[1]

In 1965 Arthur Negus fronted the pilot programme *Going for a Song*, whose popularity lasted decades and spawned many imitations. In the same year the Antiques Collectors' Club was created. As Mary Bourne succinctly summed up for an article in *The Lady*, 'In an age of speed, throwaway commodities, and machine-made articles, the old, the well-made and the hand-crafted were taking on a new perspective'.[2]

This interest in the past coincided with a growing band of young women who were eager to be educated, who wanted to learn more about their surroundings, who responded to the language of the arts, but

**Above**
Twiggy, an icon of the Swinging Sixties, which was the unlikely historical backdrop for the birth of NADFAS
**Left**
Pink topaz brooch by Andrew Grima

Benney, David Mellor and Stuart Devlin. Neo-Classicism and French Decorative art were deeply unpopular, while Op Art and Pop Art were storming the new London galleries.

It may seem strange in a period characterised by young, urban radicalism which embraced all that was new that an organisation like NADFAS, stereotyped as mature, rural, traditional and interested in the past should flourish so spectacularly. Yet amidst the growth in media and technology, the beginning of the race in space, the expansion of university education and of crippling inflation, two factors emerged that

## The Chiltern Antiques Group:
### *'A new kind of women's society'*
### **The Times**, 10 January 1966

Grasping the opportunity these conditions had created, one 'ordinary' housewife from the Home Counties took action. While confined to home, due to back problems, Patricia Fay spent her enforced leisure reading up about fine arts and antiques. Sensing that there was a wider demand for knowledge in this area, she decided to take the next step – to canvas opinion among her friends, to see if it might be possible to set up a society to share and increase this knowledge outside London. It is said that NADFAS was conceived upon the field of the Old Berkeley Beaglers, as it was to her close friends who shared a love of beagling that Patricia turned next. Audrey Chavasse, who had known Patricia since they were girl guides together, Elizabeth Watts (now Braimbridge), and Cherry Wheeler (now Aston) were all regular beaglers, and with Patricia, all young mothers in their 20s and 30s. At the invitation of Elizabeth Macleod-Matthews, Patricia organised a lunch at Chenies Manor, an elegant Tudor mansion, for her friends at which they agreed to form the Chiltern Antiques Group. They left Chenies that day having formed a steering committee, with

**Left**
Stephen Willats' minidress
**Right**
The Chiltern Antiques Group at West Wycombe on one of its first trips
**Below**
A Morphy Richards toaster with Mary Quant pattern

needed to be taught to understand it. Though the sixties have been described as swinging, many of the more restrictive and narrow manners and mores of the previous century remained, in respectable circles at least. One NADFAS member recalls that when she decided to get a job after her children had started school, it was murmured that her husband could not afford to keep her. Her generation of women had not automatically been encouraged to go to university or plan for a career. Attempting to be a good housewife and mother were still the main aims for women in their 30s and 40s. These women, who sought to understand the arts of the past, were revolutionary in their own way, even though many did not wear mini-skirts or flowers in their hair. They also represented a huge potential market, pressure group and workforce.

Patricia as Chairman, Elizabeth Watts as Vice Chairman, Cherry Wheeler as Treasurer, plus Edna Johnson, Georgette Johnstone and Audrey Chavasse. Via their recruiting activities they were able to organise an inaugural meeting at Chenies on 28 January 1965. Miss D.K. Millington gave a lecture on 'Small Antiques in our Homes' (about Victorian silver teaspoons) beginning just after 10.00 am, with coffee. Cherry Wheeler remembers how 'the invitations were so popular, it was said that … [they] were taken from people's mantelpieces',[3] while Edna Johnson related how 'The speaker was late, all sorts of things went wrong, but we were overwhelmed by the number of people who came'.[4] The results of the morning were expenses costing the best part of £5, and twenty-six signed-up members who agreed to pay an annual subscription of two guineas. Membership was limited to ninety.

The Chiltern Antiques Group first held their monthly meetings at The Old Crown in Amersham and then in Chalfont St Peter Community Centre. It was informal, predominantly female, and generally not specialist in its approach, a refreshing change from existing societies. Edna Johnson remembers how the early committee meetings were very unconventional with Patricia lying flat on the floor to rest her back. In August 1966 a reporter from *Bucks Life* wrote that:

*It comes as a surprise to find a country society with aims as erudite and interests as specialised as those of the Chiltern Antiques Group that can draw an attendance of over a hundred to a lecture that starts at 10.45am on a weekday. … [Their] main aim is the serious study of antiques through the medium of study groups, lectures and visits.*[5]

As Elliott Viney (d. 2002), another of those Berkeley Beaglers, remarked, 'the initial success of the Group transformed Patricia from a character uncertain of the way forward into a dominant leader, full of ideas, which as she now realised she had the talents and charm to make real'.[6] At their AGM the Chiltern Antiques Group agreed that 'its primary object … [was] the promotion and advancement of aesthetic education and the cultivation and study of the decorative and fine arts'.

The first foundation stone in the history of NADFAS had been laid, the formation of the Chiltern Antiques Group. Patricia was determined that from the beginning 'it would not be a group of dilettante housewives filling in their time, but a serious organisation with first class lecturers and study groups so that in due course the members would be able to serve the community'.[7]

## The Importance of Being Well-connected

The first problem for the Group was to find suitable lecturers. As Sheila Marshall, the author of the first history of NADFAS noted, in the early days Patricia was well aware that 'many lecturers were loath to waste their time on lecturing to blue rinsed lacquered ladies who probably didn't want to learn, wouldn't listen or take the fine arts seriously'.[8] Patricia thought the obvious step was to contact the Victoria & Albert Museum. There were two important results of this initiative, to meet and befriend Helen Lowenthal (1904-93) and to secure, via her, a long-term association with the museum and the support of the current, and subsequent, directors. Helen Lowenthal remembered her first meeting with Patricia: 'She came to see me at … the Museum at the end of a particularly heavy day. If she had not presented her ideas in such an organised form, I would have dismissed her as a further irritation in a difficult day'.[9] Helen was a formidable woman. After study at the Courtauld Institute of Art, and working on code-breaking in Intelligence during the War, she realised that she had an aptitude for teaching and became the education officer at the V&A. In this role she was a pioneer, building up a practically non-existent department into one which had a large staff and covered a wide field.[10] She also became Educational Adviser to the National Trust, and was, in 1952, one of the founders of the Attingham Trust.[11] It was through Helen Lowenthal's contacts that many distinguished speakers came to lecture to the Chiltern Antiques Group, and later for

Patricia Fay (left) and
Lally Robinson who
founded Thames
Antiques and Fine Art
Group in 1967, and
became the first Vice
Chairman of NADFAS

NADFAS. These were to include Sir Trenchard
Cox (1905-95), John Pope-Hennessy (later Sir
John) (1913-94), Oliver Millar (later Sir Oliver)
(1923-2007) who became Surveyor of the
Queen's Pictures in 1972 (until 1988), Helena
Hayward (a fellow founder of the Attingham
Trust, and one of the most distinguished
furniture historians of her generation), and

many others. The list of lecturers would soon
become the *Directory*, one of the most
important resources to be developed by the
Group. Sheila Marshall was right to state that
'from Helen … stemmed so many important
contacts which helped in no mean way to
give NADFAS the national status which it
enjoys today'.[12] It was fortunate timing for

Patricia, because in 1969 Helen retired from the V&A, and if Patricia had not acted promptly their paths may not have crossed at all. In the history of NADFAS so many roads lead back to Helen's initial ideas, and determination to see them become realities. Patricia was to call Helen 'the NADFAS midwife'.[13] In her turn Helen admired Patricia, who 'was blessed with radiant good looks. She had auburn hair and the kind of colouring which all Americans admire… Her effect on those whom she wanted to win over was magical'.[14] Even the critical journalist from *The Times*, Kirsten Cubitt echoed Helen's words when she described Patricia as 'pretty in the pink-lipped, grey-eyed style which gives so many Home Counties girls that minor-royal-family air'.[15]

An essential part of Patricia's success lay in her ability to, what we call today, 'network', at a high level. Her introduction by Helen Lowenthal to Sir Trenchard Cox, who had 'very recently [1967] retired as Director of the V&A … [and was] a Museum personality of note and an international lecturer', opened 'many doors for Patricia then, and has opened many more for the Association since'. [16] Trenchard Cox, who had studied at the universities of Cambridge and Berlin, and at the Sorbonne, had been assistant to the Director of the Wallace Collection, then Director of the City of Birmingham Museum and Art Gallery (1944-55), before taking up the directorship of the V&A in 1955. He has been described as 'a man of self-effacing charm and interest in his staff' and promoted women in the museum, advancing the first woman to Assistant Keeper in the early 1960s.[17]

Another crucial step was to find an influential and respected president for the Chiltern Group. Patricia's charm and persuasion worked to great effect on Mrs James de Rothschild, who agreed to fufill the role. Known as 'Mrs James', she took an immense interest in the family home of Waddesdon Manor, and its rich collections of French eighteenth-century decorative and fine arts. 'In those days no-one had heard of the Chiltern Antiques Group' remembers Janet Deramore (who was to become its vice

chairman), 'certainly none of the first class lecturers, but her name gave us instant status and credibility'.[18] At these early meetings, smoking was only allowed in question time, the audience was given permission not to wear hats and gloves and to use first names, men were not admitted to the waiting list, and stiletto heels had to be removed on visits to country houses.[19]

By the first annual general meeting of the Chiltern Antiques Group held in September 1965 the success of the venture was clear. The

MEMBERS of the Harrogate Decorative and Fine Arts Group during an illustrated lecture at the Cairn Hotel, Harrogate, yesterday. Left to right: Mr. Geoffrey Beard, who gave the lecture, Mrs. Chita Hutton-Wilson, chairman; Mrs. Joan Goldsbrough, Mrs. Zena Walker, Mrs. Bridget Dawson, joint secretary, Mrs. Elizabeth Gilman, joint secretary, Mrs. Barbara Clayton, and Mrs. Nancy Horner. (A Yorkshire Post picture.)

membership limit was raised to 150, and the pattern of lectures and visits had been set. Lectures were held between 10.30-12.00 so that members 'could drop our children at nursery school and collect them again at lunchtime'.[20] The following year more visits were arranged, to Penn House and Denham Place locally, and also to Syon Park, Southill, Hatfield and further afield. The organisation and aims of the Chiltern Group 'became a blueprint' for future NADFAS societies. A year after the first meeting, a notice in *The Times* reported the first anniversary of the Chiltern Antiques Group, and the emergence of 'a new kind of women's society'.[21]

One event Patricia organised that was a success and had long-term influence on the character of NADFAS (but was not repeated), was an 'open meeting'. The distinguished architect, author, interior designer and

**Above**

*The Yorkshire Post* reports on the launch of Harrogate DFAG. Geoffrey Beard, who gave the inaugural lecture, is pictured on the left next to Chita Hutton-Wilson and Zena Walker, fifth from the right

painter Sir Hugh Casson (1910-99) was invited to speak at Dr Challenor's School in Amersham to the Chiltern Antiques Group. He had been the Director of the 1951 Festival of Britain for which he was knighted soon after. He was an energetic, busy and famous man, and it is characteristic of Patricia's ability to network that she should have been able to persuade him to come to the school to lecture. Elliott Viney remembers that 340 tickets were sold at 5s. each, while the speaker's fee comprised two bottles of brandy and two of port costing the Group £11 10s. The lecture 'The Future of the Past' proved excellent publicity and even stimulated an article in the social columns of *The Times*. The subject of the lecture gives us an indication of Patricia's wide span of interest. Sir Hugh's job at the Festival had been to celebrate Modernism, and his designs for the Cambridge University Arts Faculty and the Elephant House for London Zoo epitomised this commitment. The Chiltern Antiques Group did not bury its head in the past, and was keen to be informed on the present as well as future trends. In his lecture Sir Hugh chided the Group for their name, suggesting that 'it implied a blind approval of all that was simply old – simply because it was old'.[22] This reprimand must surely have gone to Patricia's heart, as commitment to the present and the future in the fine and decorative arts became a recurring feature in early NADFAS policy making. Sir Hugh does not appear to have been put off by his experience, as he was later to become a Vice President of NADFAS in 1981.

## 'The whole movement looks like spreading'

*The Times*, 10 January 1966
NADFAS would have never been born if Patricia's idea had not been taken up by others, if it had not satisfied a wider demand. Before twelve months were out a second Society had started. Diana Good launched the Fine Arts Group of Thame in December 1965. She was a founder member of the Chiltern Antiques Group and was asked 'why don't you start one locally?' Diana

remembers that Patricia Fay was absolutely charming, and irresistible, and that 70 members joined at the inaugural meeting. No men were allowed, but they soon 'crept in'.[23] Patty Brooks was her secretary, and she remembers that they 'were a small and fairly informal group' and held their meetings at the Swan Hotel in Thame.[24] Lady Carrington was their first president, her husband had just completed his term as Leader of the House of Lords (1963-64). A feature in *The Times*, 10 January 1966, reported that the Chiltern Antiques Group 'is so popular that a similar Society, the Fine Arts Group, was launched at Thame last month. The whole movement looks like spreading'. Patricia Fay commented in the same article that 'We had no idea the demand would be so great, dozens of housewives seem to be looking for something intellectual to do, something to get their teeth into'. John Bly, who gave the Thame Group their first lecture, was then a young man in his 20s whose father had a house in Tring. Diana Good likes to think that this lecture helped launch his career. In 1970 this Group changed its name to the Vale of Aylesbury DFAS, to avoid confusion with another Group, the Thames Antiques & Fine Art Group, set up by Lesley Robinson in February 1967. It is said that both Groups turned up on the same day and at the same time at the Tate Gallery, and chaos resulted, prompting the Thame Group to re-title. Lesley, known affectionately as 'Lally', had moved to Buckinghamshire from Yorkshire in the 1950s and had been introduced to Patricia Fay while on a visit to Hasely Court in 1963. Sharing the same interests, with different but complementary characters, they were to make excellent working partners. As Patricia was to state later 'NADFAS might never have happened if … [I had not] been introduced… to Lally'.[25]

Other Societies followed swiftly. The first northern, rather than Home Counties Society was formed in January 1967 – the Harrogate Decorative & Fine Arts Group. On telling Patricia of her forthcoming move from Buckinghamshire to North Yorkshire Chita Hutton-Wilson (later Laurie), then 21, was persuaded to set up a new Group on her arrival in Harrogate. In September 1966 an advertisement appeared in *The Yorkshire Post* for 'any young and energetic person [who would] like to help launch a mid-week morning study group', placed by Chita. It was followed by another that read 'Lecturers required for daytime weekly study groups in Harrogate for furniture, porcelain, The Country House'. One of the ladies who offered to help was Zena Walker, who was also a friend of Patricia Fay. 'Her strong, forceful but kind personality, energy and drive ensured the growth of NADFAS outside the Home Counties', she was a founder member not only of Harrogate DFAG, but also of York (1973), Leeds (1973) and Beverley (1975) Societies.[26] The new Harrogate Group, chaired by Chita, held its inaugural meeting at the Cairn Hotel in Harrogate (where they still meet) on 25 January 1967 where they heard a lecture by Geoffrey Beard on 'Grand Interior Decoration of the 18th-century'. Despite deep snow and treacherous driving conditions, he arrived only forty-five minutes late. Chita, meanwhile, had made her first public speech to the expectant audience.[27]

Two hundred attended the lecture, and such was the success, a series of seminars for up to 15 at a time were organised at Temple Newsam House, Leeds, under the tutelage of Robert Rowe, the Director. Just over a year later he became vice president of the Group, along with George McTague, a lecturer in Fine Art for Leeds University. The monthly lectures continued with Christopher Warner talking on 'Antique Silver', May Beattie on 'Some Basic Principles in the Study of Oriental Carpets', Brian Murray on 'Some Aspects of Art Nouveau', John Bradshaw on 'Decorative Painting in 18th-Century Venice', Helen Lowenthal on 'Trade with the East and its Effect on Taste', and Arthur Negus on 'Antiques – Mainly Furniture'.

Back down south, in the Home Counties heartland, a group of enthusiasts met in a drawing room in Gerrards Cross and founded the Gerrards Cross Antiques Group in May 1967 with Ann Hopton as the founder chairman. Oliver Millar was to later refer to

these 'older' established societies as 'The Early Settlers'.[28]

## Take Off: Going National

With five Societies formed either as a result of Patricia Fay's promotion, or with related aims, the momentum was such that it was decided to hold a meeting to discuss the best way forward for these associated Groups. It was held on 26th June 1967 at Helen

The
National Association
of
Decorative and Fine Arts
Societies

Lowenthal's house at 87 Elizabeth Street, Victoria (London). Helen Lowenthal, Patricia Fay, representatives of the four other Societies (Diana Good of the Fine Arts Study Group, Thame; Zena Walker of Harrogate DFAG; Lesley Robinson of Thames Antiques and Decorative Arts Group and Anthea Smith of Gerrards Cross Antiques Group), Anne White of the Junior Museums Club, Mr and Mrs Doyle of Reigate Collectors' Club, Mrs Easterbrook who was trying to form a Group in Cambridge, Mary Petter of the Woodstock Society, Margaret Harris who was about to set up a Society in Berkhamsted, which became Gade Valley DFAS, and Ellen Mackintosh who took the minutes, attended.[29] At this meeting it was decided that the individual Groups should be formed into an Association. This was something that Patricia had been thinking about for some time, but she was worried that her own Group was not

**Above**
The anthemion pattern border on early NADFAS stationery was a precursor to the acanthus symbol finally adopted by the Association as its motif

**Above right**
Patricia Fay and the Duchess of Kent at the inaugural meeting of NADFAS

convinced of its benefits. In a letter to a friend and adviser, she declared how important she felt this step to be: 'I feel I have a difficult time ahead, but I can't let the thing sink and not go down fighting – even at the risk of unpopularity'.[30] Beneath the charm there was a will of steel, and this prevailed.

The formation of a national body to link the individual Societies together presented a new problem: what was it to be called? Husbands tended to refer to their wives and other members of these Groups, affectionately, but irritatingly as 'The Antiques'. Anne White vividly recalls the discussion that took place:

*I remember sitting round a table in Helen Lowenthal's house ... We had to think of a name and somehow hit on The National Association of Decorative and Fine Arts Societies – with the acronym NADFAS. I recollect we all repeated this several times in English and then in every other language we knew in case it might have unfortunate connotations.[31]*

Little were this Group to know that this title would inspire a whole range of emotions, amusement, confusion and respect. The established fashion magazine *Harper's Bazaar* dubbed them the National Association of Dragons and Fiery Spinsters, while Patricia reported back to her committee that someone had exclaimed 'NADFAS sounds like an amalgam of firewomen'.[32] A correspondent from *The Times* asked Patricia, rather flippantly, if the letters stood for 'The Society of Decidedly Fascinating Abductresses'.[33] The patronising author of an article in the *Sunday Express* reported that 'Keen feminists will no doubt be delighted to hear of a new kind of get-together for women. It is the National Association for Decorative and Fine Arts – the basic idea behind this ponderous title being "learning about antiques"'.[34] The reporter went on:

*I have absolutely nothing against women meeting to swap sponge cake recipes or listen to home-spun talks on loose cover making – if that's what they fancy. But the thought that so many are evidently interested in a serious study of the Decorative and Fine Arts, and now have an*

*opportunity to develop that interest, really pleases me.[35]*

The editor of *Ideal Home* found 'the title of the organisation ... a bit of a dampening mouthful', but conceded that 'there is an admirably realistic purpose behind it all'.[36] Jane Downes remembered the moment's pause at the other end of the telephone, after introducing herself on behalf of NADFAS, and the polite response 'You will forgive me if I am not immediately familiar with the organisation these initials represent'.[37]

The first occasional newsletter of NADFAS appeared in January 1968 with the names of Sir Trenchard Cox as the President and Oliver Millar, John Pope-Hennessy and Helen Lowenthal as Vice Presidents. The Chairman was Patricia Fay, the Vice Chairman Lesley Robinson, the Hon. Treasurer Mr S. Langton Forwood, the Hon. Publications Secretary Winifred Ballachey, Anne White was on the

Committee and Christopher Chavasse the Hon. Legal Adviser. This newsletter announced that:

*NADFAS was formed for the exchange of ideas and information, to issue a Directory of Lecturers and Handbook to stimulate the formation of new Societies with high standards and explore the possibilities of helping in houses and museums... By pooling our resources we can tackle any number of projects.*

All these immediate aims were to be made public on 28 May 1968 at an inaugural meeting of NADFAS. This was to take place at the V&A in the grand lecture theatre. The invitation launched the first official design of NADFAS stationery, something the reporter from the *Yorkshire Post* noted: 'NADFAS notepaper is suitably genteel: black and white tracery frames its letter-head in tasteful olive green'.[38] According to the minutes of the committee meetings devoted to organising this event, it was Lally Robinson who suggested that Graham Davis of the British Printing Corporation design a symbol to be incorporated into the notepaper headin. This was never implemented but he did design the NADFAS letter heading. The anthemion pattern border and colour were approved at the negotiated 'cut price' of £25. Here lies the origin of the acanthus symbol, part of that anthemion border, resonant of all the excellences of classical architecture, that became the acanthus leaf symbol by which NADFAS is known throughout the world today.[39]

Eleven Societies and the Junior Museums Club participated, including the recently formed Thanet and Moor Park Groups, and over 400 people came to the Lyceum Theatre, London. Her Royal Highness the Duchess of Kent attended. The Earl of Pembroke gave a talk on Wilton House and 'the problems associated with opening a house to the public, and the part that women can play in helping to preserve, foster and appreciate the nation's works of art'.[40] Sir Trenchard Cox, the new President, gave an address and Patricia Fay reported with enthusiasm on the development of NADFAS. She announced how delighted they were 'that the Duchess could grace this special day and strengthen it

for us with that indefinable influence that only the members of our royal family give'. It was an inspiring event, only slightly marred by lunch at a nearby hotel, where there was not enough food and the cloakroom facilities were inadequate. A letter was subsequently sent to the management, resulting in a partial refund.

This inaugural meeting led to coverage of NADFAS on *Woman's Hour*, when Audrey Russell interviewed Patricia. Subsequently Miss Russell became a popular lecturer for NADFAS. She was a woman of note, and a perfect ambassador for NADFAS. She had been employed as the BBC's first female news reporter and in 1944 became the first female accredited war correspondent. Patricia recognised the importance of publicity, and a series of interviews and articles appeared in popular magazines to promote NADFAS nationwide.

It is at this point in the history of NADFAS that we should consider why the idea of individual Societies, with the aim of understanding the fine and decorative arts, composed mostly of women, should have been quite such a runaway success. First it was unusual in its attempt to extend the field of interest beyond the specialist to a wider public. There were many antique societies to pre-date NADFAS, but none sought such a broad audience. The aim was not so much to turn members into amateur collectors, but to increase their more general appreciation of antiques and the arts. Second it tapped into a huge market of 'comparatively well off women with children at school all day and help in the house ... they had time on their hands'.[41] Meetings were held at first 'in the morning, while they are still fresh and their children are at school. By the time they've cooked an evening meal they don't feel like going out for a lecture'.[42] The Harrow Society was to set up it own crèche during meetings.[43] Patricia Fay noted that 'Women's changing role could be the arts world's gain'[44], harnessing the push for education, and the free time the young married mother had – she could see that their cumulative time, intelligence, enthusiasm and energy

**Above**

Patricia Fay poses at home for *Harper's Bazaar*

could be channelled into action. This was not an example of rampant Feminism, they were feminine, not Feminist, and more, as one reporter commented, an example of 'lavender scented Women's Lib'.[45] Third, and perhaps most importantly, Patricia Fay envisaged NADFAS as not only a means to provide quality lectures, but also as a way of offering practical help to the arts. 'Members could be set to work... By offering themselves as guides in houses open to the public; by caring for church ornaments and vestments; by learning to catalogue works of art; by repairing old fabrics.'[46] There was a strong sense among women that voluntary work provided a way of contributing to the welfare of society. Many of their mothers and grandmothers had been active during the two World Wars, in the Red Cross and other essential groups. The desire to serve the country was still there, but largely unfocused in peace time. Sir Trenchard Cox noted that Patricia 'had a sense of purpose which was practical as well as imaginative'. Fourth, from the beginning Patricia realised that the

Association needed to be run professionally, if it was to be taken seriously. She drew about her a group of efficient women, and made sure she was backed by respected high profile figures from the art world. As one journalist remarked these women 'who have lived in the shadow of successful husbands ... discovered confidence in themselves as organisers'.[47] Through NADFAS they became key people in their own right. Others were forceful women who already had great experience. Where else might you find working together, for example, a businesswoman who ran simultaneously two travel agencies, a small bus company and a minor airline (Ann Parkinson) and a trained pilot with a degree in medicine (Kathleen Wareham). The early days of NADFAS were marked by ladies of strong character who were often outspoken. All worked tremendously hard, in their different ways, to give NADFAS its firm foundations.

The months after the launch at the V&A were marked by meetings in members' houses to discuss the role of the chairmen of the Societies, the fees, and the ground rules. For the latter Patricia called upon Christopher Chavasse, a personal friend, a London solicitor, and Hon. Legal Adviser (who had drawn up the rules for the Chiltern Antiques Group, and whose wife, Audrey, was on the steering committee of that Society). He wisely advised 'Don't have too rigid rules ... have rules on a wide basis, allow for leeway'. The results of going national put great strains upon the Committee. Without a secretary, communication between Societies and the national officers was often difficult – there was 'no central meeting place and nowhere to store the accumulating pile of records'.[48] By the end of 1968 eighteen Societies had been formed, and the need to keep them linked put further pressure on central administration.

Through her association with the V&A Patricia was offered a space for meetings, on a regular basis, free of charge, in the Director's Committee Room. Sheila Marshall remembered the 'big windows to let in plenty of light, even if somewhat daunting to open',

and 'the headed notepaper and sharpened pencil at every seat'.[49] It was here that it was decided to appoint a paid secretary, reflective of the growing membership and workload, and an Executive Committee, appointed by the Council (composed of the chairmen of each member Society) which would 'meet nine times a year and be responsible for running the day-to-day affairs of the Association'. At the November meeting, Nadine Mitchell was introduced to the Committee, and became NADFAS secretary. She immediately set to work taking the minutes. Her energy, initiative and sheer dedicated hard work underpinned the whole structure of NADFAS, and her presence was a crucial factor in its early success, helping lay the foundations for its future strength. She was paid a modest 5s. (25p) per hour. In the same year the first regular *Newsletter* was distributed.

The Societies that had been established were drawn together for specific events. One of these was the Duke of Bedford's lecture on 28 April 1969 on 'The Stately Home Owner as a Museum Curator'. The minutes for the meeting discussing the organisation of this note that 'His Grace is doing the lecture free as he is so thrilled with the girls who are working there'.[50] This was only just over eighteen months after the Duke had hosted a Love-in at Woburn Abbey, which had attracted more than 20,000 Flower Children.[51] The Duke's mention of 'the girls' indicates that very early on in the history of NADFAS practical help in country houses and galleries was seen as an important part of its aims and work. The blossoming of voluntary work is the subject of a separate chapter in this book.

In June 1969 Lally Robinson, who had done so much to help launch NADFAS, who was chairman of her own Group at Thames, took over as Acting Chairman. Patricia had resigned due to the pressures of moving to a new home, her wish to concentrate on NADFAS volunteering, and the belief that NADFAS needed new blood to survive and flourish. The first AGM was held in October 1969, and the Constitution agreeing that 'the Association shall be called The National Association of Decorative & Fine Arts Societies', and that it should have 'as its objects the promotion and advancement of the aesthetic education of the public and the cultivation and study of the decorative and fine arts' was adopted. These key objectives were those of the Chiltern Antiques Group. By the date of this meeting 28 Societies had been established. Although the core principles and structure were the same for each Society, each had its own character. For example when Kathleen Wareham set up North Kent DFAS in November 1968 she announced in a press article that 'The new Society will not be strictly for women'. She had been surprised at the number of men who had shown interest in the Society and expected 'several retired men to attend'. She thought that the new Society might have to consider meeting in the evenings, as so many women wanted their husbands to come.[52] This was quite unusual for NADFAS at the time, and is characteristic of Kathleen's independent spirit.

## Charitable Status

One of the continuous themes that run through the history of NADFAS is the shortage of money. It was only in 1970 that committee members were allowed 'stamp and telephone expenses paid out of petty cash', and expenses 'for travelling at 6p per mile for car journeys and 15s return rail fare whichever was the least'. In April that year Patricia Fay brought Dr Henry Pulitzer (son of Joseph Pulitzer the American print journalist who established the famous Pulitzer Prize) to an Executive Committee meeting. From the minutes of this meeting it seems that he was specifically invited to come up with ideas for fund-raising. However his suggestions seem to have been a little *avant garde* for the ladies: a centre in London, perhaps rented space in a supermarket in Kensington, where NADFAS members could sell items of decorative art. The idea was never pursued.

One of the ways to enable the raising of money, for the causes that NADFAS supported, was by becoming a charity. At a 1970 Council Meeting Christopher Chavasse advocated that NADFAS become one. One Society chairman reported back from this meeting that becoming a charity:

*was the main argumentative subject. A solicitor present said that we were comparable to the National Trust now and that we had to have the machinery geared to deal with this. It saved on tax, covenants could be made, ... NADFAS had matured to this stage.*[53]

Throughout the following year preparations were made for this status, in recognition that the major object of NADFAS included the education of the public. However it seems that members of a particular Society misunderstood what the intentions of this action were, thinking that being a charity meant only collecting money for a specific cause. At the 1972 Special General Meeting, called to decide the issue, there was an

**Left** The Association celebrates its first five years with a conference at the London Lyceum.
**Far left** Patricia Fay is pictured at the event with Lord Eccles (top) and below with (l-r): Sir John Wolfenden; Ann Parkinson; Rachel Fay and Brian Thompson

Above
Patricia Fay (left),
Dr Roy Strong and Ann
Parkinson at the First
Five Years Conference

attempt to disrupt the proceedings to gain further delay. One gentleman from this Society, amid foot stamping and shouting, tried to take control of the meeting, and snatched the microphone from the proposer of the motion. Sheila Marshall takes up the story:

*Being in the 'hot seat' of Chairman was not an enviable position. At that time there was no established procedure for dealing with such a situation. I felt that the only course to adopt was to give them 'enough string to hang themselves' so the Executive Committee just remained seated and let the barrackers do their worst. About ten minutes of noise and tension ensued, after which public opinion took over. The barrackers were silenced by the other, now extremely irate, members ... the motion was carried with only two abstentions.[54]*

The happy result of the meeting was the agreement that NADFAS should become a registered charity. Charitable status gave standing to the organisation and opened the door to later royal patronage. Since each Society is autonomous, individual Societies are not registered, but may elect to be if they wish.

## The Problems of Success

Over the next few years the number of affiliated NADFAS groups grew. By 1970 there were 33 member Societies, and by 1975 there were 68. Many Societies were born out of personal connections with the founder members of the NADFAS Committee. For example Jean Ward, the first chairman and now president of Test Valley DFAS, remembers how 'Brenda Headley and I started the Test Valley Society in 1971. We were both personal friends of Patricia – Brenda having met her on a family holiday and I because our husbands were both barristers'.[55] Rosemary Horton, now president of Devon DFAS described the launch of this Society in 1975: 'I was a member of Vale of Aylesbury in 1968 ... and was asked by Nadine Mitchell to bring NADFAS to Exeter'.[56] The character of these meetings is eloquently summed up via the minutes of West Essex DFAS, founded in 1970, remembered by Pamela Percy, the chairman: 'Ladies with big hats will be asked to remove them'.[57]

In the early 1970s several Societies

resigned from NADFAS, for various reasons: Glasgow, because they wanted to keep the word 'antique' in their title; Banbury who did not want to remain part of a national organisation; Whiteknights because of the increase in subscription costs; and Edinburgh because of their unwillingness to pay the full capitation fee (although they rejoined in 1984). Much of this discontent was the result of the growing scale of NADFAS and this is something that Patricia had predicted. In her speech of resignation as National Chairman she had declared 'I am very much aware of the many administrative problems as NADFAS grows … the problems of communication with our Member Societies'. At this crucial time Lally Robinson took over as Secretary of the New Societies sub-committee. Societies also suffered from the perennial problem of recruiting officers. Patricia Fay confessed that, even in 1970, 'Our greatest problem is to get madam chairmen. They all want to join but nobody wants to take on the responsibility'.[58]

## First Five Years Conference: *Arts and the People*, 1973

**Below**
Patricia Fay receives her
OBE at Buckingham Palace

In the same year that Britain joined the European Economic Community, and women were for the first time allowed onto the floor of the London Stock Exchange, NADFAS celebrated its fifth birthday. An ambitious first national conference entitled *Arts and the People* was held at the Lyceum in London. It was a statement of confidence and commitment. Surviving notes reveal just how lengthy and detailed the planning was for the occasion. A long check list for the day includes: 'raise height of stage, remove rails, provide green baize table cloth, table in entrance for HRH to sign visitors' book, floral arrangement and cloth, six extra coffee urns for use, opening music and fanfare for HRH timing all arranged, check loos for cleanliness,' and so it goes on and on. Amongst the many messages sent wishing the team good luck was one from the president of Thanet DFAS, Edward Heath (1916-2005), then Prime Minister. In her opening speech the Chairman introduced the distinguished group of responders: Sir John Wolfenden (Director of the British Museum), Dr Roy Strong (later Sir Roy) (Director of the National Portrait Gallery), John Letts (founder of National Heritage), Lord Brooke (heir to the Earl of Warwick), Sir Francis Dashwood (owner of West Wycombe) and Brian Thompson (an entrepreneur in the stately homes business), and Roy Shaw who was to become Secretary to the Arts Council, adding:

*In case you think there is an element of "Women's Lib" in the atmosphere, because all these charming gentlemen are firmly placed behind us, I can assure you that is not the case. They are going to move forward after Lady Dartmouth has addressed us and it is not our intention to part the sexes.*[59]

This light-hearted quip was topical, the Sex Discrimination Act was about to be passed, and with it the provision for the first time of maternity leave, while the Equal Pay Act was in the process of being enforced.

The conference offered the opportunity for NADFAS members to ask the panel serious questions, about the future for volunteers within museums, whether local museums should confine themselves to local interests, the role of the mass media in disseminating art, and how to reach the young. Executive Committee Members, and invited guests of influence, like Lord Eccles (1904-99), who was then Minister for the Arts and the 7th Earl of Warwick (1911-84), were available for comment and discussion. Specially commissioned commemorative Caithness glass goblets were available for sale, an innovative and elegant fund-raising idea, overseen by Jay Atkinson. As the order form stated, the goblet 'was especially chosen to emphasise that NADFAS looks to the future by giving encouragement to the contemporary arts, as well as enjoying the things of the past'. This was not just a token comment, but reflective of visits and lectures, and a growing number of commissions that highlighted the Association's commitment to contemporary art and craft. There had been visits for example to Henry Moore's studio, and a growing number of lecturers in the *Directory*, like James Noel White, who talked on 'Modern Design'.

The conference was well covered by the national press, drawing attention to the growing role that NADFAS was playing in the field of arts and culture. There were articles in the *Daily Telegraph, The Times* and the *Guardian*. A correspondent from *Country Life* was later to praise these 'Handmaidens of the Arts', and stated 'This movement has a social significance; already the country owes a debt to the able people who administer it'.[60] During the early 1970s many other societies began to appear with an historical cultural remit. For example National Heritage, a broad-based association designed to support and encourage the work of museums and galleries throughout Great Britain, and the Historic Houses Association founded in 1973. Many of these new groups, and older established ones like the National Trust, included key NADFAS women, like Anne White, who was also a founding member of National Heritage. NADFAS had, from 1970, assisted the National Trust in an energetic drive to increase membership of the Trust, by offering to take charge of recruiting desks. As the correspondent from *Art & Antiques* stated, 'NADFAS doesn't clash with other organisations ... it works with them'.[61] The Chairman at the *Arts and the People* conference reminded her audience:

*We do pride ourselves on being an outward looking organisation, I hope that we will never look inwards and become so self interested that we forget the other organisations that have led the field in so many of the ways in which we too hope to be involved.*

It was partly for this reason that NADFAS had accepted the offer of a free stand at the International Antique Fair at Earls Court in March 1973. A note in the *Newsletter* assuaged worries about connections with 'dealers and the commercial world', explaining that presence at the Fair would 'give us valuable experience of being at an exhibition and an opportunity to talk to potential members and those already in NADFAS'. By 1973 the major foundation stones of the Association had been laid: a handbook on setting up a Society and the establishment of a directory of lecturers (1969), a regular newsletter, the adoption of a Constitution and the recognition of the importance of volunteers and tours (1969), a pilot scheme that would lead to Church Recording (1971), the acceptance of charitable status, and the launch of Young NADFAS (1972). As Oliver Millar commented in the January 1971 *Newsletter*, 'There was nothing comparable to NADFAS either in America or Europe'.

## Further Development: Official Recognition

The success of the first five years of NADFAS was officially recognised in the 1975 New Year's Honours List, when Patricia Fay was awarded an OBE for her 'contribution to the arts and the creation of NADFAS'. The *Bucks Examiner* proudly splashed the headline 'Husband finds his wife in the news'.[62] Another journalist reported Patricia 'began with £8, a typewriter and determination', ten years later, NADFAS had 13,000 members. At the time Patricia went to collect her award from Buckingham Palace there were 69 Societies, from Edinburgh in the north, to Somerset in the south, covering a huge area of the country, and active in hundreds of projects to conserve, maintain and promote local culture. A further seal of royal approval came two years later when HRH Duchess of Kent became Patron of NADFAS.

Patricia had certainly been ahead of her time in recognising the need to support the cultural heritage that lay in the country houses that were now coming under threat.

Her self-confessed 'love-affair' with the English country house, was not merely a romantic one. 1975 was the year of the *Destruction of the Country House, 1875-1975,*

**Above**
On a recruitment drive at the International Antique Fair at Earls Court in 1973

exhibition held at the V&A, a major call to arms to rescue our country house heritage.[63] In an emotional introduction to the exhibition and accompanying leaflet Roy Strong described:

*The proliferation, within a generation, of houses that open, the public-relations stunts of their owners, the firm, dignified hand of our National Trust, seem to assure us, as we thumb through the list of houses open to the public, that*

*these wonderful buildings, their extraordinary diverse contents, their magical gardens and their vast rolling parks, which Time alone can create, will stand as long as England. But will they?*

An estimated 1,400 country houses had been demolished since 1920, at an average rate of one every two weeks, and fewer than 2,000 such houses remained in England, Scotland and Wales at the time.[64] At the back of the exhibition leaflet, a section on 'what you can do to help?' included NADFAS as one of the societies to contact and join. This was not politically neutral territory, as the divided press reviews about the *Destruction of the Country House* exhibition made only too clear. Caroline Tisdall in the *Guardian* fumed that this exhibition: *could scarcely have come at a worse time. In a climate of economic crisis we can hardly be expected to have much sympathy for the lord who is forced through economic straits to "transfer his flag to a smaller house". Who can raise a tear for the withering of the great estates at a time of land and housing shortage?*[65]

Andrew Saint praised Hugh Richardson's criticism of the exhibition as a 'vehicle of elitist self-congratulation' in the *New Statesman*, and attacked John Cornforth's report 'Country Houses in Britain – Can They Survive?' for placing:

*responsibility, to general upper-class contentment, upon government … though the owners bleat much about Labour's taxation policies, they cannot have it both ways: if they want government to help, they must pay more and accept the strings.*[66]

*The Times* and *Telegraph* were more cautiously supportive.

NADFAS members had been well briefed about 'the country house dilemma' and the effects of the proposed Capital Transfer and Wealth Tax then being discussed in Parliament. At a specially organised conference, attended by Marcus Binney, one of the major organisers of the exhibition, the effects of the tax were outlined and the 'fears that they would empty the country houses of their contents in order to pay them'.[67] The audience was encouraged to take action by writing to their local MPs, signing petitions, staging public meetings, adopting a country house, and involving local press and radio. NADFAS was in the right place at the right time to raise awareness of these threats, and do something practical to help.

It was at this time that NADFAS became involved with the public fight to save the contents of Mentmore Towers from being sold off. Following the death of the 6th Earl of Rosebery in 1973, the Labour government of James Callaghan refused to accept the contents *in lieu* of inheritance taxes, which would have turned the house into one of England's finest museums of European furniture, *objets d'art* and Victorian era architecture. The government was offered the house and contents for £2,000,000 but declined (the cost of half a mile of motorway). Patricia Fay organised a viewing of the house for six NADFAS members, just before the 'sale of the century' in 1977.

In 1974 Kathleen Wareham introduced the idea of National Days, to focus on different foreign influences on the fine and decorative arts. The events were held at key country houses throughout Britain, and so helped highlight their national importance, and particularly the value of having house and contents which could be seen together. The first year concentrated on Italy. In 1975 French Days were organised across the country, at Waddesdon, Goodwood, the Bowes Museum, Lady Lever Art Gallery and Audley End. Sheila Marshall remembers:

*packing hundreds of luncheon trays for the French Day at Audley End. This was executed rather like a surgical operation, with Kathleen as the surgeon giving out instructions for the contents of each package: tomato, roll, lettuce, cheese, paté, etc ... and we, the assistants, putting them neatly into the trays provided, covering firmly with polythene, and then stuffing them into large black bags ready for dispatch in cars to Audley End. We worked until 3am and were awakened at 5am to make the journey via the Dartford Tunnel to be there on time to prepare everything for the day.*[68]

## Tenth Anniversary Celebrations, 1978

Patricia's OBE, the continuing expansion of NADFAS, and the media climate that highlighted the importance of the country house, were all good reasons to celebrate ten years of NADFAS in 1978. Of the many suggestions circulated, a grand garden party at Cliveden in Buckinghamshire, the county which had seen the birth of the Chiltern Antiques Group was decided upon. The venue was Nadine Mitchell's idea. Ten years on from 'going national' there were 93 Societies, with a membership of 17,000. 'The Almighty must have been looking after NADFAS that day,' writes Sheila Marshall. 'It was the wettest summer on record, the 20th July 1978 was the only fine sunny and warm day in weeks of rain!'[69] The day began with a sherry reception at 11.30, and a welcome address by Pamela Cowen, the Chairman, and speeches by Patricia Fay and the President Sir Trenchard Cox. An exhibition of craftwork was open to view. As the programme reminded readers 'members of NADFAS are not only interested in things of the Past; through the Present they look forward to the Future'. To further this interest the work of four contemporary craftsmen was on display, chosen with the advice of the Crafts Advisory Committee: the batiks of Tamara Miles, the calligraphy of Ann Hechle, the jewellery of Matthew Tomalin and the knitting of Florence Hall. Lunch was at 1.20 pm. The Duchess of Kent arrived at 2 pm, and tea was served at 3.30 pm. As Pamela Cowen notes:

*The real heroine was Edna Johnson, who had co-ordinated the various committees and who fell and broke her leg shortly before the event but came gamely "on parade" and presented HRH with a posy she had picked at dawn that morning in her garden.*[70]

By the time of the NADFAS Heritage Conference in May 1979, it was clear that NADFAS was a serious player in the heritage world. Through the ideas, energy and action of NADFAS this conference brought together 61 organisations associated with British heritage, including the National Trust (founded 1895), the National Art Collections Fund (1903), the Georgian Group (1937) the Victorian Society (1958), the Historic Houses Association (1973), and the British Association for Friends of Museums (1975).

**Above**
NADFAS takes action. Delivering petitions to Parliament on the 'country house dilemma'. Included in the line-up are Lord Montagu (fifth from left), Sir Francis Dashwood (sixth from left) and then Honorary Secretary Nadine Mitchell (fourth from right)

Times too were changing, in the same month as the NADFAS conference Margaret Thatcher was elected as Prime Minister.

## The Death of Patricia Fay: Time for Consolidation

These well attended, high-profile conferences and events were set against a much gloomier background. 1978 was the 'Winter of Discontent', as the impact of the oil crisis hit Britain. The National Health Service, celebrating its 30th anniversary, was also in a state of collapse. There was a postal 'go slow' which meant that NADFAS letters, AGM and other papers never arrived on time, even when posted early, while rail strikes precluded members from reaching events they had planned to attend. The Queen's Christmas speech that year reflected the

chilly political and economic climate, and contained a particularly prophetic message for members of NADFAS:

*We must not let the difficulties of the present or the uncertainties of the future cause us to lose faith. Even if the problems seem overwhelming, there is always room for optimism. Every problem presents us with the opportunity both to find an answer for ourselves and to help others.*[71]

Nadine Mitchell, who had devoted herself tirelessly to the secretaryship 'of the fledging association… died of cancer in 1978'.[72] A notice in the *Financial Times* acknowledged that 'her driving force was one of the principal factors in building up the Association from a small local Society to its present membership of 18,000'.[73] A Memorial Service was held in October at Holy Trinity, Brompton, at which Patricia, confessing nerves to her friends, made a moving speech, emphasising how much NADFAS owed Nadine. Only a year later the NADFAS community was drawn together again, in the same place, this time to remember the life of Patricia Fay, which had been suddenly and quite unexpectedly taken. The shock waves were felt throughout the Association. Patricia was only 46 when she died. Had she lived one wonders how the story of NADFAS might have differed from its present form – her initiatives, and ideals, still remain the 'backbone' of the Association. The challenge was to live up to the pioneering spirit she had instilled.

As Kathleen Wareham stated: 'The most permanent memorial to Patricia will be the continual growth of her beloved NADFAS'.[74] In the year following her death the Patricia Fay Memorial Fund was founded to 'honour and perpetuate her memory'. The first NADFAS Memorial Lecture was given that year by the distinguished NADFAS lecturer, Eve King, which accompanied a private view of the Gainsborough exhibition at the Tate, with a special luncheon.

Patricia was not just remembered at a national level, other Societies remembered her in their own way. The Chiltern Society made their January lecture The Patricia Fay Memorial Lecture. The first appropriately coincided with the Society's own 15th anniversary. At that event Sir Oliver Millar, the president of the Chiltern Society, paid tribute to Patricia, 'Few young women in our time can have done more to give pleasure through enlightenment, to so many of her contemporaries'.[75] Mary Stirling, a former chairman of the Chiltern Society, made the plea, 'Already there are new Societies, or new members of old Societies, who scarcely knew her, and it is our duty to ensure that her achievement and high ideals are not forgotten'.[76]

## Action in the Eighties

Although Patricia had gone, NADFAS did not stand still. In 1981 the conference *Action in the Eighties – Communicating the Heritage* was staged. As June Fenwick, who chaired the conference stated, 'the Eighties

were to be a troubled decade which would demand sacrifices in all areas of the arts and education'. The title of the conference could equally well have been applied to what was happening to NADFAS more generally. In 1980 the hundredth Society, Beckenham, had been formed, and the NADFAS Constitution and Rules were revised, still retaining the original objects. In 1981, the first membership cards were introduced, and the following year the first full-time paid secretary was appointed, Rowena Mitchell. In 1983 the first NADFAS diary was published, now a central feature of many members' lives. In 1984 the first Society opened in mainland Europe at Rheindahlen. As Shirley Hewett noted in the Autumn *Newsletter* of that year, with the formation of the first overseas Society 'yet another of Patricia Fay's dreams have been realised'. Sydney followed in 1985, creating what was to become a sister network of Decorative and Fine Arts Societies in Australia. This was also the year that NADFAS Enterprises Limited was created. As part of the NADFAS mission to promote contemporary craft, a 'fashion and jewellery extravaganza' was organised at the Goldsmiths' Hall, in London, under the guidance of Jean Muir (1928-95), described as 'one of London's most influential and modern minimalists'.[77] The catsuit she designed as part of Diana Rigg's wardrobe for *The Avengers*, was to become a fashion icon. The event was a glittering success.

In 1988 the 200th Society was formed, Thames Estuary, and for the first time the AGM was held outside London, at Harrogate. This was partly the result of the astonishing expansion of NADFAS, which had outgrown the V&A Lecture Theatre which was not big enough to hold the representatives of the many new Societies. The following year NADFAS was to meet in Kensington Town Hall.  From the 1960s, when heritage and antiques were only at the periphery of public concern, 'Conservation and heritage were everyday words in the vocabulary of the eighties' and NADFAS was at the centre of this new world.[78]

NOTES

[1] Sheila Marshall, *Development of a Dream*, 1982, p.1.
[2] Mary Bourne, review of *Development of a Dream*, *The Lady*, 8 May 1984.
[3] 'Chiltern DFAS 40th Anniversary Recollections'.
[4] Edna Johnson, 'The Pioneer Years', *Chiltern DFAS Newsletter*, Patricia Fay Memorial Issue, no.26, Spring 1980, p.6.
[5] *Bucks Life*, August 1966, p.12.
[6] The Chiltern Antiques Group. Patricia Fay and the Origins of NADFAS as recollected by Elliott Viney, p.1, typescript marked 'Pamela from Elliott', July 2002, NADFAS Archives.
[7] Janet Deramore, 'Chiltern DFAS 40th Anniversary Recollections'.
[8] Sheila Marshall, 'History of the *Directory of Lecturers*' from *1969*, 1987, p.1.
[9] Helen Lowenthal, 'Tribute to Patricia Fay', *April 1988*, as read by Sheila Marshall at Patricia Fay Memorial Dinner, Harrogate, 25 April 1988, NADFAS Archives.
[10] Helen Lowenthal, Obituary, *The Times*, 5 April 1993.
[11] Founded in 1952 as the Attingham Summer School Trust and named after the great neo-classical house in Shropshire at which the Summer School was first held, it offers a special insight into one of Britain's greatest contributions to Western art: the country house, together with its collections and landscape setting, as well as the development of the royal palace in England.
[12] Speech at Patricia Fay Memorial dinner, Harrogate April 1988.
[13] Chairman's Speech at the Inaugural Meeting of NADFAS, 28 May 1968, NADFAS Archives.
[14] Patricia Fay Memorial Fund leaflet c.1980, NADFAS Archives.
[15] Kirsten Cubitt, 'Fine arts and hen parties', *The Times*, 20 July 1971. This article produced 152 letters of enquiry from those interested in joining NADFAS.
[16] Marshall, op. cit., p.2.
[17] *Dictionary of Art Historians* online: www.dictionaryofarthistorians.org/coxt.
[18] 40th Anniversary, op. cit.
[19] Ibid.
[20] Kirsty Wheeler, early founder member of Chiltern Antiques Group in 'Chiltern DFAS 40th Anniversary' *Recollections*, NADFAS Archives.
[21] *The Times*, Monday 10 January, 1966.
[22] *The Times*, 3 November 1966, quoted in 'Chiltern DFAS 40th Anniversary Recollections', NADFAS Archives.
[23] Diana Good, 17 July 2006.
[24] Patty Brooks, 10 August 2006.
[25] Viney, op. cit., p.4
[26] *NADFAS Review*, 2006.
[27] Chita Laurie 'How It All Began', *HDFAG Newsletter*, November 1998.
[28] NADFAS *Newsletter*, January 1971.
[29] Viney, op. cit., p.2
[30] *The Chiltern Antiques Group. Patricia Fay and the Origins of NADFAS*, op. cit. p.2
[31] Anne White, 'The 1st Thirty Years, A Personal Reflection by Anne White, Founder Chairman, South West London DFAS', 10 January 2002.
[32] Chairman's Speech at the Inaugural Meeting of NADFAS 28 June 1968, NADFAS Archives.
[33] Marshall, op. cit., p.33.
[34] *Sunday Express*, 31 March 1968.
[35] Harrogate DFAG Archives, Scrapbook, vol.1.
[36] 'A new society', *Ideal Home*, June 1968.
[37] 'Jane Downes 1977-1981', *History of the VCC*, 1988, p.11.

[38] Anne Simpson reporting on the foundation of Harrogate DFAG, *Yorkshire Post*, June 1968. Harrogate DFAS Scrapbook vol.1.
[39] Ex.Co. Minutes, 6 Feb 1968, NADFAS Archives. It was only in 1988 that the National Chairman Shirley Hewett discovered that it was 'an ordinary border to be found in any Stationers' Directory and could therefore be used by anyone', presenting problems of protecting copyright for NADFAS.
[40] NADFAS *Occasional Newsletter*, no.1, January 1968, NADFAS Archives.
[41] N.M.C., 'Collectors, Unite!', *Harper's Bazaar*, May 1968.
[42] *The Times*, 10 January 1966.
[43] NADFAS *Newsletter*, 1 June 1970. Harrow DFAS is 'a most active Society with many young members, who bring their small children to the meetings and place them in a crèche provided by the Society. This innovation has proved very successful'.
[44] 'Chairman's speech at the inaugural meeting of NADFAS 28 May 1968', NADFAS Archives.
[45] Cubitt, op. cit.
[46] Chairman's report, 'Why NADFAS', 1967/8, NADFAS Archives.
[47] Cubitt, op. cit.
[48] Report, 1968, op. cit.
[49] Marshall, op. cit., p.4
[50] Ex.Co. Minutes, 23 September 1968, NADFAS Archives.
[51] Glenys Roberts, 'How we became generation sex', *You*, 15 October 1985, p.27.
[52] Judith Doyle, 'How to Learn More about Antiques', *Croydon Advertiser*, October 1968.
[53] Summary of Chairmen's Meeting, November 1970. Private Collection.
[54] Marshall, op. cit., p.22.
[55] Jean Ward, Test Valley DFAS, 19 July 2006.
[56] Rosemary Horton, Devon DFAS, July 2006.
[57] Pamela Percy, West Essex DFAS, July 2006.
[58] Cubitt, op. cit.
[59] First Five Years Conference, 1973, NADFAS Archives.
[60] 'Handmaidens of the Arts', *Country Life*, 18 October 1974.
[61] *Art & Antiques*, 16 June 1973.
[62] *Bucks Examiner*, 3 January 1975.
[63] R. Strong, M. Binney & J. Harris, *The Destruction of the Country House*, 1875-1975, London 1974.
[64] *The Times*, 'Lost Country Mansions', 11 October 1974.
[65] Caroline Tisdall, 'Country Homes', Review, the *Guardian*, 9 October 1974.
[66] Letters to the Editor, *New Statesman*, 20 December 1974, p.898 quoting Hugh Richardson, 'Going, Going, Gone: Another View', *New Statesman*, 22 October 1974.
[67] Margaret Flory in 'Claremont DFAS First Thirty Years', 2005, p.4.
[68] Marshall, op. cit., p.39.
[69] Ibid., p.47.
[70] Pamela Cowen, Chairman's Report 1978-80, NADFAS Archives.
[71] www.qmmemorial.gov.uk/output/page4630.
[72] Report 1978-80, op.cit.
[73] Lady Pickering, *Financial Times*, 11 October 1978.
[74] NADFAS *Newsletter*, January 1980.
[75] Sir Oliver Millar, 'Patricia Fay and Her Achievement', in *Chiltern DFAS Newsletter*, no.26, Spring 1980, p.5.
[76] Mary Stirling, 'Guardian of a Legacy' in *Chiltern DFAS Newsletter*, no.26, Spring 1980, p.8.
[77] *The New York Times*, February 1982.
[78] Cath Pepinster, 'Looking after the future by preserving the past', *Advertiser*, 16 January 1985, p.13.

# 2
# Shared Experiences:
## *Setting up a Society*

*'Societies have sprung up like mushrooms all over the country'*
Selina Sinker, 'Discovering NADFAS', *Hunting Group Review*, August 1983

The success of NADFAS, it has been said, lies in the 'blueprint' for setting up a Society that was established by the Chiltern Antiques Group back in 1965.

In reality, it is more like a great recipe that can be adapted to suit the particular cook and consumers. The organisational structure is sufficiently rigorous to provide a professional approach, something that Patricia Fay was adamant to maintain, yet flexible enough for individual Societies to adapt to their own members' requirements, and add their own ingredients. It is now time to look at this recipe from the varied perspectives of the Societies themselves, to see how the guidelines have been interpreted, revealing the common denominators as well as the unique aspects of them – the secret of the NADFAS success story. As the lecturer Nancy Armstrong observed, a NADFAS Society is 'entirely autonomous ... [and] had to be separately created and born, an enterprising chairman found, a hard-working committee formed'.[1] Each Society has its own story, linked to that

of the Association as a whole. Their stories are part of the whole story, different facets of a larger jewel. The following chapter is based on the many contributions sent in by individual Societies. It draws its structure from the common themes emerging from the material, and the detail reflects the shared experience of setting up a Society.[2]

## People: Founders
*'Many a "lesser breed" would have given up in the face of the difficulties which they had to overcome'*
**Hannah Gould, Enfield DFAS**
How then does a new Society emerge? Nearly always through the influence of a powerful personality. Many of the early Societies were founded by individuals associated with the first few groups to set up, via personal contact and mutual acquaintance. The founders were energetic, persuasive and determined to 'spread the word'. First and foremost it was Patricia Fay's own enthusiasm and dedication that helped promote the development of new Societies in

**Above**

A 'new facet of a larger jewel': Members of Sparkenhoe Arts Society – one of the most recent Societies – celebrate their inaugural meeting

the early years. In the previous chapter we have seen how Diana Good, Lally Robinson and Chita Hutton-Wilson started Thame, Thames and Harrogate Groups via their meeting with Patricia. Sheila Marshall explained that her 'own introduction to Patricia was, I am sure, typical of other people's reactions ... In 1967, we in Thanet had the same kind of idea in a more modest way of learning about the fine arts'.[3] They, like the Chiltern Group had contacted the Victoria & Albert Museum, who in turn put them in touch with Patricia. Within weeks they had received Patricia's handbook, *Managing a Decorative and Fine Arts Society*, and the *Directory of Lecturers*. Thanet Antiques and Fine Art Group held their inaugural meeting at an elegant cliff top hotel, the Fayreness in Broadstairs, Kent, on 8 February 1968, at 11.00 am. Patricia Fay came to the launch and it is said that 'she gave a splendid talk and fired all the members with her great enthusiasm'.[4] The first lecture was given on 25 April 1968 by Helen Lowenthal, on 'Houses owned by the National Trust'. Moor

Park Society followed Thanet, when Margaret Bunford got to know Patricia Fay because their daughters attended the same school. Patricia introduced Margaret to Adele Schaverien, and the two of them started the seventh Society, Moor Park.[5] Patricia's evangelising spirit encouraged others to promote the setting up of NADFAS Societies, Samlesbury DFAS for example owes its formation to a close family friendship between founder member Jo Jackson and Lally Robinson.[6]

There were many other forceful and determined ladies across the country who could see the possibilities and pleasures that NADFAS offered. Corinthia Arbuthnot-Lane, described as 'a truly remarkable lady' assisted by 'the enthusiasm of a small group of her friends' was behind the foundation of Enfield DFAS.[7] Hannah Gould, the past chairman and president of this Society, emphasises that 'many a "lesser breed" would have given up in the face of the difficulties which they had to overcome', and draws a vivid picture of the obstacles they confronted. In the early days:

*They had no finances, except what they provided, no equipment except that on loan from members. They had to find their own lecturers and try to remain solvent. They lived a "hand-to-mouth" existence, frequently unable to meet their just dues and demands to NADFAS – even having to subsidise funds to pay the rent and lecturers' fees.*[8]

Françoise White had already had an action-packed life before she turned her attention to creating a DFAS in Henley. She had been in the Belgian Resistance during the Second World War, and went on to set up the Charity *Lifeline* supporting displaced persons. She then joined the WI after moving to Chalfont St. Giles with her second husband. In 1977 'she took the WI membership with her *en masse*' when she set up Henley DFAS, recruiting, 'or some might say press ganging' her friends on to the committee.[9] From little seeds forests do grow: Henley is now the third largest Society in the country. The founder of New Forest DFAS, Patricia Hallett, 'is truly one of the people without whom NADFAS would not be the organisation it is'.[10] After an eventful life,

much of which was spent overseas, Patricia and her family returned to England and, 'once the children were grown up, I applied my time and energy to starting up branches of NADFAS in the New Forest Area'.[11] 'The determination and persistence of Enid Munson' led to the foundation of Abingdon DFAS[12], while a cliff top walk in 1978 inspired Margaret Kennedy Scott to start the East Suffolk Society.[13] Jean Pace of Teme Valley DFAS presents a wonderful portrait of their founder Helen Fielden, who had 'pragmatic motives' for setting up their Society, 'firstly, she was tired of driving long distances to hear other groups' lecturers and secondly, it was thought that the group would provide a suitable alternative occupation for the wives who did not hunt'.[14] Her meticulous notes, revealing hard work, humour and charisma, have proved a wonderful source for reconstructing the monthly running of a Society.

Those who were already busy on the National Committee, also found time to support and run their own Societies, as they still do. This is important as it keeps the local and specific needs of Societies in the forefront of national policy making. Helen Lowenthal, so influential in the early days, went on to set up the Westminster Society, advertised as 'a new art society in Belgravia' which:

*might be specially helpful to those who come from abroad and who are here for a limited period. They may well welcome an opportunity to learn more of what London can offer to the art lover, and to enjoy meeting neighbours.*[15]

The meetings were timed to fit in with embassy cocktail parties.

The advertising which Patricia promoted, with countless local and national newspaper and magazine articles on NADFAS, proved to be a promotional strategy that worked, leading to the creation of many new Societies. The stimulus for founding East Hertfordshire DFAS was 'an article in the newspaper about an Arts Group which Patricia Fay had started near Rickmansworth'.[16] Diana Straghan saw the article and telephoned her friend, Mary Beazley to ask 'if she had read it (she had!) and invited her to tea to discuss how they could form one in Broxbourne. Together they thought of six friends who might be interested, and these six were asked to write down twenty names of people who they thought might be interested'. The result was a list of sixty people.

Once the core group of Societies had been established, their success stimulated the growth of others via 'the inevitable waiting list' of existing Societies.[17] Those frustrated with being put on a waiting list were inspired to set up their own groups. There is therefore a spirit not of competition, but of co-operation between neighbouring Societies. For example

**Left**
Front cover of a history of Claremont DFAS showing Henry Holland's design for the house where members have met since 1975

THE INAUGURAL MEETING OF THE

# West Wycombe Decorative & Fine Arts Society

(MEMBER SOCIETY OF NADFAS)

will be held on

**WEDNESDAY, 17th SEPTEMBER 1975 at 10.15 a.m.**

AT WEST WYCOMBE HOUSE

(By kind permission of Sir Francis Dashwood, Bart)

## HELEN LOWENTHAL, O.B.E.

will give an illustrated lecture entitled

*THE GRAND TOUR—THEN AND NOW*

Those who wish to, may join the WWDFAS at this meeting by paying their year's subscription of £3.50 at the door. For further information apply to—

Mrs. Joan Hawkins, Old Court, Westfields, Whiteleaf
Tel. Princes Risborough 5085

DELNEVO *printers*

**Above**
Flyer advertising the launch of West Wycombe DFAS in 1975

when Basingstoke DFAS was launched, representatives from nearby Societies, particularly Newbury, attended the inaugural meeting, in acknowledgment of 'their invaluable help and advice'.[18] Bancrofts DFAS was set up in 1979, as the nearby West Essex Society had a long waiting list. Epsom DFAS was formed in 1988 in response to a plea from the chairman of Ashtead. The 'birth mother' of Arden DFAS was the Solihull Society. In 1995 Solihull 'had a large list of no-hopers patiently waiting for membership'.[19] When the 'intrepid adventurers of Ealing', four close friends, found all the Decorative and Fine Arts Societies nearby had long waiting lists, they decided to set up their own DFAS in 1998.[20]

This 'mushroom effect' means that it is often possible to work out the evolution of a network of Societies over time.[21] For example the 'clutch' of Societies in the West Surrey Area began with West Surrey DFAS in January 1969. Margaret Saunders, chairman of Shalford DFAS, explained how the great demand for Decorative and Fine Arts Societies in the area created pressure to form new ones. At West Surrey 'The waiting list grew rapidly from its inception to an embarrassing number of 300-plus'. In 1972 the Godalming group was formed, and the following year West Surrey DFAS Thursday Group (now called Shalford). By its second meeting, only a fortnight later, membership was already full. With a waiting list of over 100 by 1979, and the Tuesday (original) group having a similar list it is not surprising that Guildford Evening DFAS was started. Other local groups were formed in the following years at Farnham, Cranleigh and Woking (all within a few miles of Shalford).[22] The Wey Valley group was started from the waiting lists of both original West Surrey Societies, and uses the same venue – Shalford Village Hall.[23]

The story of the growth of the West Surrey Societies is not unique. Since 1981 four Societies have evolved from Guildford.[24] Guildford had 70 members from the Woking area and a long waiting list. Katie Butcher, its chairman, formed a steering committee, and the Woking Society was inaugurated in 1989. It soon became clear that another Society was needed and Mayford started in 1993. Such was its popularity that Geoffrey Cuttle, its first chairman set about starting a new Society in Weybridge. Even before the inaugural meeting there was a waiting list of more than 100, precipitating the formation of Walton and Hersham in 2003. 'Back in the summer of 1994, to be able to join the local DFAS the wait was several years. The idea of forming a new Society was put to Susan Oaten by Sheila Russell, they both loved the arts, as did their friends'. That summer Surrey Heath DFAS was born.[25]

The moving-on of members also had its impact. Hazel Kibble, a founder member of the West Surrey Society moved to Burton Bradstock in Dorset. The nearest NADFAS Society was Dorchester (Dorset County DFAS) in the east and Honiton in the west. Hazel's solution was to set up West Dorset DFAS in Bridport. 'On taking out an advertisement in the local paper' she was 'amazed to find so many ex-NADFAS members now retired to Dorset'.[26]

Sometimes just hearing a NADFAS lecture is enough to trigger the formation of a Society. Susan Sloan remembers that the spur to form Havering DFAS was listening to Eve King give a lecture in 1971:

*I had never heard of NADFAS until then, and I so enjoyed the lecture that I made extensive enquiries about the Society ... I approached West Essex Society ... but there was a three-year waiting list. I contacted Mid-Essex Society; there was a two year waiting list. "Why don't you start your own Society?" I was asked.*

The inaugural meeting took place in 1973.[27] When Joan Hawkins attended an event at the Vale of Aylesbury DFAS in 1975, to hear a lecture on J.M.W. Turner, she was entranced. Having volunteered to help guide at the Royal Academy, one of the early volunteer projects, she became an Associate Member of NADFAS, and at the Waddesdon 'French Day' she was pressed by Patricia to form a Society. Joan explains, 'I must tell you that Patricia was a truly wonderful person. She looked young and lovely and had a most charming manner – she really was irresistible – and to cut a long story short I eventually agreed to found what came to be known as the West Wycombe Society'.[28] Anne Hopkinson's experience was similar. When she heard a NADFAS lecture in Sheffield she was so impressed, she tried to locate a branch closer to home and failed. Her friends encouraged her to start a new Society, although others 'said at the time "It will never take off in Worksop!"' How wrong they were. Dukeries DFAS is thriving.[29]

The influence of NADFAS Area Representatives, later called Area Chairmen, was crucial in encouraging new Societies. For example when Hilda Singleton moved from Newmarket (where she had been on the DFAS committee) to North Norfolk she was persuaded by Sylvia Horwood-Smart, the member of the Executive Committee representing the Areas, to set up the Glaven Valley Society. Sylvia took her role on the New Societies Sub-Committee seriously and energetically, as she became the founder chairman of West Suffolk in 1972, Newmarket in 1976, Saffron Walden in 1978 and Ely in 1984. She was on the first committee of Bury St Edmunds in 1990, and also helped with the setting up of Colchester, Deben, Diss, Ipswich, Kings Lynn, South Suffolk, Sudbury and Wensum, as well as Glaven Valley, Societies.[30]

## The Steering Committee
*'I wonder how they will all get on?'*
**Margaret Nangle, Wey Valley DFAS**

The first practical task in turning the idea of a Society into reality involves finding a steering committee. The strategies for doing this vary from serendipity to press-ganging! The founder members of Skipton and Wharfedale DFAS were 'at the time ... attending a Leeds extra mural class on the history of art being held in Skipton and from this class drew interested members to form a steering committee'.[31] Jane Harman and Elaine Graham were 'rather dazed' after leaving a preliminary meeting to explore the possibility of setting up a DFAS in Egerton, 'finding that we were a steering committee'.[32] Elizabeth Arrowsmith recalls that Jay Atkinson, chairman of Liverpool DFAS, 'refused to leave a meeting until we had established our first committee' for Samlesbury DFAS.[33] Keith Hasnip, a former chairman of Abingdon DFAS, remembers that the first problem 'was to find a willing chairman, but once a volunteer had been found it was easy to form a ten man team, although from memory eight of these were women'.[34] Shirley Hewett, a founder of Mendip DFAS, formed in 1981, recalls that:

*jobs were allotted with some amusement; if you were the lucky owner of a typewriter you were the obvious hon secretary; if you were competent in mathematics you were the treasurer and, with*

**Above**
Founders of Felsted DFAS: Tony Eggleston, painted by Balfour Bowen; Trevor Goodman; and Charles Warren

*a very small amount of confidence, I found myself in the hot seat as chairman.*[35]

'You're about the right height' murmured the gentleman who stood beside Jenny Colmer at the first committee meeting, 'can you count?' he asked. She could, and so became the first treasurer of Cirencester DFAS.[36] The chairman of Sherborne DFAS describes the founding committee as being:

*middle-aged and exclusively feminine, though later we would recruit a male treasurer. Typically of our generation, some had given up their careers on marriage, others, mostly unmarried, had held responsible jobs. This mixture produced both enthusiasm and expertise.*[37]

At the first committee meeting of the Wey Valley Society, Margaret Nangle, the hostess 'glanced down the table at those determined faces [and] thought ... I wonder how they will all get on, especially as most of them do not know each other'. Under the leadership of Valerie Ford they did.[38]

## Creating a Membership
*'Where are we going to put them all?'*
**Peter Vermeylen, Beaconsfield DFAS**
The booklet *Managing a Decorative and Fine Arts Society* advises that 'to form a Society' approximately 150 or more members are required. So the first job of a steering committee is to entice members to join up, and various strategies are employed to do this. After telephoning NADFAS Head Office to volunteer to form a new Society in the Royal Leamington Spa area, Catherine Leahy explained that it was:

*Then the fun started. I was to gather a list of 100 people willing to join. Our Christmas card list was not very helpful, so I made a list of likely friends from the choir, church, my husband's Lions' [club] wives and neighbours.*

The Ealing ladies adopted a similar tactic, and 'scoured through their little black address books' for names of those who might be interested in forming a local DFAS.[39] At Chichester 'once the committee was formed it was agreed that each member should invite 10 people each to see if they too would be willing to become members. In a short time the Society had a waiting list'.[40] 'It was with

some trepidation', writes Peter Vermeylen, chairman of Beaconsfield DFAS, 'that those of us who had gathered to form a steering committee arrived in [the] Hall on the morning of 3 July 1986 for the Inaugural coffee morning. Our fears were allayed, our first question was "where are we all going to put them all?".[41]

Another tactic is to advertise. Sometimes this is not successful, as the steering committee of Skipton and Wharfedale Society discovered: 'After receiving information from NADFAS HQ, and a visit from Patricia Mackrill from the National Executive, an article [was published] in the local newspaper, bringing poor response'. The committee members decided that personal contact with people in the area would be more efficacious, and as a result 60 potential members emerged.[42]

Claremont DFAS pioneered a new type of DFAS, the collegiate Society, which in principle guaranteed a membership. Addressing the NADFAS mission to involve the young, the setting up of a Society based in a school was an exciting and novel idea. As Margaret Flory, the founder chairman, was a friend of the Headmistress of Claremont, it seemed natural to use the school as a venue. The Headmistress and Bursar were ex-officio members of the committee, and 'there would be no charge for the venue and up to fifty senior girls could attend [meetings, held in term] if they wished'. Although other collegiate Societies were to be formed (Rugby the following year in 1977, Felsted in 1978, Bancrofts in 1979), the experiment at Claremont was not a success, as the 'pupils found it difficult to attend week-day evening lectures because of their heavy work load [and the Society's membership understandably wanted more lectures per year]'.[43]

Many of the early Societies were exclusively female. In the early days Diana Good kept the Thames Fine Arts Society as a 'ladies only' group as she felt that we were a serious lot, joining out of genuine interest and not for social reasons, it also meant that one could go straight from the kitchen sink or garden without dressing up to impress the opposite sex – as can happen!'.[44] Others, like North Kent DFAS, encouraged the involvement of men from the beginning. It is misleading to assume that all NADFAS Societies were and are all dominated by the ladies. As the lecturer, Clyde Binfield, warns 'It is also fatally dangerous to stereotype NADFAS'.[45] Felsted DFAS was founded in 1978 by a group of gentlemen, the Headmaster of Felsted School, Tony Eggleston, with the help of Trevor Goodman, Head of Art, the NADFAS lecturer and painter, Balfour Bowen, and the retired paediatrician, mountaineer and art collector Charles Warren.[46] Robert Hartland, chairman of Chipstead DFAS, reports that:

*This Society, founded in 1988, seems to be somewhat different from most, one third of its members are men. Indeed the Society was founded by a group of men and for many years the committee was made up of men with only occasional women. In its 19 years there have been five chairmen, four of them men.*

It is also misleading to assume that areas of dense population support the largest DFAS membership. Oxford has never had a DFAS, while 'Sherborne, with only some 10,000 people, supports one of the largest NADFAS Societies in the country – over 650-plus waiting list'.[47]

## Place: Finding a Venue
### *'The only thing needed was a suitable meeting place'*
**Doreen Wadsworth, Saltaire DFAS**
Finding a space large enough to sit at least 200, that has adequate parking space, that can be booked on a regular basis with certainty for at least two years ahead, that can be 'blacked-out' for slides, that does not cost an-arm-and-a-leg to hire, and has preferably space and facilities to serve refreshments, can be quite a challenge to find. As a result NADFAS members meet in a huge variety of places, from arts, conference and community centres, cinemas, golf and rugby clubs, church, civic, masonic, college and school halls; hotels, laboratories, literary institutes, galleries, museums, racecourses and theatres – all transformed by NADFAS committee members

each month into a (usually) warm and welcoming space. Flower arrangements and embroidered lectern cloths customise the meeting place for the few hours each month that NADFAS occupies it. 'Our lecture hall is always enhanced with an excellent floral display,' writes one committee member 'as well as good coffee and biscuits'.[48] 'One of the major problems from the outset' for Beaconsfield DFAS 'was the lack of a really suitable hall in which to hold the meetings'.[49] Sherborne DFAS:

*had a year to get started, and the first problem was the venue. The Digby Hall, the main one in Sherborne, could not, at that point, guarantee us a set day each month, so we booked the smaller Digby Memorial Hall. Then we found that its blackout did not fully protect the platform from the afternoon sun, so we paid to get extra blinds made. Only five years later we needed to move to the larger hall.[50]*

The chairman of Saltaire DFAS remembers that after gathering a steering committee together:

**Above**

Members of Hallamshire DFAS at the Yorkshire Sculpture Park in 2006 considering Henry Moore's *Reclining Figure: Arch Leg* (1969/70)

*the only thing needed was a suitable meeting place ... That sounded easy enough to find, but in fact proved very difficult ... it took about two years, during which time many venues were visited and assessed. At times the outlook seemed hopeless, until by sheer good luck the newly refurbished Victoria Hall in Saltaire became available. The magnificent hall had been built in the 19th century by Sir Titus Salt in the village he had created to house his workers at his huge mills built for spinning and weaving alpaca fibre – the hall is part of the World Heritage site, and has proved a fitting venue for our DFAS.*[51]

Many other Societies gather in prestigious places, for example Stamford meets in the beautiful Georgian Theatre, now an Arts Centre. Claremont Society is named after the Henry Holland House where the group first met. The 'lectures were held in the original drawing room of the house [now the school library] and slides were projected directly onto the wall'.[52] Hampstead Heath DFAS assemble in the grand lecture room of Kenwood House. Granta originally met at the imposing red-brick College at Girton, with the College's Mistress, Baroness Warnock, as their first president. Liverpool DFAS, which started life as Merseyside Antiques and Fine Arts Society, meet at the Walker Art Gallery surrounded by local works of art. Mayford DFAS members meet in the Ambassadors Cinema in Woking with padded seats and air conditioning, while Helmsley DFAS gather in the delightful Quaker Meeting House, built in 1812. The spacious Hicks Building, part of Sheffield University, hosts Hallamshire DFAS meetings, others gather in village halls and community centres. Many committee members have to be resourceful, devising all manner of innovative systems for 'black-out' which could probably be patented! However what matters is the membership, the quality of the lectures, and the atmosphere created.

## Performance: Equipment
### 'The projectionist has had a very trying time!'
### Helen Fielden, Teme Valley DFAS

After finding a suitable venue the next hurdle is usually a technical one, obtaining access to audio-visual equipment, whether by begging, borrowing, buying or hiring. The purchase of a projector is usually the single most expensive item on a new Society's shopping list. Perhaps the most nerve-wracking moments of all DFAS groups centre on this area of 'setting up a Society'. Patricia Hallett and her committee felt that 'we were all taking a risk, but each gave a loan of £10 towards the purchase of a projector'.[53] The Upper Thames Valley Society held a coffee morning 'and this raised £70 – enough to contemplate buying a projector'.[54] Joan Hawkins remembers that 'Until we had sufficient members' subscriptions to be able to pay for all our expenses we could not afford to buy a projector .... [so] we used to hire a man who brought his own equipment. He always arrived drunk and my heart used to be in my mouth as I watched him swaying about'.[55]

The next problem is finding someone willing to take on the responsibility for this equipment. Helen Fielden's note of thanks at an 1981 meeting of Teme Valley DFAS conveys a vivid impression of the tensions of the job, without going into detail: 'The projectionist has had a trying time and I hope she will not be put off by it all and be able to forget this season's difficulties. We are grateful to her for her patience'.[56] For one Society 'Our worst "down" was when our faithful and meticulous projectionist went on holiday and forgot to tell us. Amazingly our lecture started only twenty minutes late'.[57]

As Jean Pratt of Birmingham DFAS explains from personal experience, the role of the projectionist can be enjoyable, but is certainly not relaxing. Operating the projector is only part of the job, as she is also 'at the beck and call of everybody' and is also:

*an interceptor of latecomers who erupt puffing and panting into the darkness, summoner of first aid for the faint, escorter-out of those with coughing fits; bearer of messages re sound to those behind the scenes and out of earshot; dowser of lights, and even on one occasion a straight man to a musical lady.*

The words of advice she passes on surely echo the experience of others:

*Remember to pack a nail-file (to tweak tiny switch if necessary), and eyebrow tweezers (in case of surgical operation, to remove a slide from the bowels of the machinery ...), always put the cover back on the carousel – otherwise slides have a disconcerting habit of flying about in every direction to general confusion ... Never, never, pick up a carousel of slides without turning it upside down and making sure the base plate is in the 'O' position ... to one principle I adhere rigidly ... NOT to interfere in any way, with the slides (unless catastrophe strikes!).*

But she asks:

*Are our days numbered? Our branch had its first digital lecture recently. It was a revelation ... so relaxing. ... though there were times when I felt a tingle in my hand and longed for the focus knob under my fingers! Present projectors continue to work on a wing and a prayer – serviced by good friends who are finding replacement parts more and more difficult to obtain. Inevitably, and insidiously, PowerPoint will become the norm and we, projectionists of a bygone age, will wither and die – our skills forgotten!'*[58]

## The Inaugural Meeting
### *'All should have been well'*
**Pamela Cowen, Camberley DFAS**

The experiences of Regents Park DFAS, on the day of their first lecture, must be familiar to many. 'Controlled panic set in as the date of the inaugural meeting approached. Would the lecturer ... turn up? Would everyone be able to find a place? Was the heating adequate? Would bad weather deter the less hardy? Would there be enough coffee to go round?' The lecture room of the Zoological Society also had its own unique cause of worry: 'Would the smell of gerbils (or worse?) wafting from the adjoining laboratory prove too much for the more sensitive souls?'[59]

The founding chairman of West Wycombe DFAS remembers that:

*By the time the 17 September 1975 dawned – the day of the inaugural meeting – I had 58 paid up Members and only three members on the Committee, including myself! 72 beautiful gilt chairs had been set out in the Saloon of West Wycombe Park and cars began to drive up. More and more cars appeared and Lady Dashwood became agitated. We had to rush around the house and down to the cellars to fetch more*

*chairs, as over 120 people eventually attended.*

Once the lecture was over, the committee's worries were not. The Chairman of NADFAS, Kathleen Wareham, had driven their speaker, Helen Lowenthal, down from London, and proceeded to drive to lunch which had been arranged at a nearby hotel. Unfortunately Kathleen failed to notice the lead car turning off:

*With all the other cars following ... it was some little time [before Joan Hawkins] could start in pursuit, leaving instructions to keep our guests drinking (at her expense!) till she returned with or without the lecturer. Needless to say she never found them in the maze of High Wycombe and when they [Helen and Kathleen] realised they were lost decided to return to London as Helen Lowenthal had another appointment in the afternoon.*

Pamela Cowen records how 'Foresight did not help our Saga' at the maiden lecture of her own Society, Camberley.[60] Her story is worth repeating at length, for it proves that no matter how hard you plan, something can always go wrong. However when things do go awry, the resilience and resourcefulness of the NADFAS spirit of both Society and lecturer shine through. Pamela explained that:

*All should have been well for the committee were all previously members of a neighbouring NADFAS Society, and very efficient, keen and devoted. We hired a suitable hall that also had more than adequate parking, we borrowed the projector and screen from our neighbour Society, I was to give the talk so that there would be no lecturer's fee, and the committee had prepared a good buffet lunch.*

However two days before the meeting 'the caretaker of the hall telephoned to say that there would be no electricity, but a generator could be hired locally'. This was done, but on the day when Pamela arrived at the hall she found 'all the windows had been removed ... by the double-glazing company who had unexpectedly turned up'. With great spirit she rushed round the complex of buildings to find a spare room suitable for showing slides, and found the squash court, into which all the chairs were moved. Pamela's troubles were not to end here. A test of the projector

produced a quick succession of fused bulbs, caused by the power 'pulse' of the generator. Pamela rallied, and decided to abandon her lecture on *Porcelain at the Vyne*, a lecture impossible to give without slides, for a talk on Church Recording. As lunch was concluding a helpful lady said that she had heard that the electricity would be on in 20-30 minutes, so it was back to the Porcelain lecture, only to find that the electricity was not in fact to be restored until 4 pm. Back to Church Recording. With the aid of hurricane lamps the audience found their seats, and the lights came on!

The audience of Thanet DFAS faced a rather different problem at their inaugural meeting in 1968, as 'the lecturer, when confronted with an audience of enthusiastic young women, could not get started, but once he did, stopping him became a

**Left** Kenwood House is the impressive venue for Hampstead Heath DFAS meetings, while Granta DFAS originally met at Girton College, Cambridge (pictured above)

problem'.[61] The minutes of West Essex DFAS record that after their own first meeting in 1970, it was noted that 'The cars were very badly parked and next time a member of the committee will go outside and see that it is done more satisfactorily'.[62]

Anne Stevens, the founder of the Cotswold Antiques Study Group, reported that 'Since the inaugural meeting [in January 1969] numbers have grown and we now have a membership of 130', and a waiting list had to be created. The annual subscription was two guineas.[63]

With the first lecture a success, a routine is usually created, ensuring regular smooth running of the monthly programme. The notes kept by one chairman include a check list for the person who had to step into her shoes at one meeting. They reflect some of the numerous tasks and careful preparation that are required:

*Just before the meeting, check that ... the projectionist is alright and ready to go, that Hermione will be there to pay the speaker, and will bring the new lectern and clip-on light, that Peggy is set to deal with the tea and is bringing tea/sugar/biscuits/milk ... glass cloths/fairy liquid/mop and glass for the speaker. Confirm with Lois that we can get into the cupboard that holds the china and the teaspoons, that someone fusses over the projectionist and gives him his tea, that Hermione can still meet the speaker, take the pointer to the speaker, and check with Olive if there are any notices ...* [64]

NADFAS meetings quickly settle into a pattern, combining education, entertainment and sociability in different measures depending on the character of the membership. Occasionally a group can be so absorbed that it is difficult for new members to assimilate. 'Can you be more FRIENDLY to those members you see at meetings whom you don't know?' asked one chairman:

*I don't mean KISS your next door neighbour as you do in church, or even shake hands but talk to everyone who appears to be on their own ... I know you come here partly to meet your friends and that we don't mean to be off-hand or snooty but we evidently give that impression to the outside world.*[65]

## Going Further

***'They will generally go out two or three times a year en masse to a house or a collection of especial interest to members'*** **Kirsten Cubitt, The Times, 1971**

The idea of not being satisfied with a monthly lecture was one of the novel aspects of DFAS groups, compared with other types of society. Patricia Fay stated that:

*Through our study group courses we have embarked on a long road of continuous learning and thus equipping ourselves to make a small contribution to the upkeep of historic house contents. Also in order to balance our activities, we need a relief from celluloid and sermons.*[66]

NADFAS-wide Study of Style courses were introduced in 1971, organised by Jane Osmanston, but individual Societies had been running Study Days from their beginning.

Although NADFAS groups begin with just lectures they soon become more adventurous, organising visits and study days to complement and expand upon them. As Chris Stanners explained in her chairman's Report to Chiltern DFAS in 2006, 'Study groups are a unique feature of a DFAS'.[67] It is true however that anyone 'who has not actually been involved in the running of such a Society cannot fully appreciate how much work goes into each event – lecture, local visit or full day tour'.[68] Study days often lead to visits, all part of the wider aim to broaden the membership's horizons. NADFAS groups 'generally go out two or three times a year *en masse* to a house or a collection of especial interest to members' reported a journalist in 1971 and:

*More ambitious Societies are taking parties as far afield this year as Holland and the Loire and for several days at a time, leaving homebound children and husbands to the tender mercies of 'au pairs' or the deep freeze.*

The Moor Park Society seem to have been a keen lot, as the chairman reported in their third year of existence:

*Sixteen outside visits will have taken place by the end of this year [1972]. This is a far higher number than most of the Fine Arts Societies and I am sure you will appreciate the amount of work that goes into their organisation.*[69]

**Above**

Thanet DFAS members pose for a picture for the *Kentish Gazette* on a visit to Canterbury Cathedral

lost anyone on her outings but once tried to round up the in-house volunteers of a stately home when checking the loos.[70] Mary Callander, of Edinburgh DFAS, recalls that 'several years ago I took a group from my local Society to Belvoir Castle. As I alighted from the coach I was greeted with the immortal words "It's that Lady Mary from Edinburgh with her bus of antiques"'.[71] Visits, like lectures, are planned with meticulous care. However sometimes there are problems that simply cannot be predicted. Patricia Hallett of New Forest DFAS describes the group's rather traumatic second outing in 1973:

*We set off early on a beautiful day in two coaches for the four and a half hour journey to Knole and Sissinghurst in Kent. We had difficulty in finding Sissinghurst, but Jennifer Joel came to the driver's rescue with skilful map-reading. We were also hindered by alarming grinding noises coming from the engine. The driver confessed that he suspected a broken fan belt but could replace it whilst we were visiting the gardens. This he did, as we set off for home having at that point, had a lovely day. Our luck however was to change as the clutch on the other coach began to slip and the driver said we must return to Brighton where they had agents who would repair*

**Right**
Members of Thanet DFAS are pictured on a visit to Syon House and Garden in the 1970s

By July the group had been to Clandon Park, made two visits to Spinks, had a tour of 'Roman London', explored the National Portrait Gallery and Whitefriars Glass, and visited the Fitzwilliam Museum in Cambridge and three country houses, The Vyne, West Wycombe and Rousham. Angela Bushill-Mathews of Royal Leamington Spa DFAS never

*it. They took us to a very grubby pub which was far too small to accommodate us all so we limped on to The Old Ship Hotel … whilst the drivers telephoned their depot in Bournemouth for instructions. Alas permission was refused for the roadworthy coach to go home ahead, and apparently Union Rules forbade the hire of another coach to take us on. The hours passed*

*whilst the clutch was being repaired... at last both coaches set off.*

Unfortunately their tribulations were not over, as 'at Chichester the driver, manoeuvring the Butter Cross had to reverse – alas into a brand new Rolls Royce ... we finally reached Lymington at 2.30 am'.

Outings are not of course restricted to the British Isles. The West Sussex Group enjoyed their lecture on Renaissance Art and Sculpture so much, it:

*sparked off an idea that we should visit Italy, armed with a list of what we should see in order of importance ... A group of 18 members led by Margaret Thorp set forth on our first overseas expedition. When NADFAS heard of our plans they told us that they were on the verge of starting their own tours organised by Shuna Cronin and suggested that she should break her journey from South Africa to join us in Italy where she was a great asset.*

This tour was followed by many others to France, Spain, Belgium, Sicily, Italy, Turkey, Jordan, Greece and Russia:

*For the most part things went smoothly but falls on icy pavements caused two of our members to sample a Moscow Hospital and riots in Jordan threatened our Petra visit, though the delay was compensated by a moonlit drive over the desert.*[72]

Windlebrook DFAS were tempted to go on their first foreign visit to Petra and Jordan, having been inspired by the lecture of Nicole Douek. Following an excellent study day with Edward Saunders ' ... the East Surrey Area embarked on a tour of the Baltic States visiting Lithuania, Latvia and Estonia'. The energetic and dedicated bunch had a very long hot journey from Riga to Tallinn – stopping *en route* at the lovely resort of Parnu with its fine white sandy beaches. By then they:

*were feeling pretty well cultured-out and there was nothing the local guide could do to stop the group flocking into the sea like lemmings. Casting caution, hats, bags and sandals to the wind, trousers were rolled up, skirts tucked into knicker-legs as we rushed into the waves as if we had never seen them before. Eventually we were*

**Right** Windlebrook DFAS ventured to Jordan for its first overseas visit

*persuaded to re-group, decorum was restored and the guide led us away to admire the tree lined boulevards and the many architectural delights.*[73]

Through visits such as these, the name of NADFAS spreads across the globe, highlighting the pleasure and knowledge we can gain from our artistic heritage.

It seems appropriate to conclude this chapter with the words of the indomitable Françoise White, founder of Henley DFAS. Ending her speech celebrating eight years of the Society, she asked the assembled membership 'Why shouldn't this go on forever? Ah! But this is dangerous thinking! ... When success is taken for granted there is a serious danger of apathy. Do preserve us from this danger!'.[74]

## NOTES

[1] Nancy Armstrong, Chiltern DFAS *Newsletter*, Spring 1980, p.7.
[2] The information sent in will be kept in the NADFAS Archive (catalogued under NADFAS 40th celebrations/book) and become part of the history of the Association.
[3] Sheila Marshall, *Development of a Dream*, 1982, p.3.
[4] Sheila Rule, Thanet DFAS, July 2006.
[5] Margaret Bunford, Moor Park DFAS, January 2007.
[6] Ruth Swift, Samlesbury DFAS, January 2007.
[7] Hannah Gould, Enfield DFAS, September 2006.
[8] Ibid.
[9] Geraldine Crippen, Henley DFAS, May 2007.
[10] Heather Spencer, New Forest DFAS, October 2006.
[11] Speech for Tenth Anniversary Lunch', 25 May 1982, by Patricia Hallett, founder chairman.
[12] Keith Hasnip, Abingdon DFAS, July 2006.
[13] Shelley Cowlin, East Suffolk DFAS, July 2006.
[14] Jean Pace, Teme Valley DFAS August 2006, 'An outline history of Teme Valley DFAS for 30th Anniversary lunch, 14 June 2006'.
[15] Shirley Turner, Westminster DFAS, December 2006.
[16] Diana Dale 2005, sent by David Hunt, East Hertfordshire DFAS, July 2006.
[17] Jill Hamilton-Rump, West Solent DFAS, July 2006.
[18] Peter Redman, Basingstoke DFAS, October 2006.
[19] Heather Jones, 'The Arden DFAS Chronicles', October 2006.
[20] 'The Intrepid Adventurers of Ealing', by Teresa Stella Sawicka, August 2006.
[21] The first chairman of Weybridge DFAS, Brenda Vey sent in this idea via Gillian Williams, August 2006.
[22] To distinguish between the West Surrey Tuesday Group and West Surrey Thursday Group, it was decided on the tenth anniversary of the latter in 1983 to change the name to the Shalford DFAS.
[23] Margaret Saunders, Shalford DFAS, 'Note on the History of Shalford DFAS', July 2006.
[24] Williams,op.cit.
[25] 'How a New Society is Born', from Ursula Yorke, Surrey Heath DFAS, July 2006.
[26] Hazel Kibble, July 2006.
[27] Susan Sloan, 'Havering DFAS, a brief history', October 2004.
[28] Joan Hawkins, 'The Founding of WWDFAS', West Wycombe DFAS, July 2006.
[29] Anne Coppen, Dukeries DFAS, July 2006.
[30] Sylvia Horwood-Smart to Audrey Reading, August 1998.
[31] Pamela Howard, Skipton and Wharfedale DFAS, July 2006.
[32] Elaine Graham, and Jane Harman, Egerton DFAS, July 2006.
[33] Elizabeth Arrowsmith, Samlesbury DFAS, August 2006.
[34] Hasnip, op. cit.
[35] 'A Celebration of 25 Years of Lectures, Outings and Study Days', Mendip DFAS 2006.
[36] Jenny Colmer, Cirencester DFAS, July 2006.
[37] Anne Brunker, Sherborne DFAS, July 2006.
[38] Judith Jessett, Wey Valley DFAS, July 2006.
[39] Sawicka, op. cit.
[40] Diana Taylor, Chichester DFAS, October 2006.
[41] Peter Vermeylen, Beaconsfield DFAS, October 2006.
[42] Howard, op. cit.
[43] Margaret Flory in *Claremont Decorative & Fine Arts Society, The First Thirty Years*, 2005, p.5. Margaret Flory was also Hon. Treasurer of NADFAS 1974-76.
[44] Diana Good, August 2006.
[45] Clyde Binfield to Jennifer Downey, Hallamshire DFAS, October 2006.
[46] Sybil Lock, Felsted DFAS, October 2006.
[47] Brunker, op. cit.
[48] Shirley Blick, New Forest DFAS, July 2007.
[49] Vermeylen op. cit.
[50] Brunker, op. cit.
[51] Doreen Wadsworth, Saltaire DFAS, 'Saltaire The Birth of a New Society', July 2006.
[52] Flory op. cit.
[53] Hallet, op. cit.
[54] Edith Bailey, 'How it all began in the lovely market town of Highworth', sent by Mrs Perons, Upper Thames Valley DFAS, July 2006.
[55] Hawkins, op. cit.
[56] Helen Fielden, 18 March 1981 sent by Teme Valley DFAS, July 2006.
[57] Elizabeth Kennerly, Bodmin DFAS, July 2006.
[58] Jean Pratt, 'Confessions of a Projectionist' sent by Liz Dancey, Birmingham DFAS, January 2007.
[59] Regents Park DFAS, 'The First Ten Years, 1977-1987', 1987, p.9.
[60] Pamela Cowen, October 2006.
[61] Rule, op. cit.
[62] Pamela Percy, West Essex DFAS, August 2006.
[63] Fiona Rossington, Cotswold Antiques Study Group, May 2007.
[64] Fielden, op. cit.
[65] Fielden, op. cit.
[66] Patricia Fay, 'Historic Houses European Conference', Oxford, 9 July 1975, NADFAS Archives.
[67] Chris Stanners, chairman's Report, Chiltern DFAS, 2006, Chiltern DFAS Archives.
[68] 'Regents Park', op. cit.
[69] Bunford, op. cit.
[70] 'The memories of a founding Chairman', Catherine Leahy, Royal Leamington Spa DFAS, July 2006.
[71] Mary Callander, Edinburgh DFAS, July 2006.
[72] Helen Ouin, sent July 2006.
[73] June Robinson, Area Co-Ordinator for Education, East Surrey Area, August 2006.
[74] Crippen, op. cit.

# 3

# NADFAS Takes Wing:
## The Overseas Societies

*'Now that we have 'gone international...'*
Margaret Garbett, NADFAS *Newsletter*, 1984

There were attempts to take NADFAS beyond Britain right from the start. Patricia Fay 'planned that NADFAS should extend into Europe', so, wrote Helen Lowenthal in 1988 'how pleased she would be with our increasing number of Societies abroad'.[1] In February 1968 there had been plans to form a Society consisting of different embassy wives in the hope that they would take NADFAS abroad, although nothing was to come of this. When, in 1972, Patricia Fay suggested that an international lecturer visit various Societies, she was already looking beyond the confines of Britain. Preparations began for the visit of Dr Olga Pulmanov, a friend of Helen Lowenthal from Prague. Sadly after nearly a year's work, the lecturer's visa was withdrawn a week before she left. This was a timely reminder of life behind the Iron Curtain during the Cold War. Although this foray into European connections was unsuccessful, it is clear that Patricia and her committee could see great opportunities for taking NADFAS overseas. In 1978 the Historic Houses Association asked Patricia Fay to

speak to the International Castles Institute in Utrecht, suggesting that what NADFAS was doing was of interest abroad. This was confirmed later the same year when the European League for Co-Operation on Cultural Heritage invited DFAS chairmen to their conference. Despite a great many efforts it took quite a while to launch a Decorative and Fine Arts Society overseas. When asked, at the Association's 1981 Conference *Action in the '80s – Communicating the Heritage*, if NADFAS was considering the formation of Societies on the Continent, the Chairman's answer was a resounding 'Yes, and our aims are about to be fulfilled'.

## The First Overseas Society: Rheindahlen

Three more years were to pass before the first overseas Society was actually launched in Rheindahlen, Germany. Mary Witherow has vividly related how she came, initially rather reluctantly, to be the founding chairman of the first NADFAS overseas branch.[2] In early December 1983, her husband, a senior RAF

**Above**

The Rheindahlen military base in Germany. Rheindahlen DFAS was the very first overseas Society and predominantly served RAF and army wives

Officer and a diplomat colleague, were asked to host a lunch by the Commandant of the College they were attending. The two guests were Helen Lowenthal, then Vice President of NADFAS, and Nicky Foot, the National Treasurer, who were friends of the Commandant's wife:

*My husband and his colleague, needless to say, had never heard of NADFAS, but it offered a potentially useful leading topic should it be necessary to revive what might become a somewhat stilted lunch-time conversation between total strangers.*

The conversation was anything but stilted, and all four got on very well from the start.

The conversation turned to NADFAS, and the desire to expand overseas. On learning that Group Captain Witherow was soon to be posted to Germany, the guests asked if there was a possibility of establishing a Society there. He promised to discuss this with his wife, and assess the situation once there. That afternoon Mary was astonished to be telephoned by Nicky Foot, 'of whom she had never heard, asking her to found a branch of NADFAS, of which she had never heard, at Rheindahlen, of which she had heard much but knew nothing!'. Lunch at the Royal Yacht Squadron a few days later provided the opportunity for a fuller briefing. Mary left the meeting intrigued, and undertook to investigate once in Germany. However the Witherows had yet to experience the tenacity of these two NADFAS ladies. On arrival in Germany in early January 1984, Group Captain Witherow was called in by his Commander-in-Chief to explain a letter he had received 'telling (not asking!) him that his wife was going to launch NADFAS in his Command'! The Commander-in-Chief's wife invited Mary to discuss the idea, along with the wife of the Commander-in-Chief of the British Army of the Rhine. 'If I could do it' Mary explained, 'they agreed to be the joint Presidents and would attend my first meeting… They advised me to constitute my

Committee equally from RAF and Army wives, in the spirit of "jointery" that was the cornerstone of the HQ community'. Nicky Foot had mentioned the name of a friend of hers, Penny Cann, whose husband was an Army Officer at the HQ, and Penny agreed to be vice chairman. Between them, and within 24 hours, they had a committee of ten. Within a week their first committee meeting was held!

It became rapidly clear that the special conditions of military life meant that the usual timescale and conditions of DFAS development would have to be adapted to suit the circumstances. Mary was advised that 'it would take at least two years to launch our programme of activities'. Yet, as the new chairman explained:

*We could not even contemplate such a timetable; we were, almost without exception, all in Germany for three years or less and liable to re-posting at any time, anywhere and most of my committee were anyway well into their allotted*

*span. … We had to get on with it and have it up and running in the coming Autumn, or nothing.*

By May the groundwork had been completed. It was impossible, because of the constant turnover of the population, often at notice of a few weeks, to establish a normal subscription system, so there was no capital at the start for launch. Payment had to be cash on the door, at best a precarious hand-to-mouth existence. Moreover their public relations exercise had to be sustained unrelentingly and indefinitely, so as to attract a constant stream of new members. The venue, for the first two years, was the derelict Garrison cinema. The heating system had long been de-commissioned and whilst in the Spring and Summer phase of their planning that seemed a minor problem, they had to apply considerable ingenuity (rugs, brandy, coffee flasks etc) and rugged British grit when their 'first night' came on a bitter Autumn day.

Rheindahlen DFAS was launched on schedule in October 1984 by the National Chairman, Judith Waples, only eight months after the initial meeting in England. The volunteer labour force comprised Air Commodores, Group Captains and Wing Commanders together with their Army equivalents, selling tickets, operating the sound and projection equipment and dispensing pre-lecture drinks. By the virtue of their geographical position they were able to invite German, Dutch and Belgian speakers from some of Europe's greatest museums, galleries and universities. The first lecture was by NADFAS lecturer, Sylvia Coppen-Gardner, on 'German Glass'. The Society lasted ten years, until the final withdrawal of major British forces from Germany. Mary felt that Rheindahlen DFAS had not only served the Garrison superbly, but also 'made a considerable impact on the Allied Nations as a showplace for British cultural sophistication'. The NADFAS *Newsletter* heralded 'yet another of Patricia Fay's dreams has been realised'.[3]

**Above** Rheindahlen's derelict garrison cinema was the first overseas Society's venue in its early days
**Right** The cathedral of Our Lady, in Antwerp. Antwerp DFAS was established in 1991

## NADFAS in Mainland Europe

Yet as Margaret Garbett, vice chairman of Hull & East Riding Antiques & Fine Arts Society was to comment in the same newsletter:

*Now we have "gone International" it surely means a further strain on our limited office facilities. So what is the solution? … The place of the decorative and fine arts in modern society has always been a contentious issue. NADFAS must be prepared to make its collective voice heard, to be bold in its decisions – and those decisions must be made by the movement as a whole. Our adolescent Association will soon be coming of age. When we get the key to the door we must make sure we choose the right key-hole.*

The impact of the foundation of Rheindahlen was to encourage other Mainland European groups to set up. Other German Societies were launched. Hamburg in 1988, which meets at a governmental physics research centre; Berlin followed in 1996 and Osnabruck the next year. 1988 also saw the start of Copenhagen but this Society struggled to attain financial viability and had to close after about seven years. A representative of the British community in Brussels and her husband attended the first evening of the Rheindahlen Society to assess their effort and learn how they got so swiftly into action. After lots of advice and discussion, Brussels DFAS was set up in October 1985. The Hague DFAS was established in 1990, followed by Antwerp in 1991, and now these three Societies share lecturers.

In 1992 NADFAS organised its first European conference, in Brussels, with assistance from the Patricia Fay Memorial Fund. *The Cultural Heritage of Europe: An Environment for Volunteers* brought together key speakers from diverse places including Oxford, Cracow and Greece who focused on opportunities for learning, training and discussion for volunteers. Nancy Hodgson, the National Chairman, explained that:

*we chose this title because, although we know that each country's history and culture have much in common with its neighbours, public involvement with the arts varies greatly from one country to another. Now that NADFAS has become international with Societies in eight countries – five on mainland Europe – we felt we wanted to know much more about the cultural environment of countries outside Britain.*[4]

The Conference was largely made possible thanks to the co-operation of Brussels DFAS, and one of their patrons, the Prince de Ligne, welcomed the participants:

*At the end of the last two World Wars this country was liberated by the British Army thus saving most of our fine arts. Today again the peaceful British army of volunteers are here to help us maintain … some of our treasures. You might not find it difficult to enrol a large quantity of volunteers to look after other people's treasures. It is not, I'm afraid, the same in our tradition or mentality. Therefore your presence here today is ever so important to show us by your example.*

As a direct result of this conference Professor Ostronski from Poland, one of the speakers, was sponsored by NADFAS to make a lecturer's tour of Britain.

Since the formation of Rheindahlen in 1984, the number of Mainland European Societies has grown to ten. A cluster of Spanish Societies began in 1988 when Susan Brodie became the first chairman of Costa del Sol. The story of its foundation reveals the close ties between the British and European Societies. On the day that Susan was to be elected to a local DFAS in England, her husband Philip had a heart attack. This shock resulted in their moving home to their *finca* in Spain which they had bought in 1984. Four years later, 'after her old NADFAS chairman reminded her that she had been asked to look into the possibility of starting a branch in Spain' the inaugural lecture of the Costa del Sol Society took place.[5] Nerja followed in 2002, and De la Frontera in 2006.

The Hague group were formed as a result of the NADFAS representative Joan Lefroy contacting various interested members of the expatriate community, who soon formed a committee. As Judy Kahn explained 'The original committee was full of strong personalities and meetings were long and lively. Indeed agreeing on a Constitution for the new Society took as much time as setting up an emergent nation'. It soon settled into a regular pattern, although 'it became clear that all those fascinating voluntary activities were beyond our scope'. Fifteen years on, and with relatively few problems (like the loss of a harpsichord between Delft and The Hague, though the musical lecturer went on with hardly a hiccup), a member was heard to say recently, 'When you come here, you feel you've been out'.[6]

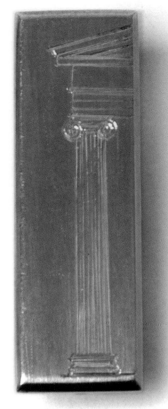

The Antwerp group were set up in 1991, with the help and encouragement of BRIDFAS, the established Belgian DFAS in Brussels, who allowed the Antwerp group to use already-booked lecturers to 'test the water' in March, April and May of that year. One of the founder members of Antwerp DFAS (ADFAS), Elizabeth Turnbull, contacted possible 'culture vultures' with an encouraging result and the British Consul offered the use of a venue, free of charge. The inaugural meeting was sponsored by the Paribas Bank and took place in the elegant Osterriethhuis, in which the Bank's collection of rare artworks is housed. One of the remarkable achievements of the Antwerp Group was to set up their first Volunteer project the following year, cleaning the silver reliquaries in Saint Andries church. To see people giving up their time freely was such a rare event that ADFAS received wide publicity in both newspapers and television. The work was finished a year later, and from this beginning the Volunteers have made a name for themselves, cleaning gold embroidery and making discoveries in the archives.[7] A Society was formed in Paris which, unlike many of the other Societies in Mainland Europe, has a high proportion of nationals amongst their membership. They have two prestigious Honorary Presidents, one is Madame Georges Pompidou, and the other is Lady Holmes, wife of the British Ambassador in Paris. For their tenth anniversary the Society held a dinner at the Musée d'Orsay and members were entertained by students from the Academie de Musique, Paris. Although some of the European Societies find it difficult to keep going, maintaining the membership, and finding the money to meet the lecturers' fees and transport, they have great

**Left**
AADFAS lapel brooch designed by Juliet Michell, now made by Jane Bowden of Zu design
**Bottom left and right**
Pencil and watercolour design and finished silver and gilt brooch by Shannon O'Neill, commissioned by NADFAS for the AADFAS Chairman

determination. Their presence is an important element within the concept of NADFAS.

## International Exchange

In 1990 NADFAS launched its first international exchange. While on a sightseeing trip to Hamburg, the NADFAS lecturer, Douglas Mackay, kindly offered to help arrange a small study trip to the UK for members of the Hamburg Society. In mid September 1990 a group (two Australians, a Greek, five Germans and five Britons) travelled from Hamburg to England, where members of Reigate DFAS acted as hosts. NADFAS lecturers turned out in force to make this a very special trip. Visits were organised to Knole and Penshurst with the Mackays, to the Turner Gallery at the Tate with Clare Ford-Wille, to Sissinghurst and The Wallace Collection with Wellesley Clinton, and to the Royal Academy with Eveline Eaton. This 'was a unique chance of furthering international

understanding on a more personal level – the common ground being provided by NADFAS'. The following year 15 Reigate DFAS members visited Hamburg. Since that first trip Hamburg has made five more very happy and successful exchanges with NADFAS Societies, Brussels in 1991 and 1992, Copenhagen (formed in 1988 but since closed) in 1993 and 1994, Canterbury in 1996 and 1997, York in the spring and autumn of 2000 and Malvern Hills in 2004

and 2005.[8] Through these activities the fostering of international relationships has become part of the NADFAS vision.

## Beyond Europe

The mid 1980s seem to have been a particularly ambitious time for NADFAS, as there were not only European Societies opening, but also ideas for moving beyond Europe. In 1984 Valerie Woodford suggested exploring the possibility of 'taking NADFAS to Saudi Arabia in order to feed the culture starved ladies who tend to live on International Compounds'. She was based in Jedda at the time, 'the commercial centre of Saudia Arabia, with a population of 1.2 million, two British Embassies and a university, and due to its geographical location alongside the Red Sea, it was a very popular place to live.'[9] Valerie welcomed constructive criticism and advice on her plans, and although she could promise nothing, endeavoured to 'do the best I can for the name of NADFAS'. Sadly nothing did come of the idea, but it reveals the enthusiasm and ambition of members to take NADFAS into the global picture.

In 1992 two South African Societies were set up, in Johannesburg and Cape Town. However due to monetary problems and, at times, the political situation, their membership had to be suspended. There were in fact more arts societies in South Africa hoping for membership, and the door is always open for their return should circumstances change.[10]

## The Australian Connection

Only a year after the launch of the first Mainland European Society, the first Australian Decorative and Fine Arts Society was founded by Patricia Robertson who discovered NADFAS on a visit to England. With the encouragement of the National Chairman, Judith Waples, and with much hard work and the support of a dedicated committee, the first Society was launched in Sydney in 1985. By 1989 there were enough Societies (1985 Sydney, 1986 Canberra, 1987

Armidale and Melbourne, 1988 Bowral, Newcastle, Sunshine Coast and Sydney morning session, and in 1989 Toowoomba) to form the Association of Australian Decorative & Fine Arts Societies (AADFAS) with Patricia as the first Chairman. In 1992 the Australian member Societies, as they had already set up their own Executive and Council, became a Group Associate Member of NADFAS, and, in effect, a sister organisation. In 2001, Patricia Robertson was awarded the Medal of the Order of Australia for her services to the arts through AADFAS, an acknowledgement not only of her dedication but also of the contribution of the Association to the cultural life of both urban and rural Australia. It was through Patricia's inspiration that voluntary conservation and guiding work was undertaken by Society members and resulted, in 1994, in the establishment of AADFAS Volunteers, whose work is similar to the Heritage Volunteers in the United Kingdom and Mainland Europe (see Chapter 5). The work of AADFAS Volunteers is highly valued by significant organisations such as the National Trust of Australia (NSW). AADFAS guides work at the Johnston Collection in Melbourne, a fine Italianate villa bequeathed to the people of Victoria in 1996, which houses a fine collection of eighteenth century English furniture and portrait miniatures, and at the Bundanon Trust on the south coast of New South Wales. This unique 'living arts centre' celebrates not only the work of the artist Arthur Boyd and his forbears, but also that of other Australian artists. It houses an education centre and facilitates a regular programme of artists in residence. Volunteers also support Beleura House and garden in Mornington and Barwon Grange, Geelong. Pauline Hopkins, who was Overseas Area Representative from 2001-2005, remembers visiting the Grange, 'a lovely old weatherboarded house built in 1855 and now owned by the National Trust of Australia, where Geelong Heritage Volunteers were working and their positive commitment was gradually returning the house to its former glory'.[11]

Through AADFAS Volunteers a number of Church Recording Groups have been established. The first Church Recording of the Parish Church of St Mary's, Kangaroo Point, was completed by the Brisbane River Society in 2002 just as NADFAS achieved its 1000th Church Recording in the UK and a copy was presented to the Bishop of London at the service of celebration.

The Association of ADFAS also encourages the promotion of arts for the young through scholarships and grants to suitable institutions and art colleges, by subsidising students at vacation schools or by introducing visual art to rural children at art venues. Twenty (out of a total of 30 Societies in Australia) provided approximately A\$30,000 (£13,000) in 2006 to fund a variety of Young Arts programmes ranging from youth orchestras, theatre, ballet and music scholarships, providing art books and equipment in schools, and activities in museums, galleries and historic houses.

Another successful innovation has been ADFAS Travel founded in 2001, which promotes excursions both overseas and in Australia. Tours to study indigenous heritage and art have proved extremely popular, including visits to see Rock Art in the remote Kimberley area of North Western Australia, to Uluru and to Wilpena Pound. The 2007 programme includes visits to South America, Eastern Europe and Morocco, and in 2008, Southern India and the Far East are among the planned destinations.

By 2008 there will be member Societies extending from Adelaide in South Australia to Cairns in northern Queensland. Membership exceeds 5,500 and several Societies hold both day and evening lectures. There is also an Associate Member Society, Friends of the Art Gallery of Western Australia in Perth. Lectures are held once a month for at least eight months of the year and because of the vast distances between centres visiting NADFAS lecturers are invited either to the Southern Circuit, from Adelaide to Sydney, or the Northern Circuit, from Sydney to Queensland. A third lecture circuit is being planned as new Societies are being established. It is difficult to capture the very

special experience of lecturing to AADFAS, flying thousands of miles, then travelling via road, rail, and eight-seater planes, across desert, through the Bush, to reach diverse venues. Whereas London to Glasgow by road is 400 miles it is 1,400 miles from Adelaide to Sydney. All lecturers who have 'gone over' are united in appreciating the exceptionally warm and generous hospitality. The Chairman of AADFAS in 2007, Naomi Williams, refers to a letter of thanks written

by lecturer Edward Saunders on returning to England after his fifth Australian tour, as a way of conveying something of the experience:

*What was so amazing about the month was that nothing, absolutely nothing went wrong! Trains, buses ... planes and cars all went perfectly ... No businessman, no tourist, no ordinary visitor can ever have the diversity and range of experiences which are offered on the lecture circuit and although it can be demanding, with a succession of two-night stands, the momentum and exhilaration of moving from one venue to another, of getting off the*

**Above and left** AADFAS enjoys close ties with the Bundanon 'living arts centre'

*plane/bus/train and seeing another smiling face and being given another warm welcome is incredibly rewarding. Was I tired when I got back – Yes, very much so! But was it worthwhile – Yes, a resounding Yes! I loved every minute of it!*

While the visiting lecturers travel thousands of miles, AADFAS members often clock up vast distances to get to the meetings, too; some might drive several hours in order to get to the venue, and across beautiful if sometimes difficult terrain. This means the lectures are rather special events. Many members stay overnight, and nearly all are accompanied by generous and convivial

The relationship between British and overseas Societies is often close, and this was recognised in 1997 when Sheffield DFAS was the first Society in the UK to twin with a Society from abroad. This idea arose as a result of Jo Mason's visit to Australia as Overseas Area Representative earlier in 1997, and the Society has been delighted to welcome members of Bowral to Sheffield over the years and Sheffield members have been warmly received in Bowral in return. Other Societies have adopted this mutually rewarding idea, helping stretch the hand of friendship and support for the arts across the world.

**Left**
Melbourne's Johnston Collection benefits from the work of AADFAS guides and Volunteers
**Far left**
Patricia Robertson, founder of the first Australian Decorative and Fine Arts Society

parties that create a particularly warm and welcoming atmosphere. These characteristics of Australian Societies mean that planning can be particularly complicated, taking into account dramatic climate differences, distance and variable road and air conditions. No wonder the meetings have an element of excitement, for lecturers, organisers and audience.

One of the most important activities to have been undertaken in recent years has been the establishment of a forward planning committee to investigate and take recommendations for the future development of the Australian Association. The committee's paper, entitled *AADFAS – Towards 2010*, was adopted as policy in 2006 and provides a blueprint for the future.

### 'If Australia can do it, so can we'
**Fran Reed, Chairman, Canterbury NZ DFAS**
The success of AADFAS encouraged the creation of the first DFAS in New Zealand in 2002. Fran Reed, the chairman of Canterbury NZ DFAS, remembers 'When visiting a friend in London in 2000 I picked up her NADFAS magazine and read to my amazement, that there were 18 to 19 DFASs in Australia. My immediate reaction was, that if Australia can do it, so can we, and I started the "ball rolling"'.[12] She contacted NADFAS and was sent the information pack on setting up a new Society, and received lots of help from the Australian Association. Fran says that the beginning was very similar to those Societies formed in the UK, '... the main difference being that we were 12,000 miles away from the central body', and she was the only

person on the steering committee who had heard of NADFAS! As Pauline Hopkins, then Overseas Area Representative, comments, 'setting up a Society in New Zealand was something new for NADFAS – Australia was well established and quite a different story'. She was delighted to be able to work with the group at Canterbury in Christchurch to form a constitution and guidelines, and realised that 'we had to get this right as it would be set in stone for any future Societies which hopefully would form in New Zealand'. By July 2006 Canterbury NZ DFAS had a small waiting list, and had put in place their Youth Art programme. By paying for transport and entrance fees for classes from primary schools in less advantaged areas to attend the Schools Education Programme at the new Art Gallery, they have introduced 1,700 children to the world of art, children who would probably never have been taken to an Art Gallery.

The second New Zealand Society, Auckland, started in 2004. David Leyland, who became chairman, joined a couple who had been NADFAS members in England, an antique dealer and her friend who had attended the Canterbury NZ meetings, and Anne Gambrill, who had heard of it through her Christchurch friends. During a visit to England, David Leyland spent a whole day with Pauline Hopkins working on the blueprint for the Auckland Society. The founding group each put up a subscription and at least 20 names and by August the committee had doubled. They booked the University as a venue and after mailing out invitations had requests for 280 tickets. Unfortunately the venue only took 240. At the (inaugural) lecture the treasurer took a year's subscriptions, and the Society was launched. However, soon after and much to the committee's horror, the Leylands announced their plans to return to England, so the committee had 'all the money and no chair!' Anne Gambrill valiantly took over, and spent 'hours in the early New Year finalising the 2005 programme', before facing the organisation of the 2006 lectures. With the sterling support of NADFAS, the Australian

Association and the lecturers' sub-committee of Canterbury NZ DFAS all went well. The Society has 250 members and a small waiting list.[13] In August 2006, the third New Zealand Society was set up in Wellington. The inaugural lecture was given by Anne Anderson, on Art Deco. The membership of 65 to 70 is small, but the Society is 'perfectly formed and going from strength to strength'.[14] Plans for a fourth Society in Nelson are nearing fruition. The prospective chairman is Sally McDonald who was a member and programme secretary of North Somerset DFAS during a ten year stay in the UK. On returning to New Zealand she was 'desolate without NADFAS', and was thrilled when she heard one was proposed in Christchurch. She was on the committee there until she moved to Nelson. Although the new Society is not 'signed and sealed' things are progressing well.[15] By September 2008 there will be 10 European, 30 Australian and 3, probably 4, New Zealand Societies, taking the message and vision of NADFAS around the world.

NOTES
[1] Helen Lowenthal 'Tribute to Patricia Fay, by Helen Lowenthal April 1988', read by Sheila Marshall at Patricia Fay Memorial dinner in Harrogate, 25 April 1988, NADFAS Archives.
[2] Mary Witherow, Founding Chairman, 'NADFAS Branch 'Overseas 1' Rheindahlen, Germany', sent by J. Perons, Upper Thames DFAS, July 2006.
[3] NADFAS News Autumn/Winter 1984, front page.
[4] Conference on 'The Cultural Heritage of Europe. An Environment for the Volunteer', Brussels, 1992, NADFAS Archives.
[5] Newsletter of the Costa del Sol Decorative and Fine Arts Society, no.22, Winter 2004, p.8.
[6] Judy Kahn, 'Pastime with good company (Henry VIII). The first 15 years of DFAS', DFAS of the Hague Newsletter, 2006-7, p.2.
[7] 'ADFAS – the Antwerp Decorative and Fine Arts Society – a brief history', sent by Marion Lawrence, August 2006.
[8] Vicki Wohlfarth, Hamburg DFAS 'Exchanges and Donations – BRIDFAS of Hamburg's contribution to the NADFAS Heritage', October 2006.
[9] Valerie Woodford, June 1984, Private Collection.
[10] Chairman's Report, Anthea Johnston, 1994-1996, NADFAS Archives.
[11] Pauline Hopkins, July 2006.
[12] Fran Reed, Chairman, 'Canterbury DFAS, the first Overseas Member Society of NADFAS in New Zealand', July 2006.
[13] Anne Gambrill, October 2006.
[14] James Wilkins, August 2007
[15] Kate Siebert, Overseas Area Representative, NADFAS, August 2007.

# 4

# Listening to the Lecturers: *The Heart of NADFAS*

*'The lecturers are the centre of NADFAS'*
Nannette Foster, in 'The History of the *Directory of Lecturers* from 1969', 1987

From the beginning Patricia Fay was determined that NADFAS should not just be 'another lecture society'. One of the distinctive qualities of the Association was its determination to deliver first class lectures to the member groups; introducing, developing, maintaining and constantly reviewing a 'stable' of top quality speakers. Their knowledge, ability to communicate and professionalism mark a gold standard in the world of the arts. This is made possible by a rigorous selection procedure, evaluation of performance at each lecture, a businesslike contract between Societies and lecturers, a decent fee and warm hospitality offered by Societies to the lecturers. It is not unusual for long lasting and mutually respectful relations to develop between lecturers and Societies.

## Developing the *Directory*

The core of every DFAS meeting is the lecture. The quality of the lecture sets the standard for the meeting, it is an essential part of what NADFAS is. The search for good lecturers has always been a hot topic among Societies. One chairman reported:

*My vice chairman discovered the most wonderful lady who had a detailed list of all the lecturers they'd had in the last 12 years, catalogued under graded headings of excellence. Whilst she kept her occupied in a corner, I copied down as many as I could. All the time she was murmuring "of course, it's confidential".*[1]

In 1969 the first *Directory of Lecturers* was a duplicated booklet. An indication of the importance of creating and managing this list was the setting up of a special sub-committee devoted to it in 1970. It was agreed that the list should be restricted to chairmen and committee members of Societies, as it was 'discovered that many were having it photocopied and distributed around'. The first *Directory* contained the details of 56 lecturers and by 1972 there were more than 90 names. It now contains over 300.

The Annual Directory Meeting (ADM) where programme secretaries can hear new lecturers, and details of new lectures by established NADFAS speakers, as well as meet the lecturers who attend, is one of the most

**Above**
NADFAS lecturer Sheelagh Lewis with one of her beloved Persian rugs. Having joined the *Directory* in 1972 Sheelagh became one of the most popular lecturers on the circuit

important events in the NADFAS calendar. In 1981, 94 lecturers attended the ADM with a total audience numbering 265. At the last ADM in 2007, 148 lecturers presented themselves to an audience of 643. The excited buzz of conversation at lunchtime covers a multitude of subjects from ancient Chinese art to the use of concrete in architecture. The ADM is an immense exercise in teamwork that brings together the many aspects and personalities of NADFAS, in a unique way.[2]

In 1971 a booking form based on that used by East Hertfordshire Society was suggested, which eventually emerged as a printed form two years later. This was invaluable as a clear professional contract that gave both Societies and lecturers confidence and commitment. There were attempts to link lecturers and Societies together from the early days. In 1971 the first sherry party for chairmen, programme secretaries and lecturers was held at the Institute of Recorded Sound in London.

Each DFAS committee goes to great

lengths to ensure each lecture goes well, as Oliver Millar remarked: 'As a lecturer to many Societies over the years I can bear grateful witness to the efficiency and hospitality with which lecturers are always treated.'[3]

## The Early Days

Peter Darty is one of the 'founder' lecturers for NADFAS, in fact he was giving lectures to Patricia's Group before the National Association was formally created. He remembers the early years, when there were few lecturers, who as a result had to talk on a very wide range of topics from the Renaissance to Posters. The only places, he says, where students could study art history were the Courtauld and Newcastle University. Lecturers had to do without microphones. As the halls got bigger to accommodate larger audiences, this became a problem. At a *Directory* Meeting in the spring of 1974, it was reported that 'The question of a microphone is becoming important. I receive increasing complaints that lecturers cannot be heard'. The early projectors were the push-pull variety, which required someone to load one slide at a time. Those were the days when you had to say 'next slide please!' These were nearly half the price of the state-of-the-art Kodak carousel, which was launched in 1961. The lively Education Department at the V&A was a great centre for recommending lecturers, under the enthusiastic guidance of Madelaine Maidstone. It was through her that Peter Darty met Patricia Fay, who he says was born in York, and trained as a dental nurse before her marriage to the barrister Charles Fay. His lectures, many based on his own textile collection (which members sometimes modelled) were, and still are very popular. They were refreshingly different from the more formal art history being taught at the time, and one of the ways of 'opening windows' into a different world for his audience. NADFAS members were also involved in repairing nineteenth and twentieth century costumes from his collection, including originals designed by Bakst for the Diaghilev Company.[4] Peter also accompanied NADFAS Tours and recalls the disbelief of his entourage when visiting a chateau in northern France in the 1980s, he looked up to see a helicopter, and informed the group that the owner of the castle, Laura Ashley, had flown in to welcome them.[5]

The former students of the Study Centre for the Fine and Decorative Arts, set up in London by Erica O'Donnell in the early 1970s, also became a source of NADFAS lecturers. It was a pioneering course that enabled those interested to study furniture as well as paintings, silver as well as sculpture across the ages. Patricia's time as a student on this 'Diploma Course' meant that she had access to a network of contacts who taught there, including the early lecturer Eve King.

Prospective lecturers were advised:

*NADFAS lecturing requires special skills, since, although many members are knowledgeable they are nevertheless not university students geared to take exams. They need to be instructed in an interesting and entertaining way. However, the facts must be correct. The lecture must be good and be coloured (where possible). Lectures should not be entirely read since this can become very monotonous.*

Lecturers were asked to:

*consider their audiences with care … They are a varied group with a wide range of occupations and educational experience and different from Society to Society. Most are probably middle-aged … but we have young mothers and many pensioners. The lecturer should not be deceived by the elderly front row … [as the audience] often does contain keen, critical, and appreciative people … on the whole one hopes that in the choice between Arthur Negus and Kenneth Clark the right policy will be found.[6]*

Looking at lecture programmes from the later 1960s and 1970s one can see the huge range of topics offered right from the start. This was all part of the NADFAS vision. For example, in their first year the Thanet Group heard Helen Lowenthal on 'Houses Owned by the National Trust', Mrs E.F. Gordon, Conservation Officer from the V&A, on 'Furniture Construction', Helena Hayward on 'Georgian Silver', Oliver Millar on the 'History of the Royal Collection', Ian Lowe from the Ashmolean in Oxford on 'Worcester Porcelain', and Arthur Negus on 'Furniture and Other Antiques'. There were many distinguished speakers, from a dazzling range of backgrounds. Early supporters of NADFAS, like the Duke of Bedford, gave talks to many groups to assist fund-raising, and as a way of thanking NADFAS for all the voluntary help the Association gave them. The graphic artist and textile designer Enid Marx (1902-98) appears, probably best known for her 1930s designs for London Transport fabrics, and Stella Mary Newton (1901-2001), who had careers in the theatre as an actress, a costume designer and a West End couturier, and set up the History of Costume Course at the Courtauld in 1965. For NADFAS she talked on the evolution of dress. Wellesley Clinton, an expert on furniture, and Nancy Armstrong, famed for her book on fans, appear frequently on Society programmes, as do Mary Stoyle and Eve King. Eve King was one of the first lecturers for NADFAS. She was clearly a charismatic speaker who won over her audience with her unbounded

**Above**

A member models for Peter Darty, one of the founder lecturers for NADFAS, at a meeting in Alderley Edge in 1977

lecture to her Group, and so Eve's long relationship with NADFAS began.[7]

Kathleen Wareham had her own lecture on the History of NADFAS up to the early 1970s, as well as lectures on the City Livery Companies. There is also a clear indication that NADFAS searched for lecturers who could talk on contemporary topics, like W.J. Strachan on 'Henry Moore, Barbara Hepworth and Contemporary Sculpture', Elizabeth Gordon on Picasso with a lecture entitled 'How seriously should we take him?', and later Geoffrey Opie on the Bauhaus and other modern movements in design, Jacques Paul on Le Corbusier, and the ever popular Valerie Woodgate on modern and contemporary fine art. Trenchard Cox, Helen Lowenthal and others made continual pleas for DFAS Groups to consider 'modern' subjects.

## The Trial

NADFAS lecturers are renowned for their calibre, and this is because they go through a strict vetting process that has evolved over time, and remains unique to the Association. In the early days of NADFAS a lecturer had to be heard speaking in public, before being recommended to talk to a Society. Sheelagh Lewis remembers joining NADFAS as a lecturer in 1972, after chatting with Patricia Fay at a Chiltern Group meeting. Sheelagh was well prepared as she recalls that 'after a local fund raising event in Hertfordshire the vicar's wife invited me to the Enfield Society saying "You must join the NADFAS lecturing team". She was warned 'They will come and spy on you and if you are good enough invite you to join the *Directory*'.[8] Sheelagh became one of the most popular lecturers on the circuit, learning much from Helen Lowenthal, who became her mentor. By 1983 she had lectured on Persian rugs to all but eight of the 175 Societies, and settled into a regular routine of giving about 40 lectures a year.

This 'hearing' now passes the potential NADFAS lecturer on to what used to be termed the 'Trial by Tweed', officially called the Selection Session. Prospective lecturers are required to give a 20-minute mini-lecture to a

enthusiasm for art. She had trained at the Courtauld with such great figures as Niklaus Pevsner, Ernst Gombrich and Rudolf Wittkower. Eve met Patricia Fay when she began attending the Decorative and Fine Arts Diploma Course at the V&A, where other students included Princess Michael of Kent and Giles Waterfield, who was later to become Director of the Dulwich Picture Gallery and a Vice President of NADFAS from 1998-2006. They paid 7s. 6d a time to hear lectures, and Patricia thought what a good idea it would be to found a local, rather than London-based Society for the appreciation of the arts. Patricia asked Eve if she would

panel made up of members from various sectors of NADFAS, including an already accredited lecturer. This was instituted in 1976 when an Advisory Committee was set up, under the chairmanship of Nannette Foster and comprising Patricia Fay, Helen Lowenthal, Lally Robinson, René Marcousé, Jay Atkinson, Helena Hayward, Kathleen Wareham and John Cushion. At first it was staged at the British Institute of Recorded Sound, then later at the Royal Institute of British Architects which had more suitable black-out and sound facilities. Later on regional venues were organised across the country. Nannette recalls that: 'We took some excellent lecturers at this time – Douglas Skeggs, Patrick Conner, Marie Conte-Helm, Kenneth Cotman, David Durant, Clare Ford-Wille, Trevor Goodman, Elizabeth Gordon, Richard Grasby, Ruth Hayden, Reynold Higgins and many others'.

For those who are experienced lecturers from outside NADFAS, the 'trial' may seem galling, but it sets a standard that is valued throughout the lecturing world. A note from one Society chairman to Nadine Mitchell, NADFAS secretary, stressed the importance of 'The necessity to maintain a high standard and "weed" the *Directory* in the light of experience is an essential service by NADFAS to member Societies and one in which NADFAS must not fail them'.[9] The lecturer David Cross remembers his trial rather vividly. As he entered the room:

*some panellists were still making notes and I was asked to wait for a sign. After a while the sign was given, the lights went off and I began. Having practised, I kept to the time, completed the quarter lecture, and showed all 15 slides. Then the lights came on again, and I was asked to come and sit opposite the panel at a long table. Several straightforward questions were followed by a really arcane googly from the elderly clergyman who was evidently no beginner in the art of the 18th century. He demanded to know why I had not referred to the iconography of the relatively (to me) obscure figures lurking behind the main sitter in Reynolds's 'Mrs Siddons as the Tragic Muse'. Initially back-footed by this question, I rallied, deciding he was merely trying*

*to establish his cultural bona fides with the panel and gave a reasonably straight answer to the question. The tweedy ladies nodded and smiled and said I would hear from them in due course. A week or so later I was welcomed into the fold.*[10]

In 1981, the annual and affectionately named, 'slave market' was introduced. New lecturers are invited to give a three (now two) minute introduction at the *Directory* meeting. This is a mutually rewarding exercise, as programme secretaries get to hear new talent, and the lecturers are given a chance to get bookings before they are known throughout the network, and 'word-of-mouth' recommendations can circulate. Judith Jessett, chairman of Wey Valley DFAS, remembers with amusement Antony Hopkins's introduction at the *Directory* day: 'I hadn't realised that I had to satisfy 630 women in three minutes. NADFAS women terrify me'.[11] Even before the invention of the Lecture Report, committee members made comments about the lecturers, not just at the *Directory* meeting, but after each lecture, to help other Societies select good speakers, and in booking repeat performances. They make amusing if not particularly politically correct reading: 'v. detailed and amusing. Good clear diction well arranged too much to absorb as very wide subject'; 'professional, erudite, charming'; 'enthusiastic, professional, informative, lucid, audible'; 'slides v.g.'; 'good but tricky'; 'mixed reports'; 'very pretty'; 'nice but dull'; 'gets in a tizzy, handle with care'; 'slides good, good dry sense of humour but too long'; 'some liked, some didn't – superior'; 'slides jammed and ruined the projector – v. rude'; and 'affected manner but the audience enjoyed it'. Most, of course, were full of praise and admiration, and many lecturers became firm regular favourites.

## The Programme Secretaries' Point of View

Organising the lecture programme is often challenging, but rewarding. The announcement made by one DFAS chairman reflects just one of the problems a programme secretary can experience: 'Next month's lecture will be slightly different from

**Above and above right**
Nannette Foster,
Chairman of the first
Advisory Committee to
the selection of lecturers,
and Oliver Millar

the subject on the programme. I have had rather a lot of trouble over it as the first lady went off to Italy. She recommended someone who couldn't come, who recommended someone else who couldn't come who recommended the textile conservation centre at Hampton Court'.[12] At another Society AGM, the chairman explained:

*I do hope you don't think I'm trying to run this thing single handed – or just with Olive, but I am torn between just getting on and finding lecturers the best way I can … It is really that my ideas and enthusiasm run away with me, and not that I mean to be autocratic.*[13]

I wonder how many lecturers are recognisable from the following shorthand adopted by one Society chairman in the 1970s: 'born China, designer of Pilkington glass, lecturer worldwide, married to a diplomat' (Patricia Jellicoe); 'lectures in Britain and abroad on historical architecture,

journalist, historian and author, broadcaster on radio & TV.' (David Durant); 'widely travelled, lectures for NADFAS Tours, the National Trust, colleges and schools and is president of a NADFAS branch (Mary Stoyle); 'art historian, lecturer at V&A Study Centre, guest lecturer on tours to India, Middle East & Soviet Union' (Yolande Crowe). What an amazingly diverse group of people NADFAS lecturers are!

The sound system is another common cause of anxiety. Think of the lecturers who coped with the early days of Gravesend and District DFAS. Valerie Martin explained:

*We decided right from the beginning that we should have the best equipment possible and so purchased the top of the range projector and screen. This meant that for the first year we had to use the rather old sound system that was in the hall. Unfortunately it must have used a frequency very similar to that of a local taxi firm,* and on one or two occasions during the learned talk, coming through loud and clear would be a request to send a taxi to take Mrs Jones to the hospital or to take Mr Smith to the station.

## The Other Side of the Lens

Then of course, there is the projectionist's view of the lecturer:

*Lecturers vary but are usually kind, understanding and helpful, occasionally nervous, and one or two, like the projector, have their peculiarities! "Do not move at all!' said one, quivering in anxious anticipation at the thought. "You'll shake the table and make the slide wobble and I can't have that – my slides are works of art!" I promised. He lectured – superbly – his slides were indeed wonderful – and they, and I, remained motionless throughout! There was, of course, the lecturer who, in his exuberance, knocked over the lectern, his notes, the jug of water and dislodged the microphone, and the one with whom I engaged in a sort of song and dance routine – he needed two projectors, which we had, but only one remote control. Not wanting to keep saying "Next slide please", as he felt this made his lecture disjointed, he pressed a rolled umbrella into service. As he clicked and tapped, I nudged the next slide forward and a fine double act developed.[14]*

More dramatically, Phillip James, formerly Art Director of the Arts Council of Great Britain, was nearly blown up when giving a lecture on Henry Moore. The fault in the electrical system brought home the need for the Society to insure against damage.[15] Another lecturer set fire to his notes. Adjusting the papers on the newly purchased lectern he must have edged them too near the halogen bulb. One of the committee: *suddenly … noticed smoke rising up from the lectern. The lecturer seemed oblivious to what was happening so I leapt up and pulled out the plug, much to his amazement. … afterwards, when we were able to inspect the damage, we found that he had bent the lamp so close to his*

notes that they were burned brown and the lamp had burned a hole right through the casing that went round the edge of the lectern – the lamp had to go.[16]

*The Harrow Decorative & Fine Arts Society*
*Welcome you to an evening lecture*
*'The History and Treasures of Woburn Abbey'*
*by*
**His Grace, The Duke of Bedford**
*on Saturday, May 20th, 1972*
*at Harrow Technical College, Watford Road, Harrow*
TICKET £1.50
PARKING FACILITIES
BUFFET 6.30 p.m.
LECTURE COMMENCES PROMPTLY 8.00 p.m.
ALL PROCEEDS TO ST. PAUL'S CATHEDRAL RESTORATION FUND

## The View from Behind the Lectern

NADFAS lecturers are a resourceful and adaptable lot. Being able to speak knowledgeably and clearly, with amusement yet erudition, is only part of their job. The first challenge for the lecturer is often getting to the venue. David Battie had a problem finding his way to a Wey Valley DFAS meeting, as the Society's 'instructions and his navigation did not quite tally'.[17] 'It is often thought' writes Eric Shanes, 'that we NADFAS lecturers receive payment for speaking':

*That is only partially true. In these days of privatised railways and gridlocked roads we only receive half our fee for the talk we deliver, and the other half for the ingenuity we display in getting to the hall on time. And sometimes we are unsuccessful. Such failure has befallen me three times, twice because all trains were cancelled and once because of motorway immobility caused by a crash somewhere miles ahead. At times like these one really needs improvisatory and map-reading skills of the highest order. But what has proven truly wonderful about NADFAS audiences is that they do not display hostility when a lecturer walks into the hall about twenty minutes after the start-time. Instead, we receive a huge round of applause for demonstrating the bulldog spirit and getting to the lecture-hall at all.*

David Cross remembers being met by his hostess at a railway station in Sussex, and they were just about to drive off when he suspected all was not quite in order. He enquired 'You do want a lecture on Ruskin tonight, don't you?' The lady looked startled and replied 'Oh, we thought you were speaking on the Newlyn School.' 'Ah,' he said 'please stop the car and wait a moment.' He got out of the car and looked across the

**Above**
The Duke of Bedford, an early NADFAS supporter and lecturer, during a visit to Harrow DFAS in 1972. He is pictured with Mayoress Valerie Haslam, Valerie Woodford, chair, and Robby Brown, vice chair
**Above right**
NADFAS lecturer and *Antiques Roadshow* regular David Battie with members of Beaconsfield DFAS

before laser pointers).

Heather Jones from Arden DFAS says 'the most memorable of all the lectures seem to be those with a comic or entertaining element'. She vividly remembers that:

*Peter Medhurst gave a delightful lecture on the origins of the Christmas Carol. As the origins lie in dance – he had to dance and this he nimbly did. The stage, on which he had to lecture, play the piano, sing and dance, had a great part removed for an orchestra performing later that day. To have the stage restored had met with refusal so our hero risked limb, if not life, cavorting in the near dark around a gaping black hole. What*

station to see Tom Cross, not a relative but a fellow NADFAS lecturer, getting into another. He dashed over and gestured to his hostess and explained 'wrong car'.

Behind many a lecturer's calm façade there are fearful moments, as recalled by Sheelagh Lewis. 'Was I wearing the correct outfit, would the car get me there on time, would I get a puncture, would I find the venue, had I got the correct slides, would the projector jam, would the microphone work?'[18]. Lecturers do not just have to be good communicators, they have to be adaptable. Eric Shanes writes:

*Like all my colleagues, I have talked in some curious venues. One that sticks in my mind was a modern church whose architect's favourite book was obviously Herman Melville's 'Moby Dick'. As a result, one lectured from an overhanging pulpit shaped like a ship's prow. I felt like Captain Ahab up there, with a long lecturing stick substituting for a harpoon (this was in the days*

*a trouper! Health and Safety – Where were you?*[19]

Although nearly all NADFAS lectures are accompanied by slides, a lecturer sometimes has to do without them. It may come as a relief to many that problems with the projecting equipment were a common cause of worry even in the early days, when technology was simpler. A letter from Nannette Foster, then chairman of Westminster DFAS, to Helena Hayward in 1986 reveals an embarrassing accident with the projector:

*I am writing at once to say how terribly sorry and upset I am to hear of your trouble with the projector … and was horrified to hear of the burning of some of your slides … we are still completely mystified as to what happened to our recently overhauled projector, it is now in the hands of yet another 'expert' but we also intend to buy another projector. This one seems to be fated but we had great hopes that having spent £100 on it recently it was in complete working order.*[20]

Fiona Pragnell of Sevenoaks DFAS remembers:

*One night when we were listening to a marvellous talk on, I think, the First World War. We suddenly had a major blackout in our area. After a few minutes the lecturer continued without slides, and gave us a quite memorable and inspiring talk. This is the stuff real NADFAS lecturers are made of.[21]*

When the Sarratt electricity supply failed at 10.30, half an hour before Rickmansworth DFAS's illustrated lecture, there were no slides or microphone. The lecturer, Nicola Smith, disappeared into a quiet back room and revamped her talk to cope – which she did magnificently. Naturally the electricity came back on at 12, just as she finished.[22] When Colonel Willcox came to talk to the Wey Valley Society he was well prepared. When the projection equipment failed, 'in typical army style he happened to have his own equipment in his car', to the relief and appreciation of everyone.[23] Much to the alarm of the audience of one Society, when a slide became jammed in the projector, a flustered and apologetic projectionist was reassured with [the words of the lecturer] 'Don't worry, it's not the worst thing that has happened, once someone died in my lecture'.[24] The chairman of Moor Park Society had to report that in 1972 the 'February lecture on silver by Miss Sylvia Coppen-Gardner... had to be cancelled as we could not use the projector because of the power strike', a grim reminder of the political situation at the time.[25] Sylvia is remembered by many for her trademark style in dress, wearing a different coloured stocking on each leg.

Think of the lecturer for Cirencester DFAS 'coping with 80°F. whilst giving the lecture *In the Bleak Midwinter*'.[26] This roll-call of problems might give the impression that a lecturer's life is not a happy one, but this would be totally wrong. The benefits of NADFAS lecturing are many. The lecturer, if good, is nearly always appreciated. Julia Macleod, chairman of Sevenoaks DFAS, vividly remembers one such expression of satisfaction. After a lecture on Goldsmiths' Hall by the curator, Rosemary Ransome Wallace, who 'was a young attractive blond', there was a lengthy period of questions:

*Finally the chairman called for one last question and a very elderly gentleman stood up. "I hope you don't object to my question, but how old are you?" he said. When she told him, he said: "Well, I think you are bloody marvellous!"[27]*

The lecturer James Taylor remembers a very moving moment, one of those occasions when lecturing is more than usually rewarding:

*After finishing the first slide lecture I noticed in the front row a gentleman holding a white cane. I approached him to see if he had enjoyed the talk. He had seen none of the pictures. I wondered how he could have enjoyed the experience without the gift of sight. He told me he loved the enthusiasm and knowledge of the NADFAS lectures. For him the speakers created "word pictures that brought the subjects to life".[28]*

The lecturer, while experiencing NADFAS *en masse*, also has the opportunity to get to know individual committee members via the hospitality system that has developed from the early days. After travelling for hours a lecturer can be met with a 'cup of chocolate and a hot water bottle, or a five course candlelit meal'.[29] In the visitor books that hold a record of all the lectures and lecturers for Chichester DFAS from its first meeting in 1978, one lecturer in the first year noted 'Your standard of hospitality makes taking a fee as well seem positively immoral'.[30] Part of the attraction of NADFAS lecturing is the fascination in staying in such a variety of homes, meeting interesting people, and being introduced to the arts and architecture of the area. In a letter to another host a NADFAS lecturer wrote:

*I did enjoy my outing; the countryside was so stunningly beautiful and it was a great pleasure staying with you, to see your house and garden and all the splendid things in both. I felt as though I had been lucky enough to have a mini holiday and returned much refreshed.[31]*

What do the lecturers see when they face their audience? Clare Ford-Wille, who has been lecturing to NADFAS since 1978, thinks that 'Because...[the NADFAS audience] know one another and meet regularly in the same place, this gives a more relaxed spirit'.[32] A letter

**Above**

The renowned textile designer Enid Marx was a distinguished early lecturer for NADFAS

archaeologists, architects, art historians, curators and auctioneers; who are specialists in anything from Auerbach to Zoffany, pre-dynastic pottery to plastics. The *Directory* has maintained its selectivity and standard of excellence, while broadening the field of its expertise. So many key 'experts' feel that lecturing to NADFAS is a worthwhile and rewarding activity that quite a number have become involved with their local Societies, not only as members but as presidents and chairmen and, on occasion, they have been the driving force behind the foundation of a new Society. Lecturers and Societies have the same mission, to share their passion for the arts with the widest possible audience.

from the distinguished, and well-seasoned, NADFAS lecturer, Clyde Binfield, conveys the essence of what NADFAS collectively is:

*There is something quite terrifying about a gathering NADFAS audience. On the whole well dressed, articulate, determined to be entertained but also ready to be critical if not instructed as well. But in fact, what an extraordinarily interesting lot they are – from a lecturer's point of view, there is bound to be in every audience someone who genuinely knows more about your subject than you do yourself. That is very stimulating. It is of course, demanding – how do you get across to them, as well as to those who are there, just as justifiably, for the ride? But that is part of the lecturer's challenge in communicating, and it is part of the NADFAS mission in promoting knowledge of, enjoyment of, concern about, determination to do something about, the whole range of fine (and applied) arts and their content. I use the word "mission", that is vital. It is as vital as enjoyment, the two should be inseparable, but the mission should never be lost sight of.*[33]

Forty years on, and NADFAS still has an enviable *Directory of Lecturers* who come from a wide range of fields, including

NOTES

[1] Helen Fielden, 18 March 1981, sent by Teme Valley DFAS, May 2006.
[2] Annual Report 1994/95, NADFAS Archives.
[3] Chiltern DFAS Newsletter no.26 Spring 1980, p.5.
[4] NADFAS *Newsletter*, January 1976.
[5] Telephone interview, August 2007.
[6] 'NADFAS Educational Aims', 1976, Chiltern DFAS Archives.
[7] Telephone interview, August 2007.
[8] Sheelagh Lewis, August 2006.
[9] Ibid.
[10] David Cross, December 2006.
[11] Judith Jessett, Wey Valley DFAS, July 2006.
[12] Fielden, op. cit.
[13] Heather Jones, 'The Arden DFAS Chronicles', October 2006.
[14] Jean Pratt, 'Confessions of a Projectionist' sent by Liz Dancey, Birmingham DFAS, January 2007.
[15] North Kent DFAS, May 1970.
[16] Jill Pearson, Gravesend and District DFAS, July 2006.
[17] Jessett, op. cit.
[18] Lewis, op. cit.
[19] Jones, op. cit.
[20] Shirley Turner, Westminster DFAS.
[21] Fiona Pragnell, Sevenoaks DFAS, July 2006.
[22] Jean Butler, Rickmansworth DFAS, July 2006.
[23] Pratt, op. cit.
[24] Jenny Colmer, Cirencester DFAS, July 2006.
[25] Margaret Bunford, Moor Park DFAS, Chairman's Report for 1971-72, p.1.
[26] Colmer, op. cit.
[27] Jacqueline Pembroke, Sevenoaks DFAS, 'NADFAS: Reflections on the early years' by Julia MacLeod, Sevenoaks DFAS 1980-1986.
[28] James Taylor, January 2007.
[29] Cross, op. cit.
[30] Diane Taylor, Chichester DFAS, October 2006.
[31] Shirley Valentine, NADFAS lecturer, to Helen Fielden, Teme Valley DFAS, 20 September 1981, Private Collection.
[32] Clare Ford-Wille, August 2007.
[33] Clyde Binfield to Jennifer Downey. Hallamshire DFAS, October 2006.

# 5

# Handmaidens: *Practical Help for our Heritage*

*'It is important to see that members are given more opportunity to "do" rather than "look"'*
Patricia Fay to the Duke of Bedford, 1969

A fundamental part of Patricia Fay's vision of NADFAS was its practical potential. As early as 1967 she had stated that 'In fifty years' time we shall be judged not by our number of members and lecturers, but by what we have achieved in the houses and museums'.[1] One of the major objectives of NADFAS, as outlined in the Constitution of 1968 was, and still is, 'the giving of aid to the preservation of our national artistic heritage for the benefit of the public'. This assistance comes via two main routes: the raising of funds to support the purchase and conservation of objects, and the supply of volunteers to physically carry out cataloguing, cleaning and conservation, as well as guiding. The latter was to be the most original and pioneering aspect of NADFAS, and grew so quickly that 'two mighty branches of the NADFAS tree' emerged from this root, Volunteering and Church Recording.[2] Both these movements were part of Patricia's belief that 'It is important to see that members are given more opportunity to "do" rather than "look"'.[3]

## The Birth of the Voluntary Conservation Corps
*'With my hand on my heart I declare that the idea of members forming a volunteer group to give practical help, was in our minds right from the start'*
**Helen Lowenthal, 1988**
When Patricia Fay conceived the idea of NADFAS it is clear that the concept of volunteering was integral to it from the very beginning. As Helen Lowenthal was to state, the idea of giving 'practical help, was in our minds right from the start'.[4] She had already witnessed the impact of museum volunteers in the United States, and was aware of the potential of Patricia Fay's fledgling idea. Nadine Mitchell, the new secretary for NADFAS, and a friend, were already at work at Woburn Abbey in 1967, repairing curtains, which the 'public thought ... was part of the entertainment like the zoo'.[5] The minutes of a NADFAS Committee meeting on 6 February 1968 held at Helen Lowenthal's house reveal that with 'Sir Trenchard Cox [they] discussed briefly the conservative attitude of museum

**Above**
Harpenden VCC team in
1984 cleaning the
chandeliers at Chicheley
Hall, Newport Pagnell

officials in general and particularly in the case of voluntary help in museums and houses as proposed by NADFAS' and recognised that 'there were very real difficulties to contend with, such as Union problems', and as a consequence, 'every care should be taken to exercise great thought and tact in our operations'. Helen Lowenthal then invited Barbara Wriston, the Head of Education at the Art Institute of Chicago, to give a lecture to NADFAS at the Victoria & Albert Museum on 12 May 1969 on the role of the volunteer. The ground was being laid for action. It was at the first National evening event for NADFAS in 1969, hosted by Dr (later Sir) Roy Strong at the National Portrait Gallery, that the first request for volunteers was made. Dr Strong called for help in the Gallery archives, indexing portraits in books and catalogues and filing the resulting slips. Pamela Cowen was one of the six who volunteered, and '28 years later .. [she was] still there. … We file men before women and women if married under their last married names (but Elizabeth Taylor has bucked the

system and goes under "T" for Taylor)'.[6] Lest anyone think that this task was simple, Pamela added:

*Diana, Princess of Wales's stepmother illustrates another problem. Apart from her marriages there are her changes in title: before her divorce and marriage to Earl Spencer Miss McCorquodale became the Hon. Mrs Gerald Legge, then Lady Lewisham, then Countess of Dartmouth. Subsequently she married (and divorced) a French count, so you need to be alert filing copies of portraits.*

Dr Strong was one of three newly appointed directors of London galleries, the others being at the Tate and National Gallery. Their appointments heralded a new approach to museums, making them more accessible to the general public, and opening their doors to outside help. NADFAS was in the right place at the right time to do something innovative, useful and practical in helping custodians of our national cultural heritage.

The early days of the Volunteering are vividly evoked by Phyllis Dryden-James, a member of North Kent DFAS, who with Adele

Barton worked hard to organise the first teams of Volunteers. She remembered that 'It was whilst in Committee in July 1970 that the Chairman, Kathleen Wareham, looked across at me and said "You, Phyllis, will be in charge of Stately Homes!" To put it mildly, this command took my breath away'.[7] Phyllis however, was only momentarily daunted, as she drove home from the meeting she thought '*What* was I going to say to the owners of Stately Homes? *What* did I know of members and *what* did I know members could do?'.[8] She wrote to Chevening House, Knole, Hever Castle, and Penshurst Place, to the National Trust and the National Maritime Museum offering limited and amateur help. Only a fortnight later a letter from the National Trust asked if about six helpers could mark all the furniture with their catalogue numbers at Knole. During an exploratory visit Phyllis learned that they would:

*have to crawl under billiard and other large tables and up-end settees and large chairs ... We would work on Monday and Tuesday morning when the house was closed to the public and it would be as well if we could finish before mid-November as there was no heating in the house.*

With three members and two husbands the project began in the middle of August. In three weeks the NADFAS Volunteers had completed the task that had been estimated to take three months. In April the wife of the agent at Chevening visited the Society, this resulted in 18 members working in the library, cleaning the books; followed by the refurbishment of the volumes in the Royal Academy Library. When Gabrielle Taylor from *Woman's Realm* visited them at the Academy in March 1974 she was impressed by 'the six dedicated members ... busy on their once weekly stint ... cleaning and cataloguing the fifteen thousand art books ... working under the expert eye of librarian Philip James'.[9] The books had to be cleaned with a lactate solution, dried, treated with a special polish from the British Museum, and left to dry off until the Volunteers arrived the following week to polish them, then return them to their proper shelves. The journalist

was even more impressed by Margaret Farquhar, another North Kent DFAS Volunteer working at Hever:

*As she tied a tough blue and white striped apron around her waist and pulled on her rubber gloves ... and then with her companion ... disappeared round the pergola, bearing a red plastic bucket on one arm and a step-ladder on the other, and headed towards the lakeside Venus.*

She explained that Lord Astor had written asking 'Could we scrub the statues in his Italian and Rose gardens?'. Phyllis remembered that 'He liked the paying public to see us working'. In 1970 the North Kent Volunteers coined the term 'Voluntary Conservation Corps'. Nancy Rhodes, whilst working at Chevening had asked 'We need a name – what about Voluntary Conservation Corps?'[10] So that day, the VCC was born. As with the acronym NADFAS, there was sometimes confusion about what the letters stood for. When Virginia Evans, then Chairman of the VCC, was introduced to HRH The Duke of Gloucester at Cardiff, he looked at her badge and asked 'Does that stand for the Veteran Car Club?'.[11]

The success of the early work by the Volunteers meant that in 1973 the VCC was nationally co-ordinated, with Patricia Fay as its Chairman, and an inaugural meeting held that year at the British Institute of Recorded Sound in London to explain its work to the appointed VCC representatives, country house owners and museum directors. The panel consisted of Lord Astor of Hever, Helen Lowenthal, John Fuller, Librarian at the V&A, and Adele Barton of North Kent DFAS. As Patricia Fay announced at the *Historic European Houses* Conference in Oxford 1975, at first neither country house owners nor museums 'seemed over-enthralled at the idea of lots of lovely NADFAS ladies invading your territories'. Yet she told them:

*The discovery and mobilisation of NADFASIANS could be a small contributory condition of your survival. ... If you think our work is worthwhile, we can expand and develop. What we need is your co-operation, encouragement and a willingness to experiment.*[12]

Patricia was frustrated because she had

**Above**

The smart emerald and gold NADFAS Volunteers badge, supplied as part of the original *How to Start a Voluntary Conservation Corps* pack

willing Volunteers, but not enough projects to keep them occupied. Fortunately there were a few far-sighted individuals who recognised the potential these ladies offered, among them the Duke of Bedford, Lord Astor, Sir John Pope-Hennessy and Dr Roy Strong.

'What these women are doing' announced Patricia:

> is truly astonishing. Collectively they give the image of privileged wives. In point of fact, many are women of stature, in their own right, as well as fulfilling their roles as wives of peers, politicians, judges, captains of industry etc. they are not afraid of hard work or soiling their clothes.[13]

It was perhaps these words that inspired the editor of *Country Life* to christen these ladies 'the Handmaidens of the Arts'. Far from being 'just a lecture society' or concerned only with looking, Patricia emphasised that 'members of NADFAS are prepared to work very hard, quite unpaid, to preserve and restore, wherever they see old or neglected objects facing destruction for lack of care'.[14] This offer of help came of course at a crucial time in the history of the country house. Changing social patterns, particularly since the Second World War, made the keeping of large resident staff, equipped with the relevant skills, rarely viable. So the role of the independent professional and the skilled volunteer became increasingly significant.[15]

## Forging Links

The growth and success of Volunteering relied on the many connections NADFAS made with country house owners, and other heritage-orientated organisations. As early as 1971 a member of the NADFAS Executive was appointed to the Council of the Historic Houses Association, in recognition of the growing power and influence of NADFAS. Winifred Ballachey, an Executive Committee member who had recently retired from the staff of the National Trust, was given the task of collating information from museums, churches, libraries and the National Trust, with the idea of expanding NADFAS conservation work.[16] In the same year

NADFAS was asked to support the recruitment drive for the National Trust. In January 1976 a seminar on *The Conservation Role of the Volunteer in Historic Houses and Museums* was organised by NADFAS at the Royal Commonwealth Society, in conjunction with the Crafts Advisory Council and the HHA, and over 300 attended. The speakers from various museums, historic houses and the Department of Education expressed their thanks in public to NADFAS for the work done by their volunteers. The following year, via Jane Downes (who had become VCC Chairman in 1977), links were consolidated with the National Trust Historic Buildings Department. The NADFAS Volunteers had come a long way in a short time. The initial 'cold reception' to the first offers of help, which had so angered Helen Lowenthal, had turned into a warm vote of thanks for their services.

The *Heritage Co-ordination* conference in May 1979 was a milestone for the VCC, it was a NADFAS sponsored day led by Pamela Cowen. For the first time a VCC Chairman sat as an equal on the conference committee with members from most of the national amenity societies. In 1982 NADFAS was nominated by the National Trust as one of the organisations able to appoint a member to its Council and Sheila Chapman, as National Chairman, became the first NADFAS representative. By 1983 NADFAS VCC were active at 68 different sites, from Anglesey Abbey to York Minster. Over 100 groups within the 150 member Societies were occupied with work ranging from cleaning books at Penshurst Place to repairing the armour at Chiddingstone Castle. There was every cause to celebrate the 10th Anniversary of the VCC that year, when a party was organised at the Royal Society of Arts to which 120 people came. Only a year later 115 groups representing 1,200 members were actively Volunteering. In answer to the growing demand for information a 'How to Start a Voluntary Conservation Corps' pack had been assembled, and new emerald and gold badges supplied to indicate (and advertise) the NADFAS Volunteers at work.

## The Importance of Training

### 'Training my dear, that's what they need, training!'

**Helen Lowenthal to Virginia Evans, 1981**

Patricia Fay knew that it was simply not enough to just offer help. She recognised that there would be two major prejudices held against the VCC. First, as amateurs they lacked the professional knowledge to undertake their tasks and, second, they would be perceived as flighty middle-class ladies who would quickly tire of tedious, regular work. The answer to both was to provide training and for the groups to prove their worth. They were the early ambassadors for NADFAS and it was crucial that mistakes were not made, or prejudices confirmed. As Helen Lowenthal reminded Virginia Evans, then Chairman of the VCC, 'Training my dear, that's what they need, training!'. Leaflets advertising the VCC and magazine articles stressed that 'No project is undertaken without training, and all the work is done under the guidance of art historians and experts'.[17] Perhaps to compensate for misconceptions amongst the professionals NADFAS Volunteers worked extremely hard to overcome the stereotype and became renowned for their stamina, reliability, and efficiency.

In the early days Roy Strong emphasised the need for discipline if Volunteers were to be taken seriously, and their work to be respected. Talking about the first NADFAS Volunteers at the National Portrait Gallery he said: 'I remember I was very fierce with them to begin with and I said to them "You can only come and work here if you absolutely guarantee to keep hours and come regularly and not fall by the wayside".[18] I said "If you do you will go"'.[19]

In the early days some sceptical curators and house owners waited with ill-concealed anticipation for evidence of an unpunctual workforce plagued by migraine to offend permanent staff! This failed to happen.[20] As one journalist explained, the offer by the VCC of help:

*was one the Horniman Museum thought it might refuse. There were reservations about letting in a group of people who would need training from scratch and who could turn out to have a less than professional approach.*
*They were fears museum staff were delighted to find unfounded.*[21]

From the start training was seen as central to the success and growth of volunteering. Helen Lowenthal and Helena Hayward assisted with the training of the first guides for Ham House and Osterley Park from the Chiltern, Thames and Gerrards Cross Societies, under the guidance of Maurice Tomlin from the Furniture Department of the V&A. Training days were organised at the V&A, the first by Elizabeth Greenhill on the preservation of old books in January 1970. Many others followed.

By the mid 1970s such was the demand for volunteers, the VCC realised the need for more formal and continuous links with advisory experts. In 1976 the Advisory Council for Volunteers was set up, comprising Helen Lowenthal, John Fuller from the V&A, Robert Rowe of Temple Newsam, Derek Shrub of Sotheby's, and Arnold Wilson of Bristol City Art Galleries. As the official leaflet stated, the VCC is: 'one of the most important divisions of NADFAS. No other Association gives members this opportunity to learn a new skill, or re-learn an old one and, in this way, make a practical contribution to the conservation of our heritage'.

In 1978 the first representative meeting was held for the VCC to assist the dissemination of information amongst the growing number of volunteer groups. In 1981 NADFAS secured the help of Dr Nicholas Pickwoad, who advised the National Trust on the keeping and care of books. He agreed to offer the volunteers basic training. By degrees a group of experts was recruited to give training in the handling of a variety of materials: paper, wood, ceramics and glass, silver and metalwork. Virginia Evans, who became the Chairman of the VCC in 1981, approached West Dean College the following year, and the result was the first residential training course for 12 in 1982 on the 'Care and Cleaning of Porcelain and Glass' with Judy Larney, their resident tutor. This was

**Above**

Roy Strong and Kathleen
Wareham (far left)
cataloguing photographs
at the National Portrait
Gallery, one of the first
voluntary projects
undertaken by NADFAS

followed in 1983 with 'Conservation,
Mounting, and Framing of Works of Art on
Paper for Display' with Jane McAusland, and
in 1984 'Identification, Cleaning, Care and
Repair of Oriental Rugs' with Majid Amini.
Some of these tutors became official advisers
to the NADFAS VCC. Although trained it was
'important, however proficient we became
that we were not, as amateurs, trying to
emulate the professionals'.[22]

Any NADFAS Volunteer project requires
expert advice from the outset, to ensure that
the proposal would be within the capability
of the Volunteer group following suitable
training. In 1997 national training days were
started and offered to Volunteers currently
working, or about to start work, and were
paid for by NADFAS. The first were offered in
book care, and preventative textile

conservation, the latter held at the Textile
Conservation Centre at Hampton Court.
These courses reflected the most popular
work undertaken by NADFAS Volunteers.
Training days also began to be organised at
Area level, and to suit specific projects. As
Isobel Lattimore, then Chairman of NADFAS
Volunteers, confidently stated 'We have
systems in place to monitor all the
Volunteers' activities and are very concerned
that nothing is done to jeopardise the
heritage we are all trying to save'.[23]

The *Volunteers Handbook*, an important
benchmark in the history of the VCC, was
originally conceived by Michaela Jenkerson-
Kenshole (who became VCC Chairman in
1985) to be an aid to both those interested in
being a Volunteer, and to introduce the
trained conservator to some of the

experiences of a Volunteer. The contributors to the *Handbook* included some of the most distinguished conservators, archivists and librarians in the country, Dr Nicholas Pickwood, Dinah Eastop from Hampton Court, Dr Roger Pringle from the Shakespeare Birthplace Trust, and Dr Jonathan Ashley-Smith, Head of Conservation at the V&A. In this first NADFAS *Volunteers Handbook*, published in 1991, Kenneth Hudson commented that:

*I believe that voluntary work in museums is going to become steadily more widespread and more important. It gives a lot of pleasure and satisfaction to the people who carry it out, planned and properly organised it allows things to be done which would otherwise have to remain undone and it can bring a breath of fresh air into an atmosphere which can all too easily become stale and oppressive. There is not the slightest reason for volunteers to feel unwanted or inferior. The world is going their way.*[24]

How right he was.

## Praise and Problems
### '... not a threat but a caring band of willing people'[25]
**Volunteers Handbook, 1991, Margaret Beard**
However it was not all plain sailing. As Michaela Jenkerson-Kenshole explained:

*Even allowing for the enormous growth of NADFAS, the actual number of members actively engaged in Volunteer work is still a small percentage, and much continues to be asked of them in commitment, achievement of a high standard of work, and responsibility for the reputation of NADFAS as a whole.*[26]

This statement is as true now, as when it was made in 1985. Finances were always difficult, and generous support from the Patricia Fay Memorial Fund, in acknowledgement of the founder's special interest in Volunteering, was crucial to the survival of the VCC. Training, which is central to NADFAS voluntary work, has to be paid for. By the mid 1970s the success of some of the early projects was beginning to take effect. When Patricia Fay addressed the *Historic European Houses* Conference in 1975 she boldly remarked to her audience of country house owners and heritage professionals:

*Some of you are gradually shedding yourselves of your understandable prejudices against voluntary help ... We are, I think, in a similar situation to that of Florence Nightingale and her nurses to the medical profession over a century ago. This country needs your survival; not as isolated showmen and showhouses, but to establish yourselves as cultural and loving spiritual centres, involved with the people ... Unless more challenging opportunities can be found for these women, much of their talent will drift away.*

This was fighting talk, but there were still other problems on the horizon.

Some conservation professionals were not too happy about volunteers taking on projects. The later 1970s were a time of severe cuts in museum expenditure, and job losses. When Norman Brommelle, Keeper of Conservation at the V&A, and a Vice President of NADFAS between1975-89, left the VCC Advisory Panel, his successor, Dr Jonathan Ashley-Smith was not so enthusiastic about NADFAS Volunteers. He warned the new VCC Chairman, Jane Downes, that 'we could no longer depend on practical instruction from his department for VCC Study Days as he thought there were very few categories of job that we could properly undertake'.[27]

At the *The Use of Volunteers in Museums and Art Galleries* conference in 1985 it became clear for the first time 'the hostility felt by Union members from some of the large museums in London' towards NADFAS Volunteers, exacerbated by high unemployment in this and other professions. When Marjorie Somers-Cocks wrote an article on NADFAS she was keen to state that the Volunteers, 'in no way ... take the bread out of the mouths of paid workers'.[28] June Fenwick emphasised to the Association of Independent Museums that 'VCC Volunteers never seek to take the place of professional conservationists, only to give them assistance where it is needed'.[29]

Two action points were taken to address these problems. Only when a project had

**Above**
Osterley Park was one of the first stately homes to benefit from specially trained guides and volunteers

been carefully assessed by a professional conservator would specific training be arranged, and an Indemnity Form was introduced, detailing training procedures and supervision. The ever-increasing role and range of work undertaken by the VCC culminated in a change of name, when in 1989 the Voluntary Conservation Corps became the NADFAS Volunteers. Projects were no longer largely limited to conservation, as conservation itself was becoming much more professionalised, with:

*an increased number and quality of initial training courses and the development of professional bodies, … the rate of change has increased as better-educated conservators have reached prominent positions, able to influence opinion-formers, decision-makers and budget-holders … the changes that have taken place in NADFAS Volunteers are part of this general progression in conservation.*[30]

The NADFAS Volunteers became Heritage Volunteers in June 2001. It was felt that the new title explained their particular role more clearly within the context of NADFAS and the outside heritage sector where they are acknowledged as a leader in heritage volunteering. Previously, there had been

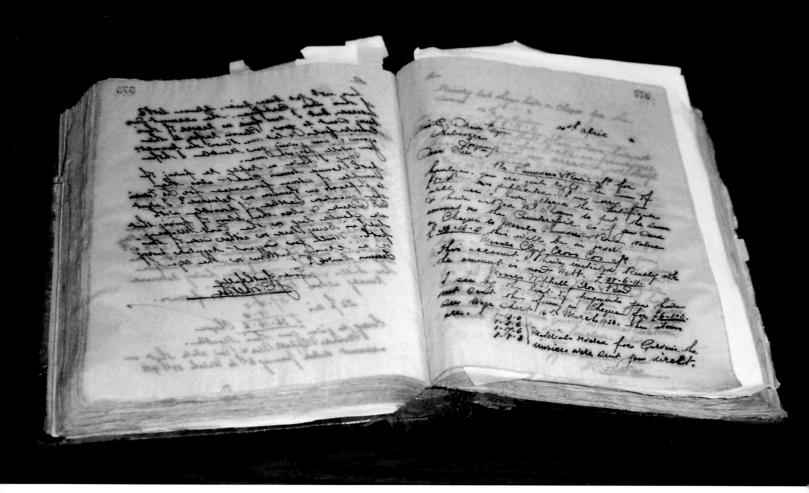

confusion between the many people who give voluntary help, namely volunteers, and NADFAS Volunteers.[31]

## Some Projects

The importance of Heritage Volunteer projects can surely be calculated by how many of the early projects have led to long-term and continuing relationships between NADFAS Volunteers and country house owners and museum and gallery curators, librarians and archivists. For example York DFAS started work refurbishing the books at Castle Howard Library in 1975, and they are still there today.[32] The North Kent group, once ensconced in the Library at the Royal Academy, were asked to make a card index of all the 25,000 volumes, and after that asked to 'man' the Private Rooms at the RA which were opened to the public for the first time in 1974. As Irene Martin remembers, 'This was indeed a mammoth task!'. Patricia Fay organised a meeting and 150 NADFAS members arrived, some from as far away as Bournemouth. When the meeting was over Patricia handed Irene her file and said 'Here you are Irene, it's all up to you'.[33] Seventeen

Societies became involved, and this was the first of many guiding assignments that North Kent DFAS Volunteers undertook. In 1991 two members of the Society had completed over 20 years' service for the RA.

Some early projects also developed national collaboration between NADFAS Volunteer groups and others to realise vast, scholarly and important undertakings. The Furniture History Society's *Dictionary of English Furnituremakers*, published in 1986, was compiled over a period of seven years by nearly 400 researchers, of which 70 were NADFAS Volunteers. This was, and still is, the definitive reference work on furniture makers active in England between 1660 and 1840, and is an indispensable source for identifying makers known hitherto only by faint inscriptions, faded labels, or scattered references in country house archives. The Society for the Preservation of Ancient Buildings also owed much to NADFAS volunteers for research towards the *Domesday Survey of Barns*, published in 1984. These projects show NADFAS at its best pooling labour, working to high standards under professional guidance to achieve outstanding

**Above and bottom right**
Books of bound letters at Castle Drogo gave up some exciting secrets for Taunton DFAS Volunteers

**Top right**
Stamford DFAS Volunteers working on the Phillips Collection were surprised to find that the spine of one volume had been patched using a back issue of *The Times* dating from 1854

and nationally important results, contributing to the wider and deeper appreciation of our heritage.

The following sections on the major types of work undertaken by Heritage Volunteers can only convey a glimpse of the astonishing range of tasks carried out. It serves to highlight the flexibility, tenacity and professionalism that have become the bywords for Heritage Volunteers. All show the qualities of 'self-discipline, commitment and diplomacy' the essential requirements of a NADFAS Volunteer.[34]

## Guiding and Stewarding

*'Be cautious... Be prepared for Disaster... Be enthusiastic'* [35]
***Volunteers Handbook**, 1991, Barbara Askwith*
The 'favourite job with NADFAS members everywhere … is guiding … as they also have to learn to cope with the unexpected – such as the short-sighted visitor who inquired about the giant spider in the hall. It turned out to be the bell-pull!'.[36]

The key skills of the guide are 'caution in answering queries on staff and security, being prepared for disaster, and maintaining enthusiasm'.[37] As Norman Hudson was to comment, 'Guiding might seem as though it should be straightforward to anyone who has done their homework. But without proper instruction it could dissolve into a scene from

the latest comedy'.[38] As early as 1975, NADFAS guides were active across the country. Thanet DFAS Volunteers were working in Canterbury Cathedral and Quex Park, while Croydon DFAS helped man Quebec House. The Edinburgh group was at No.7 Charlotte Square and Gladstone's Land. Goodwood House and Parnham House used Volunteers from West Sussex DFAS. Ham House and Osterley Park were stewarded by Thames DFAS and the Sevenoaks Volunteers were at Knole and Leeds Castle. North Kent and Enfield DFAS groups could be found at Westminster Abbey. The Chiltern Volunteers were at St George's Chapel Windsor, and Thames DFAS was represented at West Wycombe Park. All over Great Britain, country houses and ancient buildings were able to respond to the growing demand for public access by turning to NADFAS for help. By 1983 the VCC leaflet listed 19 separate places where NADFAS Volunteers were guiding, and the list continues to grow. Some projects were substantial feats of organisation, like the 150 Volunteers mobilised to run the Royal Armouries Information Centre in the 1980s, for 363 days a year. Patricia Fay herself volunteered at Knebworth, during her secondment from London Polytechnic as part of her Diploma course in Historic House Management. The manager David Condy remembers that she not only guided, but also devised a customer survey, designed information 'bats', cleared away cups and saucers in the cafe, and drove the miniature railway, which she managed to de-rail!

## Cataloguing

*'... completed this task in a fraction of the time it would otherwise have taken'*
**Roger Pringle, Director of the Shakespeare Birthplace Trust, 1991**

For many museums, archives and country houses the task of listing, indexing and researching their collections represents an urgent but almost unrealisable task. The more immediate pressures of keeping open prevents work on these longer term and time-consuming projects. In many cases it is only the trained volunteer who can provide the regular time, and cumulative expertise required for cataloguing. An early triumph was the discovery in Reading Museum of 30 letters from Auguste Rodin to an English sculptor, unearthed by a Volunteer from Hart DFAS in 1978. As a result of the Harrogate VCC working at Temple Newsam, a reserve collection of 2,500 ceramic items, part of the Smithfield Collection, which had lain in boxes since the beginning of the twentieth century, was put on public display. This led to many other projects at Temple Newsam, including packing the Harding Collection for removal to the cellar, while the Long Gallery ceiling was repaired. Seven Volunteers from Horsham DFAS worked in the 1990s at the local museum preparing its ceramic collection for exhibition. The cataloguing involved washing, describing, ascribing, dating and valuing each piece. Some of the ceramics had not been handled for over 25 years. This exercise was part of a larger project dating from the 1980s which had begun with costume. As the curator Jenny Knight stated 'the main advantage in using NADFAS is that they are trustworthy, reliable and dedicated'.[39] Volunteers at the

Shakespeare Birthplace Trust indexed the local newspaper, the *Stratford-upon-Avon Herald*, and listed the receipts and vouchers from the papers of the Leighs of Stoneleigh Abbey between 1600-1800. The archivist was eternally grateful to the 'brave band of NADFAS Volunteers apparently immune to the very cold conditions ... who completed this task in a fraction of the time it would otherwise have taken'.[40]

The excitement of being involved in cataloguing does not wane over time, as the experience of Katharin Dalton, chairman of Taunton DFAS, at Castle Drogo, proves. She was just finishing transcribing the second book of bound letters of the site agent responsible for the building of the Castle when she idly checked right to the end of the book. There she found tucked inside the back board four original letters, one being from the owner Julius Drewe. The Volunteers had been handling the book for three years and had no idea there was anything hidden at the back. Moreover the manager of Castle Drogo had recently told Katharin that the National Trust did not possess any of the original letters. So the find was a treasure in its own right.

Distance and difficult access does not put NADFAS Volunteers off. The project to catalogue the three libraries at Mount Stuart House on the Isle of Bute first required a feasibility study [taking] into account the 40-mile drive from Ayr's environs to Wemyss Bay and the 30-minute ferry crossing to Rothesay. The Volunteers were invited to live in-house on once monthly three-night visits. As Ellice Miller from Ayrshire DFAS explains, 'as we work six hours a day, in one and a half hour stretches, travel, eat and relax together, it is essential for the team to get on well'.[41]

Cataloguing projects have also resulted in the emergence of whole teams of Volunteers contributing to much larger surveys that have an impact on a whole subject area. When five members of West Sussex DFAS went on a course to Juniper Hall in 1975, led by Joan Harding, the result was the creation of a vernacular building recording group. She had become aware that although larger buildings were well recorded little was known about the construction of domestic buildings which, at the time, were rarely listed and were becoming much altered and even destroyed to make room for development. Fired up by their tutor the five Volunteers set up the Vernacular Buildings Study Group under the aegis of West Sussex DFAS. They report that their:

*highlight was when the secretary of the Royal Commission for Historic Buildings sent us a student studying vernacular building as part of*

and more have all come under the careful care of NADFAS Volunteers. In fact, there are few types of object that have not been tackled by them, including seals dating back to the 1200s at Arundel Castle by Arun DFAS Volunteers, while the gentlemen of Sevenoaks DFAS worked with arms and armour at Knole and Chevening House.

As Helen Lloyd, the Housekeeper to the National Trust, stated, 'working as a Volunteer on preventative conservation … is

**Above**
Joint effort: Volunteers from Arden DFAS and Stratford DFAS show off their handiwork – a set of fine canvaswork covers for the dining chairs at Coughton Court
**Above right**
Malvern Hills DFAS textile volunteers hard at work on a copy of a William Burges design quilt for the Marquis of Bute's bed in Cardiff Castle

*his degree, to record a house with us. He later wrote to tell us that together we had achieved an "A" for the project.*[42]

Perhaps one of the most unusual cataloguing projects is being currently undertaken by a member of East Hertfordshire DFAS, who measures toothbrushes one afternoon a week at Hertford Museum, part of the collection of the local brushmakers Addis.[43]

## Cleaning and conserving
**'It gives a new meaning to the words "dirty pictures"'**
**Jill Barlow, Cheltenham DFAS, on cleaning documents at Gloucestershire Record Office, 1998**
Armour, books, glass, gravestones, maps, paintings, paper, silver and statues, textiles

not a glamorous occupation. It is certainly not for the faint hearted and unfit'.[44]

A typical example of co-operation between NADFAS and a museum was the project undertaken at Skipton's Craven Museum to conserve the Museum's large unused store of period clothing.[45] Training was arranged for the volunteers from the Skipton & Wharfedale DFAS by the Museum and Art Gallery Service for Yorkshire and Humberside, and part of the cost for the training came from the Patricia Fay Memorial Fund. They are part of what was called 'the emergency help squad'.[46]

Edinburgh Antiques and Fine Art Society Volunteers helped at the Edinburgh Museum of Childhood for several years, working on the collection of dolls. Their work included mending and darning split seams, stitching backing supports and even cleaning their faces, with Ponds cold cream.[47]

In 1992 the Antwerp Volunteers began their first project, cleaning the large silver reliquary in Saint Andries church. A year and 550 hours of work later it was completed, under the guidance of Antwerp's leading precious metals expert Patrick Storme. This task has led to further work including the cleaning of gold embroidery, and the 'rescue of fallen street madonnas'. Although other mainland European Societies have ventured into Volunteer work, Brussels with a library and Hamburg stewarding, Antwerp DFAS is the only one to have set up an 'official' Heritage Volunteer Group, and their success will, it is hoped, stimulate more of these Societies to take up this pioneering and important work. As has already been mentioned several Australian Societies have active Volunteer projects, taking Patricia Fay's mission to 'do' rather than to 'look', to the other side of the world.

## Books
### *'The temptation to settle down for a quiet read is always great'*
**Helen Ouin, West Sussex DFAS Volunteer, 2006**

Of all the variety of cleaning and conserving work, that related to books and textiles features most prominently. The Athenaeum Club, Balliol College Oxford, Carlyle's House, Ightham Mote, the National Maritime Museum, the Royal Zoological Society and Wells Cathedral all have something in common. They all have libraries which have benefited from NADFAS book cleaning projects. The refurbishment of libraries has been one of the most popular tasks undertaken by NADFAS Volunteers. Between 1975 and 1988, 121 libraries from The Alpine Club to the Yorkshire Archaeological Society have received attention from NADFAS Volunteers. In some cases the process of cleaning is the first time that many of these books have been looked at in detail for centuries, and the scrutiny often results in exciting discoveries. Volunteers from Hampstead Heath DFAS were asked in 1991

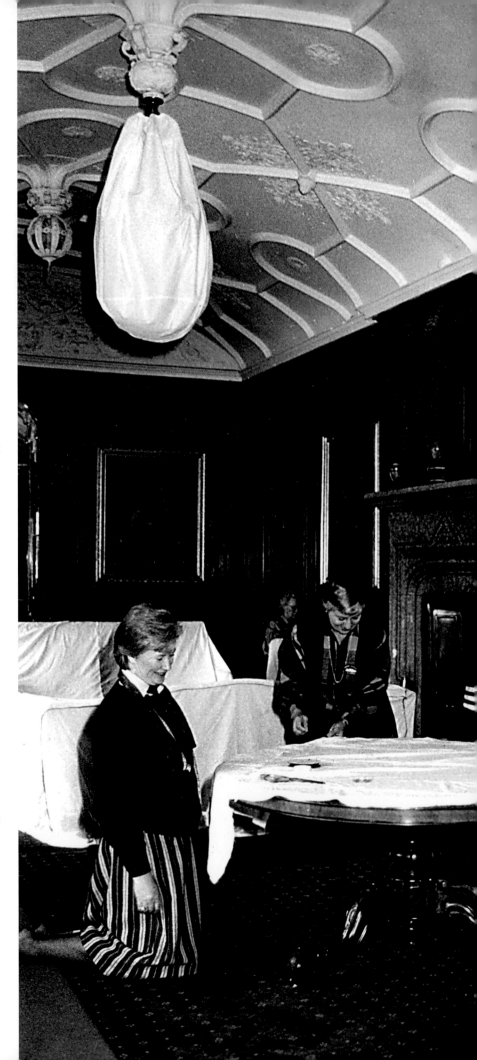

to help 'dust the books' in the Adam Library, which houses a large part of Lord Iveagh's collection at Kenwood House, where the Society meets for its monthly lectures. 'On inspection it was clear that much more was needed than a mere dusting' and so began a project of systematic conservation and recording. Ten years later, the job was completed. During this time a fascinating discovery was made. The Volunteers were asked to empty a large breakfront bookcase before it was moved from the Lecture Room to a new site. Inside were documents relating to the Iveagh Bequest as well as a pile of prints and oversized books, which had lain hidden for decades.

A group of seven volunteers from Stamford DFAS started work in their local Town Hall in September 2000. One of the team explained:

*We set to work on the town's Phillips Collection, a fine collection of old and precious books principally relating to Stamford that were purchased by public subscription and placed in the care and custody of the corporation after the death of Joseph Phillips in 1905.*

They dusted, treated, glued, polished, mended split hollows, sewed, crafted 'made to measure' book boxes and melinex covers and generally cared for these fine old books. This job completed, the group moved on to the conservation of statute books and charters housed in the safe of the Town Hall. Whilst examining one of the statute books which was badly in need of repair to its broken spine, 'we realised that this repair had been done once before. Not by a NADFAS Volunteer, I hasten to add! The spine had been previously repaired using the front page of *The Times*, issue no. 21,710'. They traced this issue to Saturday 8 April 1854, and had a photocopy of this front page made, and enjoyed picturing the scene of those who repaired the book in 1854 using the daily paper to do so! 'Recycling is not a new idea!'[48]

Four Devon Volunteers work at Exeter Cathedral Library, and in 2006 celebrated ten years of book restoration by adjourning to the Champagne Bar at the Royal Clarence! Volunteers from the Sidmouth, Honiton and

Devon Societies are combined in four teams working at the Devon & Exeter Institute, called 'one of the city's best kept secrets'.[49] With a grant from the Patricia Fay Memorial Fund in 1993 these volunteers have been trained to work on the 36,000 books in the cathedral library. The main problem with working on books, as Helen Ouin, a member of the West Sussex DFAS Volunteers remarked, is that 'the temptation to settle down for a quiet read is always great'.[50] NADFAS Volunteers have also come to the aid of two of the most distinguished libraries in the land, in each case following a disastrous fire. In 1993, the South Mercia Area mustered a very large number of

Volunteers to help at Windsor Castle in cleaning the books in HM The Queen's Private Library. The 46,000 volumes were not in themselves damaged by the great fire of 1992 but had to be moved in order to permit the re-wiring which followed. Five Societies, Chiltern, Chalfont, Henley, Aylesbury and West Wycombe, each provided a group to work on one day a week and this mammoth task was completed well within the time expected by the Librarian. In the case of the

**Left** Thanks to the efforts of South Devon volunteers (pictured) the worn protective sheets at Saltram House were replaced by smart new linen covers
**Above** One of two canvaswork window seat cushions presented to the Museum of Edinburgh, Huntly House, designed by Maureen Johnson. This one depicts the Old Town and was executed mainly by the Heritage Volunteers of Edinburgh DFAS in 2007

Hampton Court, in 1986, VCC members from Claremont and Runnymede Societies were involved, not in conservation, but in creating a record of the fire damage by cataloguing and mounting thousands of 'before and after' photographs taken by the architects in charge of the restoration works.

## Textiles
### *'Dirty, dusty, fiddly, but fascinating, work'*[51]
### Julia Macleod, Sevenoaks DFAS, 2006

Textiles, like books, occupy a special place within the history of DFAS Volunteering. The needleworking skills of countless ladies have been applied to the rescue of fabrics, from curtains to altar cloths, and also to the making of replicas, which 'once disparaged, is now rapidly becoming an acceptable part of conservation', and is approached with as much knowledge and expertise as the care of the originals.[52]

At the Horniman Museum work on Indian textile examples is 'slow exacting work that means spending hours to tease back into shape a couple of inches of material that may never go on exhibition anyway'. The Volunteers work under the direction of two conservators who trained them. They had to learn what cloth was used to make the fabric, to recognise the stitches, to flatten and straighten the material and 'to handle it before we were allowed to work on it'.[53] Such time consuming and skilled work is often a luxury for many a country house collection and museum, and many fine examples of needlework have languished in a store room for lack of attention.

A more unusual use of Volunteers' skills is deployed in the making of replicas. The Malvern Hills DFAS Textile Volunteers group made a beautiful copy of a William Burges design quilt for the Marquis of Bute's bed in Cardiff Castle. This four-year project means that the visiting public can appreciate the glow of the bright colours without further damage to the original. The rich yellow quilt makes a bold and important design statement in the dark green of the bedroom. This same group is in the final stages of replicating hangings for the smoking room. With both

projects careful attention has been paid to sourcing the correct fabrics, threads, spangles and fringes. Another Heritage Volunteers project involved the re-creation of a period bedroom for the Topsham Museum in Devon. The plan was to re-create a period room as a teaching aid, with the brief to make a set of needleworked bed-curtains in seventeenth-century style, which could have been embroidered by the ladies of the household of a middle class merchant with thriving Amsterdam connections. The joint Bedfordshire & Hertfordshire/South Mercia Area Projects at Chiltern Open Air Museum included making replica clothes for school children to use on visits.[54] Ladies from two NADFAS groups, Arden and Stratford, combined their skills to produce a set of fine canvaswork covers for the dining chairs at Coughton Court.

An interesting combination of conservation and new-making was involved in the rescue of the altar frontal at Christ Church in Kensington. This project was initiated in 2003 by The Patron of NADFAS, The Duchess of Gloucester, who attended this church.[55] Originally worked in the 1900s, it had been remade in the 1960s using a poor quality fabric. Volunteers from three different Societies from the West Mercia Area were invited to redesign and remake the frontal putting the motifs back onto new green silk. To complete the work, the small pieces not used in the new frontal were incorporated into a simple matching pulpit fall. In acknowledgment of their excellent work, The Duke and Duchess invited the volunteers to a re-dedication service, followed by a private lunch.

Another aspect of textile-related conservation is the making of protective covers. The Dukeries DFAS are currently making sun curtains for 14 huge windows at Hardwick Hall, the fine Tudor house famed for being more 'glass than wall'. This is not a new venture as they have already made about 90 linen covers for the furniture. The before and after photographs of the work of South Devon DFAS Volunteers are self-explanatory: ugly, cumbersome sheets were replaced by elegant, effective covers for the furniture at

Saltram House between 1993 and 1995, the work of 17 teams.

As fabrics are prey to light damage and wear, one of the most essential conservation tasks is repair. The Sevenoaks DFAS Volunteers were plunged in at the deep end when their first project was to help restore the King's Bed at Knole, under the direction of Philippa Lawrence. A workroom was set up under the eaves at Knole, where a rota of enthusiastic needlewomen was organised from several societies around Kent.[56] Julia McLeod recalls how she was keen to help, but having little experience of needlework, was given the task of unpicking large amounts of untidy and rather crude Victorian repairs. Thick black thread, attaching gold and silver brocade to disintegrating backing cloth, had to be removed.

In the 1970s Volunteers from Societies in the Merseyside Area restored the upholstery on the chairs at the Lady Lever Art Gallery by mounting them on a scrim backing to protect the tapestry from further damage and by covering it with a fine silk net: 'It's a technique learned from the advisers at the V&A. We wouldn't touch it unless we had good advice'.[57]

The Glaven Valley DFAS needleworkers began to mend the William Kent upholstered furniture in the South Dining Room at Holkham Hall in 2002. As well as the silk velvet upholstered chairs and soft furnishings in the State Bedroom, they also worked on the silk embroidered cover of the state bed. As with many of these ambitious undertakings, collaboration with other DFAS groups was required to complete the task. King's Lynn DFAS Volunteers willingly came to their aid.

A more unusual aspect of textile associated work is the creation of new work to enhance existing exhibits. The Kennet DFAS Volunteers have been embroidering runners, which will decorate the bed cover of the newly restored state bed at Lydiard Park. They are finely embroidered with silk, the designs based on

**Left** Dukeries Heritage Volunteers polishing antique kitchen utensils at Hardwick Hall

panels within the fifteenth century window in the adjoining dressing room. The project has taken over three and a half years to date and the results will be future museum treasures, proving that high quality handcraft skills have not died, but live on to be appreciated by future generations.

## Conclusion

Little can Patricia Fay have known how varied the tasks of her NADFAS Volunteers would be, from cleaning Lord Uxbridge's wooden leg to restoring an elephant's boot.

In the later 1980s NADFAS Volunteers entered new territory when they became involved in garden history. As Heather Prescott, the Garden Advisor for the NADFAS Volunteers, reminded readers of the *Volunteers Handbook* in 1991, 'great gardens are a notable form of decorative art' and have become a rapidly growing area for volunteers to become involved with. Research into 'lost' gardens via old maps, auction catalogues and estate letters assist in their reconstruction. In 1993 the Garden History Project linked Yorkshire and Warwickshire Volunteers with the Centre for Historic Parks & Gardens at York University. Volunteers have been active at Chelsea Physic Garden, Claremont Landscape Garden and Hatfield House. The horizons of the Heritage Volunteer are always expanding.

The work of the Heritage Volunteers takes NADFAS all over the country; it is one of the important public faces of the Association, and demonstrates how members can contribute to the preservation, appreciation and understanding of our cultural heritage.

As NADFAS grows the impact of Volunteering grows too. Heritage Volunteer projects often develop into long-term relationships with country houses, museums, galleries and archives. As Virginia Evans, Chairman of the VCC, reminded readers of the NADFAS *Newsletter* in 1980, 'Some VCC groups have been adopted by their houses or museums and become so integrated that they are part of the "family" or "administration".

At Castle Howard, for example, Volunteers have been helping with the care and refurbishment of the books and documents for 15 years. The Curator there, Christopher Ridgway, states quite clearly that 'their work is absolutely essential and is often of the highest quality and dedication'.[58]

The importance of their work as part of maintaining a collection was borne out in 2000 when Volunteers found outbreaks of mould in part of the Library which required immediate attention and helped prevent disastrous damage to the collection. They create networks of help that often involve many sites, and reveal the diverse range of skills that the Heritage Volunteer has to offer. For example the North East Cheshire DFAS volunteers work at Tatton Park, Bramhall Hall, Tabley House, Gawsworth Hall, Dunham Massey and Lyme Park, clean books at Capesthorne Hall and catalogue at Manchester City Art Gallery. Projects undertaken include the making of festoon blinds, costumes for adults and children, curtain repairs, cushion covers, altar cloths, fire screens, case covers, and the design of crewel work curtains. Sherborne DFAS Volunteers report that:

*Their projects have been many and varied from refurbishing and cleaning a brass chandelier and making cotton covers and padded coat hangers for the copes at Sherborne Abbey to repairing books in the Library at Sherborne School and stewarding at Montacute House, Sherborne Abbey and Sherborne School.*

Their current project is the refurbishment of the archives following a flood at the Fleet Air Arm Museum in Yeovilton.[59]

The impact of NADFAS Volunteering was summed up by Sir Peter Wakefield, Director of the National Art Collections Fund (NACF) – now The Art Fund – when in 1987 he noted:

*In my travels round the country I have seen something of the wide range of tasks that NADFAS has shouldered in promoting both the enjoyment and care of our inheritance of works of art. On my visits to some of the far flung museums and galleries which the NACF has assisted I often stumble across a NADFAS group that has been helping in some way, whether guiding, cataloguing, or conserving objects in the museum's care.*

In 2007 there were 213 Heritage Volunteer groups involving around 2,500 members in over 350 projects.

The Charity Commission requires that the result of any project undertaken by Heritage Volunteers is able to be seen by the visiting public. So the fact that the Volunteers are doing this work often means that more items are put on show, which in turn raises awareness of the riches to be found in our historic houses, museums and galleries.

Heritage volunteering does not stand still. Like the Conservation profession it assists, it must keep abreast of new developments in practice, taking the lead from the experts. When the United Kingdom Institute for Conservation (called ICON) was set up in 2005, it brought together many existing groups, and set new standards for accreditation and training. The emergence of ICON and a new Centre for Conservation Research based in Winchester, led to the updating of the volunteer guidelines to match these new standards of practice. Heritage Volunteers are aware that if they are to continue to be useful, they must be up-to-date in their knowledge. This striving for professionalism has been a hallmark of the Heritage Volunteers since their beginnings in the 1970s and still continues in their work today.[60]

## NOTES
[1] Sheila Marshall, *Development of a Dream*, 1982, p.14.
[2] Michaela Jenkerson-Kenshole, draft of article for *Church Recorders Newsletter*, Summer 1987, NADFAS Archives.
[3] Marshall, op. cit., p.14, Patricia Fay to the Duke of Bedford, 1969.
[4] *History of the VCC*, 1988, p.7.
[5] Ibid.
[6] Pamela Cowen, 2006.
[7] Phyllis Dryden, North Kent Voluntary Conservation Corps, photocopied booklet, n.d. NADFAS Archives.
[8] Ibid.
[9] Gabrielle Taylor, 'The Caretakers', *Woman's Realm*, 23 March 1974.
[10] *VCC*, op. cit., p.9.
[11] Ibid., p.16.
[12] Patricia Fay, *Historic European Houses* Conference in Oxford 1975, NADFAS Archives.
[13] Ibid.
[14] *Country Life*, 18 October 1974.
[15] Diana Adams, 'A Helping Hand', *Historic House*, Winter 2004, p.29.
[16] Sheila Marshall, 'My recollections of the beginning of NADFAS Conservation', NADFAS Volunteers Silver Jubilee Newsletter, Spring 1998, p.5.
[17] 'Don't Just Sit There', *Harpers & Queen*, January 1974.
[18] First Five Years Conference proceedings, 1975, NADFAS Archives.
[19] Ibid.
[20] 'NADFAS – Potential army of volunteers, *Association of Independent Museums Magazine* (AIM), July 1980.
[21] Lesley Adamson, 'Museum piece', the *Guardian*, 28 January 1976.
[22] *VCC*, op. cit., p.13.
[23] Isobel Lattimore, 'NADFAS and its Training of Volunteers', *Historic House*, Spring 1998, p.41.
[24] *Volunteers Handbook*, 1991, p.3.
[25] Ibid., p.1.
[26] *VCC*, op. cit., p.20.
[27] Ibid., p.10.
[28] Marjorie Somers-Cocks, 'Sightseeing in Britain with NADFAS', *Diplomatic Service Wives Association Spring Magazine*, 1986.
[29] AIM, op.cit.
[30] *Handbook*, op.cit., p.14
[31] Heritage Volunteers Annual Conference in October 2001, NADFAS Archives.
[32] 'History of York DFAS', Charlotte O'Gram, York DFAS, July 2006.
[33] 'North Kent DFAS, A Short History 1968-1993', p.82.
[34] *Handbook*, op. cit., p.5.
[35] Ibid., p.13, Barbara Askwith.
[36] Taylor, op.cit.
[37] Ibid.
[38] Ibid.
[39] Jenney Knight, 'NADFAS Contribution to Horsham Museum', Silver Jubilee Newsletter.
[40] *Handbook*, op.cit., p.10.
[41] Ellice Miller, 'Operation Outreach – NV's on an island', Jubilee Newsletter, op.cit., p.29.
[42] Gillian Wilson, West Sussex DFAS sending reminiscences of Helen Ouin, 18 July 2006.
[43] *Heritage Volunteer*, 2006, p.7.
[44] *Handbook*, op. cit., p.12.
[45] *British Association of Friends of Museums Yearbook*, 1986-7.
[46] Jill Parkin, 'The art of waiting', *Yorkshire Post*, 29 July 1987, p.11.
[47] Petrina Fortune, 'New Toys for Old', Jubilee Newsletter, op.cit., p.10-12.
[48] *Heritage Volunteer*, October 2006.
[49] James Cornish, 'Shelves of hidden history', *Express & Echo*, Monday, 26 August 1996, p.12.
[50] Wilson, op.cit.
[51] Julia MacLeod, Sevenoaks DFAS 1980-86, July 2006.
[52] *Handbook*, op. cit., p.9.
[53] Lesley Adamson, 'Museum Piece', the *Guardian*, 28 January 1976.
[54] Nancy Hodgson, Jubilee Newsletter, op.cit., p.28.
[55] Kathleen Hollands, 'Loose threads', *NADFAS Review*, Spring 2007, p.35.
[56] MacLeod, op.cit.
[57] Taylor, op. cit.
[58] Sally Whittal, 'NADFAS Volunteers', *Historic House*, Winter 2000, p.19.
[59] Anne Brunker, 'The beginnings of Sherborne DFAS', July 2006.
[60] Diana Adams, op.cit.

# 6

# Recording Angels:
## *NADFAS Goes to Church*

*'When the History of NADFAS is written the Church Recording Scheme will be seen as one of the most significant activities NADFAS undertook'*

Ann Parkinson, 1989

### The Evolution of an Idea

In 1977 the Victoria & Albert Museum staged the touring exhibition *Change and Decay: The Future of Our Churches*. It provided for our churches, what the *Destruction of the Country House* exhibition had for our stately homes – a wake-up call to their neglect and decline, and the accompanying loss of 'the community's greatest visual expression of itself across the centuries'. In the *Change and Decay* catalogue the Director, Roy Strong, reminded us that our churches faced not only declining belief but 'outright redundancy and demolition'. Between 1968 and 1976 the Church of England had declared 592 churches redundant. Yet, as Roy Strong emphasised, their fabric is an essential part of our history, 'telling us of prosperity and depression, of war and peace, extensions in size reflect rise in population, the names on the headstones reveal families who for generations moulded the life pattern of the land around'.

But all was not gloom and doom. Six years earlier another V&A exhibition had stimulated the first attempt to systematically record the contents of these precious treasure houses of our past. The work of these early Church Recorders was deemed important enough to be represented on a stand in the *Change and Decay* exhibition. Church Recording dates back to 1971 when Shirley Bury, then Assistant Keeper in the Metalwork Department of the V&A was organising an exhibition entitled *Victorian Church Art*. Meeting with Helen Lowenthal, then a NADFAS Vice President, on a train to Amersham *en route* to give a lecture, she mentioned the confused state of the parish churches she had visited in search of nineteenth-century works for the exhibition and how some objects had vanished without trace. Although by Common Law each church has a list of its contents, these were rarely kept up-to-date, often inaccurate, incomplete and only brief. Helen took the problem to Patricia Fay, and so the idea of Church Recording was first mooted.

In true NADFAS style the idea soon moved from the abstract to practice. In

**Above**
Freda Campbell (left)
and Nadine Mitchell
provided the crucial
early momentum
for the Church
Recording Scheme

October 1971 a meeting at Hambleden Church was organised by Freda Campbell. As a clergyman's wife and member of the NADFAS Executive Committee she was well placed to draw together members of Chalfont, Chiltern, Gerrards Cross, Harpenden and Thames Societies, from the early NADFAS heartland. From this meeting three teams were set up, and staff from the V&A agreed to help decide the format of the Records, 'on the line of the Royal Commission set up in 1911', and identify suitable churches in Buckinghamshire.[1] NADFAS gave them £25 for this pilot scheme. The following month the Vicar of Chalfont St Peter hosted a meeting of 30 volunteers when it was decided to seek the advice of Sir John Pope-Hennessy, then Director of the V&A and Vice President of NADFAS. Three key issues emerged from discussion at this meeting: the need to develop a system of identification of objects, the form of publication and the requirements of security. With the enthusiastic support of the V&A's librarian, Charles Gibbs-Smith, a card index

system was devised, and tested. By July 1972, Chalfont St Peter, Hambleden, (Buckinghamshire) and Nether Winchenden churches had been recorded using this new format. This system was soon to grow into a fully fledged *Manual for Church Recording*, and has been continually updated ever since.

Recording the contents of churches evolved quite naturally out of volunteer work, but soon took on a major role in its own right, requiring a specially trained workforce, handbooks, newsletter and representation at NADFAS headquarters.

## Reception
***'...doing a great service to the Church and the Nation'***
**Bishop of Oxford, 1973**
At first Church Recording was received with varying degrees of enthusiasm, from interest to outright opposition by the various Diocesan Advisory Committees. One misunderstanding, in 1968, resulted in a sharp letter from the Bishop of Buckingham to NADFAS, regretting that he had: 'heard

one or two stories of your members taking the bull by the horns and going on without permission. This can only lead to a wholesale repudiation of the work you are trying to do by the Parish Authorities'.[2]

Duly chastised, a letter was written to go to all incumbents to point out the Recorders' responsible attitude, and how much they needed their backing. The Bishop of Oxford, who felt very strongly about the benefits of Recording, also drew up a note as a further means of reassurance, it was circulated to all incumbents and secretaries of Parochial Church Councils in the Archdeaconry of Oxford, introducing NADFAS, 'They are doing a great service to the Church and the Nation, and I hope you will give them a warm welcome'.[3] Initially the Recorders were members of what was called the 'NADFAS Recording of Church Furnishings'.

## Consolidation

**'Church Recording sounds dull ... but once you start it becomes almost like a drug, and there's no end to the pleasure of discovery'**
**Ann Parkinson, Woman's Weekly, 1975[4]**
By 1973 the Church Recorders were officially established with Ann Parkinson as their first Chairman, while Patricia Dirsztay became organiser. It was calculated that an aspiring Church Recorder needed to allocate at least two mornings per month and allow for homework, to become a fully fledged 'Recording angel'.

By 1974 groups had formed in the Dioceses of Chelmsford, Canterbury, St Albans and Southwark and by the end of the following year over 59 churches had been recorded. This is an extraordinary achievement within two and a half years. Much of this early success was due to the hard work and enthusiasm of Nadine Mitchell, NADFAS secretary, whose labours behind the scenes kept everything running smoothly. By then a clear brief had been developed for the Church Recorders:

*to catalogue every item of furnishing within a Church. This includes metalwork, stonework, woodwork, textiles, documents and registers, paintings and windows, musical instruments,* *memorials and monuments. Every possible detail of the age, history, designer or manufacturer, and donor is researched using the libraries of the V&A and the Council for the Care of Churches (CCC), local diocesan archives and parish records and magazines. Each item is measured (unless it is impossible) and weighed in the case of silver. The state of preservation is noted, and the more important items photographed or drawn. The position in the Church (or Vicarage or bank – or "under the Churchwarden's bed"... ) is also recorded.[5]*

The negatives (and now the digital images) were lodged with the CCC but, since 1997 have been sent to the National Monuments Record Centre (NMRC) which is part of English Heritage. The number of copies made of the Records for each church varies from four to six, depending on the region of the United Kingdom (or Isle of Man), and on the denomination of the church. For the vast majority of Anglican churches in England five copies are made; one each for the church, the National Art Library at the V&A, the Cathedral & Church Buildings Library (CCB), the NMRC, and the County Record Office. The Board of Finance of the Church of England and NADFAS no longer retain copies, these now going to the CCB Library and the NMRC respectively. Originally it was not possible to record any church without having obtained permission on three levels, from the Bishop of the Diocese, the Archdeacon who is responsible (among other things) for the maintenance of the fabric of the churches within his Archdeaconry, and the local Incumbent and Parochial Church Council. Today usually only the two latter authorities need to give their consent. The Records are not only for the church, they provide a cornucopia of information for a wide range of academic and amateur interests including ecclesiastical, social, local, family, art and cultural history. A list of the names mentioned is placed at the beginning of each Record to facilitate genealogical history researchers. They

**Above**
Early Church Recording work was first made public at the V&A's *Change & Decay* exhibition, whose catalogue is pictured above
**Right**
St. Margaret's, Lee, Blackheath, London – the 1,000th church recorded

are a record of both secular and ecclesiastical art and as such a list of artists and craftsmen is compiled as part of each Record. The process of Recording often reveals specific references which are valuable to other fields of research. For example the Royal Armouries is sent information on any funerary armour that is found. The collation of details of maker's marks on stained glass, highlighted as important by Michael Archer from the V&A from the early days of Recording, resulted in a book called *Stained Glass Makers' Marks*, compiled by Joyce Little (the Bedfordshire & Hertfordshire Area Representative for Church Recorders), and first published in 1993. She happened to have an Amstrad computer and was as a result able to take on the complex task of compilation. A second edition, compiled by Joyce Little, and edited by Angela Goedicke and Margaret Washbourn, and retitled *Stained Glass Marks and Monograms*, was published in 2002. It remains the standard work of reference on the subject. Details of seamen's memorials are dispatched to the Maritime Museum at Greenwich while information gleaned from portrait memorials and old photographs are sent to the National Portrait Gallery. The potential value of the Records is thus priceless.

In 1975 Pamela Cowen took over as the Chairman of the Church Recorders. Training, standardisation in the vocabulary of Recording and the perennial shortage of funds were to be the first issues to be tackled. In the same year Dorothy Brining became the first Church Recorders Treasurer. Pamela acknowledged the hours and hours of typing and the checking of entries that Church Recording requires, the work of those who went uncredited and unrewarded except for the lasting thanks of the Church Recording Committee. 'Recording needs patience, a willingness to double check facts, the skill to write unambiguous English using unfamiliar words like orphrey and aumbry, and a supply of warm underwear.'[6] 'We all learnt through each others mistakes' wrote Pamela, and she circulated some of the more amusing blunders. Her three favourites were the description of a brass, removed from its

original matrix and placed in the floor of the nave as a 'widow set in stone'; the ensign of an RAF Squadron which merited 'this flag actually flew in the Battle of Britain', and an alms dish which in its well had 'a bishop engraved in ostrich feathers'.[7] Behind the humour lies a determination to keep up standards, and maintain a high level of professionalism.

One of the problems that the V&A staff could not help the Church Recorders with was joining the EEC, and 'Going Metric', which as Pamela Cowen recalls:

*caused quite new hazards as we are mostly of an age to be "set in our ways" and it was easy to put the "dot" in the wrong place or use the wrong abbreviation. When checking the Records, we often found a communion cup would be 2.05m high while a bookrest was measured as 1.75cm.*[8]

In 1980 Ann Wickham, who had led her own Church Recording group at Claremont, became Chairman of the Church Recorders. She rationalised the administration by dividing the country into geographical areas, each with its own representative to liaise between groups and the sub-committee. The enquiry made by Norfolk Museums Service to NADFAS in 1985 is indicative of the growing status and reputation of Church Recording. The Assistant Keeper asked for comments on a form he had produced for cataloguing the church plate of the Norwich diocese. In the same year the Chairman of the Church Recorders, Jane Wright, was invited to contribute to a conference held at the Goldsmiths' Company in London on inventorying. These requests show a growing acknowledgement of the high standards and experience of NADFAS Church Recording, and the move towards wider collaboration and the sharing of knowledge between organisations, and fostering links with them.

'Certainly from 1980 to 1983 …. the percentage of Church Recorders was a steady 4.5% of the total NADFAS membership.' The problem was 'how to convince the remaining 95.5% … to start Recording'.[9] While the number of those who actually do record churches remains small, their responsibility is great.[10] The words of Roy Strong on the fate of the country's churches echo the role of the NADFAS Church Recorders – 'The future of our parish churches belongs to that gloriously British eccentricity, the determination of the few'.[11]

## Training
### *'We only record what we see'*
**Ann Wickham, 1982**

As NADFAS Volunteers are 'striving for professional standards' training is key to projects undertaken by NADFAS Church Recorders. This training comes in many ways, and has evolved over time. In the early days the V&A conservation staff helped teach the Recorders about the various ways of identifying church furnishings. Shirley Bury guided them through silver, and John Cooper supplied a bibliography for metalwork, Michael Archer used the Museum's collection to build up expertise in identifying stained glass, Tony North and Claude Blair advised on base metals. Simon Jervis came and studied a church with them, giving them on-site guidance on cataloguing the woodwork, while Santina Levey provided expertise on textiles, and Charles Avery on the sculpture.

In 1977, national 'Looking at Cathedrals' and 'How to Look at Churches' days started. The following year a landmark reference book was published, Patricia Dirsztay's *Church Furnishing: A NADFAS Guide*, followed by *Inside Churches: A Guide to Church Furnishings* in 1989. This latter publication has undergone two revised editions in 1993 and 2001, giving an indication of its importance as an essential working reference book. These publications have been dubbed an antiquarian's Mrs Beeton. Both rapidly became the 'bibles' of Church Recording groups. Accurate, methodical and systematic Recording is a skill in its own right. 'We only

Above
Nadine Mitchell
(in background,
second from right)
busy with fellow
Church Recorders

record what we see, we don't give professional opinions or quality judgments. A recorded object is not small or large or beautiful or ugly – it is.'[12] One of the important skills of Recording is not to work when overtired. Pamela Cowen remembers an entry which she checked, that read: 'St Peter holding a sword in his right hand and with a cigarette behind his left ear'.[13] The usefulness of training, and keeping up with research has always been acknowledged. The value of seminars was highlighted when one Recorder, who had been at a V&A seminar in 1976 remembered the notes she made on Nuremberg brass dishes, and the request to inform the Museum if any were found. One turned up unidentified in a church she was Recording, and was subsequently dated to c.1500-1550.

Training continued to be central to Church Recording. In 1996 Angela Goedicke, after retiring as Chairman of the Church Recorders, became the first Church Recorders Training Officer, a job which she still does today. She has held training days all over the country, assisted by another former Chairman, Patricia Brown, until her untimely death in 2006. As Angela has been involved almost from the start of Recording, first with Harrow Church Recorders group, then joining the Committee in 1982, as editor of the *CR Journal (Newsletter)* from 2002, and as Chairman, she is in a position to know exactly what form of training the Recorders need. The success of Church Recording owes much to Angela, and demonstrates the unstinting dedication characteristic of key figures within the Association.

Jane Wright, who had been Church Recording from the early days, became Chairman of the Recorders in 1984 and took over the co-ordination of the first residential training course for Church Recorders Group Leaders. Jane and Angela Goedicke had assessed the viability of staging a two-day seminar, but neither perhaps realised the success it was to be. Jane remembers that 'The response from the Group Leaders to the initial invitation to the Seminar [to be held at Hengrave Hall] was overwhelming and in the end fifty-five out of the sixty-two leaders were able to come'. The preparation of sample pages of Recording for the Seminar revealed inconsistencies in the *Manual* and the necessity for amendments stimulated its revision, a major task in its own right, but a healthy indication of the sustained professionalism of Church Recording.

Another important way of teaching Recorders, and bringing them together to share their skills, observations and experiences, is through National Study Days. First introduced in 1982 at Harefield Church, their success ensured that they have remained part of the training for Church Recorders ever since. Jane Wright and Sheila Chapman took over their organisation until Jane died in 1993, and Sheila handed over to Jane Hedley in 2004. Some of these days have been very memorable, including one held at Taylor's Bellfoundry in Loughborough where the group witnessed the casting of a new bell for a church in Birmingham.

## Finding the Funding

As with all early NADFAS enterprises, the lack of money was always a problem, but one faced with determination, imagination and hard work, and innovative and effective fund-raising events. The success of Church Recording meant, of course, a concomitant increase in costs, of photography and the duplication of copies. In the early 1970s, '3p a mile was paid for petrol, and without photographic expenses the average church cost £6 to record'.[14]

Without the support provided via fund-raising events, most notably those at The Vyne and at Phillips Auction Rooms in 1975, progress would have been slowed. A Kodak Award of £650 to buy cameras, cover photographic expenses, and training, funds from the Esmée Fairbairn Trust, and the Royal Commission of Historical Monuments agreement in 1976 to process films free, provided not only much needed funds but also official recognition of the importance of Recording. Smaller sums were given by the Diocesan Advisory Board, and Christie's, every penny counted. In 1983 the Church

Recorders were awarded a further grant of £2,000 from the Pilgrim Trust for photographic expenses, building on the £1,000 given three years previously by the same Trust. In 1993 the Goldsmiths' Company gave £2,500 a year for three years to support Recording, and continued giving grants for photography until 2004. In 2006 Ecclesiastical (formerly Ecclesiastical Insurance Group) shared the cost of producing the new *Church Recorders Handbook*, and in 2007 gave £2,000 for photography. The previous year £3,000 was given by an anonymous donor, which was put towards the new 'Sample Pages'. Cumulatively these grants make the continuation of Church Recording possible, and are an acknowledgement of the importance of the activity.

## Spreading the word

Disseminating news and information among the growing band of Church Recorders meant that some form of regular communication between them was required. In 1975 the first *Bulletin* appeared. Ann Wickham introduced the first *Church Recorders' Newsletter* in 1981 which replaced the *Bulletin*. In the first edition she reported that 'We have recently engendered a new collective noun, "A devotion of Church Recorders" from a grateful Rector in Devon'. The pages of the *Newsletter* are full of reports relating to the rescue and discovery of important church artefacts, thanks to the vigilance of Recorders throughout Britain, and beyond. In 1991, the *Journal* was started which ran parallel to the *Newsletter* until 1998, when the latter ceased. In 2002 *News & Views* was introduced and remains the chief means of disseminating information about Church Recording. In what other publication could one read of such varied and important discoveries, including unidentified chalices, chasubles and wall paintings? The following examples illustrate only a small number of the exciting finds. Sandwich Evening Group discovered in a chest of drawers a cloth-covered folder enclosing four sides of manuscript on parchment with faded illumination. It turned

out to be an 11th century fragment of the Treatise of St Augustine on the Psalms. After the Dissolution it had been used as a binding for a later volume. Other 'finds' include a previously unknown pattern of medieval floor tiles;[15] a signed pane of glass by Peter Cole, a mid-eighteenth century craftsman who specialised in mending medieval glass in the area;[16] a Viennese chalice of 1761; and a chasuble identified by Watts & Company the ecclesiastical outfitters as being of outstanding design and its whereabouts previously unknown. The Dover & Deal Group found a 'rusty tin box' containing a beautiful heavy brass 'Magic' Lantern c.1890 with a plaque attached reading 'Church Army Lantern', and with it two boxes of glass slides of 60 hymns and Sunday school verses. A member of the Exmoor Group learnt that some papers had been found in a kiln sealed off at the back of a local shop.

*Amidst paint tins, Victorian lavatory bowls and cans of varnish, important material came to light relating to John Toms, who had his workshop on this site from 1836 until his death in 1869. He had been a key player in the Victorian revival in the art of stained glass.*[17]

Amongst the debris was found a series of full-scale glass cartoons, and his estimate book for work carried out in the 1850s to 1860s.

## The Problems of Church Recording: Tales of the Unexpected

Church Recording is not without its hazards, the most common being the cold. Other problems experienced have been of a more unexpected sort. Bowdon & District Group were 'fortunate that Thursday was not a working day for the group' when they would have been caught up in the chaos caused by the IRA bombs in central Manchester in 1993.[18] In the same year Warminster Recorders were puzzled when their photographer failed to turn up to work at Edlington Priory Church. They eventually

**Left** Chairman Church Recorders 1983-1988 Jane Wright (top), Audrey Barrow and Pat Coulton carrying out the very first NADFAS recording at Hambleden Church, Bucks

discovered that he had met with an accident. At his previous venue, seeing the cover off the clock in the ringing chamber, he had decided to take a couple of photographs of the mechanism. He apparently fell, struck his head and passed out; some time later he was taken to hospital where he spent several days recovering.[19] The new Blackheath Recorders faced a rather different challenge: their first job. They were all slightly daunted by the fact that their first task was to record all twentieth century acquisitions in St Paul's Cathedral.

Church Recorders have to be of an unflappable nature. The South Suffolk Group found a skull complete with a few teeth in a small alcove in the vestry of St George's Sudbury.[20] A little research indicated that it was the head of Simon of Sudbury, who became Chancellor of England in 1380. He had been beheaded by Wat Tyler's men and his head returned to St Gregory's, the church he had rebuilt. It had been kept there ever since, although this gruesome reminder of him had long been forgotten.

## Some Important Discoveries

Some of the most exciting discoveries have to remain unsung. As Pamela Cowen remarked in her salute to the Church Recorders in 1990, 'the most exciting discoveries can only be proclaimed anonymously; since theft and vandalism make security the watchword'.[21] A report in *The Art Newspaper*, however, gives a flavour of the range and importance of some of their finds:

*In Kent for example they spotted an unrecognised stained glass window designed by William Morris. Recorders at Barnston Church in Essex, recently discovered a 'lost' window by the Pre-Raphaelite painter Edward Burne-Jones. A Leeds group tracked down a seventeenth century jewelled chalice and a communion cup which had been deposited in a bank vault during World War II and later forgotten by the church authorities. Its presence had been highlighted as it was mentioned in an ancient parish list discovered by one of the Recorders. Similarly, a record of silverware in a county archive, led to its discovery in a wall safe at the back of a cleaner's cupboard in the local church. In Warwickshire, a* carved wood panel reminded a Recorder of a Poussin painting, and investigation revealed that it was copied from the artist's original 'The Finding of Moses'.[22]

Another recent discovery was a rare printed Bible, a James Baskerville edition of 1763.[23] These finds were made public to advertise the benefits of Recording.

There are many cases where these finds have led to their safe-keeping within museums, where they are accessible for the appreciation of a much wider audience. The Recorders working in St David's Ashprington, Totnes, found part of a medieval wooden screen gate, stored in a passageway by the Sacristy. Close inspection of the panels revealed traces of original paintings of Saints. These gates are all that is left of a screen that was still in place in 1846, though damaged. They can now be seen in the Royal Albert Museum, Exeter.[24]

Some discoveries are of international importance. Ashstead Church Recorders found a linen napkin whilst working at the Church of St Mary's, Headley, in Surrey in 1999. It was unearthed in a cardboard box in the vestry safe. All that was known was that Mary Stydolf, Patroness of the Living and wife of William Stydolf 'Esquire to the Body of King Charles I' had given it to the Church in 1666. She had at the same time given money for the repair of the chancel, a new stone font with a cover, and had embellished the pulpit. She also supplied the communion table with a cloth covering. The Recorders contacted experts in the field, who revealed that the cloth was an extremely rare survival of a papal banquet napkin, made in 1624 and bearing the arms of Maffeo Barbarini which he bore as Pope Urban VIII (1623-44). It was made in Kortrijk in the Spanish Netherlands of linen damask. Such 'napkins seem only to have been woven for the great'. Among the few inventories in which they are found is one relating to the goods of Mary Queen of Scots dated 1561. There are few surviving examples. Until this banquet napkin of Urban VIII was 'discovered' by the Recorders, no sixteenth-or early-seventeenth-century linen damasks that had been woven

for the princes of the church and state in the Iberian peninsula or in Italy were known to scholars. It has now been restored and mounted and can be seen in the Treasury at Guildford Cathedral.

Other discoveries have led to the uncovering of exciting new local information which is priceless. Keen-eyed recorders from the Wantage Group encouraged the churchwarden at St Andrew's Letcombe Regis to apply some Brasso to a black panel above the vestry door, thus revealing the family tree of the Godlake family made in the mid-nineteenth century.[25] The North Devon Group found a seating plan for St Mary's Atherington, which was thought to have been lost. Gade Valley Recorders discovered documents in a church chest that included the bills for the floor tiles, supplied by Maw & Company and Minton Hollins & Company, right down to the cost of carriage to the nearest railway station. This type of information is a treasure trove for the historian, and plays an important role in scholarship. Church Records are often the first port of call for researchers. For example, work on the early twentieth century ecclesiastical goldsmiths Barkentin & Krall, began with a trawl of the Church Recording volumes to find churches that possess examples of their work.

## Recorders to the Rescue

*'We have found three bishop's mitres'*
**David Holmes, Church Times, 2002**[26]
The crucial importance of thorough cataloguing emerges most dramatically in cases of theft and vandalism. Many a vicar and police officer has blessed the presence of a Church Recorder's photograph with detailed description, enabling tracing, conservation or reproduction. As one journalist observed:

*Although their main aim is to add to knowledge about church furnishings, the Recorders turn out to be Miss Marples when thefts occur. Their inventories are often the only means of identifying missing property'.*[27]

In 1982 'over 400 churches in Kent alone [had] … been burgled during the last twelve

**Above**

In this cartoon
Ken Wolverton ARPS
offers a lighthearted
take on NADFAS
Church Recording

months'.[28] Church Recorders' photographs made possible accurate repairs and restoration for a vandalised stained glass window in Axminster Church and a memorial window, shattered by burglars, in a West Surrey church.[29] The work of Harpenden Recorders assisted the restoration of a stolen lectern[30], while the Welwyn Garden City Recorders helped with a photograph of a 'pair of handsome chairs' subsequently stolen from the chancel.[31] These are just a few examples of the countless times Church Recording has come to the rescue.

The activity and interest of Church Recording groups also provides a stimulus to others. The value of objects, historically, socially and culturally are highlighted by the attention paid during Recording. In the Kent Area the activities of the Dover & Deal Recorders galvanised the parishioners into action, who subsequently found a 'beautiful old font which had been discarded and placed in a shed in the churchyard'. The Thanet Group wrote a guidebook for the church at Monkton, and made 'local people more aware of their church and are helping it come alive again'.[32]

Church Recording can also lead to international communication and the sharing of knowledge. Woking Recorders corresponded with archivists at Nienburg in Germany over a link with some armorial glass.[33] The Harpenden Recorders ended up helping a member of the Hellenic Navy identify medieval graffiti on a ship from St Leonard's Flamstead, assisting his research into the development of ship-building.[34]

## Milestones

At the 10th anniversary Thanksgiving Service held at St Paul's Cathedral in March 1983, Dr Robert Runcie, Archbishop of Canterbury and a Vice President of NADFAS, referred to the Church Recorders as 'the "shock troops" of conservation'. 'Because it is not possible to conserve what we don't know about', he added, 'a surprising number of treasures and furnishings of our churches and historic houses are yet to be found in any inventory'. Over 500 attended the service, celebrating 190 completed Church Recordings. He remained an admiring supporter of the Recorders, offering them Lambeth Palace as the venue for their 15th anniversary celebrations. Five years later, Lord Runcie, now retired, joined the Recorders at their 20th Anniversary service in St. Albans Abbey.

Another milestone came when the Church Recorders received very public and high profile recognition as one of five winners of the National Art Collections Fund Awards for 1990, which honoured their invaluable work since 1972. By 1998, 750 of Britain's churches had been recorded. As an enthusiastic journalist reported:

*Like the work of the Mothers' Union or the Women's Institute, theirs is sterling work, but, owing to their genteel self-disregard, it often goes unsung. There are 2,500 Church Recorders, divided into one hundred and fifty groups in England and in Scotland and Wales.*[35]

The 25th anniversary was celebrated with events in the Abbey at Dorchester-on-Thames, and in Hereford Cathedral when the NADFAS President, Timothy Clifford, joined the Recorders and gave an address. The Patron, HRH The Duchess of Gloucester attended a day in Manchester at Chethams School and the Cathedral.

The completion of the 1,000th Record in 2002 was that of St Margaret's Church, Lee, Blackheath, London. A service of Thanksgiving was held in the church of St. Bartholomew the Great, Smithfield, London, in the presence of the Rt. Revd. and Rt. Hon. Richard Chartres, Bishop of London. Marianne Eastgate, group leader of the Brisbane Recorders was also present because at roughly the same time, the Australian Association of Decorative and Fine Arts Societies (the Australian sister of NADFAS) celebrated the completion of Recording their first church, St Mary the Virgin at Kangaroo Point, Brisbane.[36] It is one of the oldest churches in Brisbane, and has unusually early examples of Australian workmanship in

stained glass and silver. A copy of this Record was presented to the Bishop at the same service. Church Recording has become an international campaign to help preserve local heritage, and through it Recorders and researchers from all over the world are brought together.

The 30th anniversary in 2003 was also tripartite. The Duchess of Gloucester attended the celebration at Chichester. In Norwich a two-day exploration of the city's churches was organised. In Chester a lecture on the recent archaeological discoveries brought the celebrations to an end.

At the end of 2006 there were 187 Church Recording groups, including nine from Scotland, Ulster, Wales and the Isle of Man supported by 204 DFAS groups (some groups are sponsored by more than one DFAS). At the time of writing this book Roger Allen, the

**Above**
In what was an astonishing find, a linen cloth unearthed by Church Recorders working on St Mary's, Headley, turned out to be an extremely rare papal banquet napkin

**Right**
This fine medieval screen gate is now in safe keeping at the Royal Albert Museum, Exeter, having been discovered by Recorders working at St David's, Ashprington, Totnes

current Chairman of Church Recorders, reports that a total of 1,338 Records have been completed. While the greatest number, by far, are Church of England buildings, this also includes churches and chapels of the Church in Wales, the Scottish Episcopal Church, the Roman Catholic, Presbyterian, United Reform and Unitarian Churches, and some non-denominational chapels. Although only a minority of NADFAS members are Recorders their work continues to be one of the 'jewels' in the NADFAS crown.

As the Bishop of London, a Vice President of the Association since 2003, reminded his NADFAS audience in 2002, the Recorders put on file 'the treasures and memories of the whole community stored up in our churches … Memory and modernisation are not opposed… Any society which has lost its memory is in a sad, distracted state'.[37]

## NOTES

[1] Ann Parkinson, *Church Recorders Newsletter*, 1989, p.5.
[2] *History of Church Recording*, 1986, p.20.
[3] Ibid., p.20.
[4] Irene Heath, 'Out of Town', *Woman's Weekly*, 7 June 1975, p.6.
[5] Lecture transcript by Ann Wickham, 1982, NADFAS Archives.
[6] Pamela Cowen, *CRN*, 1990, p.3.
[7] Pamela Cowen, *History of Church Recording*, 1988, p.28.
[8] Ibid., p.27.
[9] Ibid., p.37.
[10] *CRN*, 1993, p.2.
[11] Roy Strong in Marcus Binney and Peter Burman, *Change and Decay: The Future of Our Churches*, 1977, p.9.
[12] Wickham, op. cit.
[13] History, op. cit, p.28.
[14] *CRN*, 1989, p.5.
[15] *CRN*, 1990, p.12.
[16] *CRN*, 1993, p.15.
[17] *CRN*, Autumn 1988, p.7.
[18] *CRN*, 1993, p.26.
[19] Ibid., p.32.
[20] *CRN*, Autumn 1994, p.21.
[21] *CRN*, 1990, p.3.
[22] Simon Tait, 'Art sleuths discover churches' lost treasures', *The Times*, 30 May 1990.
[23] Martin Bailey, 'How Britain found out what was in its churches' *The Art Newspaper*, June 1998, p.4.
[24] *CRN*, 1993, p.28.
[25] *CRN*, 1991, p.27.
[26] Bill Bowder, 'Church Records are "the community's memory"', *Church Times*, 28 March 2002, p.7.
[27] Bailey, op. cit.
[28] Wickham, op. cit.
[29] *CRN*, 1985, p.10.
[30] *CRN*, Autumn 1986, p.12.
[31] Ibid.
[32] *CRN*, 1985, p.11.
[33] *CRN*, 1993, p.29.
[34] *CRN*, 1990, p.12.
[35] Bailey, op. cit.
[36] 'NADFAS records its 1,000th church', *Country Life*, 25 April 2002, p.107.
[37] Bowder, op. cit.

# 7

# Sowing the Seeds:
## *NADFAS for the Young*

*'Our cultural heritage is only safe if young people are encouraged to appreciate it at an early age'*
Anne White, foreword , 'History of Young NADFAS', 1987

Right from the beginning Patricia's plans for NADFAS included attracting the young to the arts. From within her own Antiques group formed in 1965 two young mothers, Judith Constantine and Pamela Foster-Browne, had organised a visit in the school holidays for their two five-year-old daughters, inviting others with young children along.[1] Patricia had also met Anne White, a vivacious journalist and mother of four children under nine, who had formed the Junior Museums Club in London during the winter of 1964/5, when she took her own daughters to attend a session. She must have been impressed, as Patricia invited her to attend the 1967 meeting that led to the formation of NADFAS. Her club was a pioneering idea, inspired by the child

friendly activities of museums in America which she had visited.[2] In November 1972 the NADFAS Council agreed that the Association should explore the formation of junior groups, and asked June Fenwick to take on this task. She had been on the Executive Committee as Joint Chairman of Events, and had been asked if she was interested in either representing NADFAS for European Architectural Heritage Year or developing the role of junior groups within the Association. As she had already expressed her views on the latter, she was more than happy to take her ideas further. June recalls, however, that 'There was not a strong feeling among Council or Members of the Executive that a junior membership was either vital or practical at

**Above**

Anne White with some of her junior charges in the 1960s

*members' children aged ... between 8 and 16. It would be exciting if we could start to explore the potential that these young people represent.*

She suggested 'that each NADFAS Society should arrange at least one event each holiday for children'. As Anne herself reminded NADFAS members:

*It was June who single-handedly ... brought Young NADFAS into being. Her ideas on giving children the intellectual tools and articulate language to identify, correlate and enjoy the visual arts around them are still the basic ideals of Young NADFAS.*[4]

Three NADFAS Societies, Hart, Runnymede and Moor Park already had groups of 'juniors' for whom they arranged holiday outings and lectures, so it is not surprising that one of them, Hart, was the first to respond to the call for setting up 'Young NADFAS' Groups. June realised that the word 'junior' was perhaps a little outdated, and the contemporary emphasis on Youth led to the title Young NADFAS, embracing at first, young people between the ages of 9 and 14, and now an age range of 8-18. A handout was prepared for interested NADFAS groups which advised: start locally, use children's own suggestions and pass on your ideas to others. By November there were five Young NADFAS Groups, and enquiries from 12 other Societies, which at the time represented almost one third of the total number of existing Societies.

The first Young NADFAS flyer was distributed in October 1973, and included suggestions for activities and outings, like brass rubbing, a visit to Tom Rowland's antique furniture restoration workshop, and a list of lecturers willing to talk to the young, and ended with 'all this is only the beginning, but an exciting one'. Another of the many memorable early events was a day potting and painting with Anne Reyntiens and her husband Patrick, the acclaimed stained glass artist, at their home in Burleighfields. In April 1974 Runnymede DFAS, inspired by the leaflet, went to rub the brasses at Eton College Chapel with Jerome Bertram. It was the first Young NADFAS event, and one that was to become popular.

that time'.[3] It was June's determination and commitment that drove the idea forward. Like so many others June turned to Helen Lowenthal for advice, and Nadine Mitchell for practical administrative support. Having heard Anne White speak to her own DFAS group at Runnymede, she agreed with Nadine that they should ask her to write and present a paper to NADFAS on 'Interesting Children in the Arts'. In this paper she remarked:

*If we were to take the average age of our members we might find it fell between 30-40, and therefore it is reasonable to suppose that in each Society there are a high proportion of*

Harrow DFAS Christmas newsletter of 1976 included a report from Andrew Ellis aged 12 who wrote that as a result of a trip to the Norman church at Aldenham he had learnt that 'the use of outline figures in brass as memorials began in Germany c.1200 and were first used in this country in 1277'. Andrew then proceeded to give clear instructions on how to rub the brasses! The experience had clearly left a deep impression on him. The promotional leaflet that had stimulated this Eton Chapel visit came under fire from one Society, questioning the 15p charge for it. With no funds of its own Young NADFAS had seen the charge as a means of raising funds. However, as a result of this complaint, the leaflets were made free and, at the same time, went pink, to give this 'branch' of the Association a distinct identity. The choice of colour was a practical one, as Nadine Mitchell had a stock of pink paper to spare! Another fund-raising activity was the commissioning of Young NADFAS badges from Sally Rodda of Condé Nast Publications. 1,000 were ordered at a cost of £149 and resold to make a few pence profit per badge.

### Early Years

The early years of Young NADFAS were characterised by a ferment of ideas and possibilities. The idea of involving children in museums and galleries and encouraging them to feel at home with, and appreciate, Art was relatively new. Few institutions had education departments and little was offered by them that catered specially for children. Links were soon made with other organisations which offered advice and support, like Young Rescue which involved youngsters in archaeological digs. Members of Young NADFAS were invited to join their excavations. It was felt that Young NADFAS should encourage ideas, and that it was important to involve the young in any branch of artistic development. As these were early days with few examples and rules it was emphasised that the progress of each project needed to be mapped to help the growth of others. An approach was made to the Royal Institute for British Architects (RIBA) resulting

in the creation of Awareness Trails by Young NADFAS Groups, stimulating interest in the built environment. June Fenwick also approached the newly formed Historic Houses Association with the idea of organising special arrangements for young parties in country houses. In 1977, which was designated Heritage Education Year, Young NADFAS organisers were included among the groups of teachers and education advisers, showing how far they had advanced both in profile and confidence. In 1978 a representative from Young NADFAS, Sheila Chapman, was invited to join the National Trust Panel for Youth, and the following year Young NADFAS became a Schools Corporate Member of the National Trust, as well as

**Above**
A group of teenagers enjoys the first Young NADFAS overseas trip, to Paris, in 1975

joining the Groups for Education in Museums. All these connections underpinned the central aims of Young NADFAS, pleasure in education, history as excitement and adventure out of the classroom, a proper relationship with schools and co-operation with hard-pressed owners of historic houses. It was agreed that 'Any person with the right degree of helpful enthusiasm and empathy with the young can deal successfully with a Young NADFAS Group'.[5]

## Coming Together

Although it was the initiative of individual Societies to set up their own Young NADFAS Groups, there evolved quite naturally various ways in which both children and the

organisers from these different groups could meet. There was the *Newsletter*, the annual holidays and national days, and the organisers' workshops, which later became training days.

In 1974 the first Young NADFAS *Newsletter* for group organisers appeared and, in 1986, the first *Newsletter* for the young members themselves was produced. Sue Young compiled, edited, and printed the broadsheet known as the *Artichoke*, 'an amusing pun, describing the leaves clustered around the central core, as the Young NADFAS Groups are to NADFAS'.[6] In 1996 the magazine changed its name to *Image*, and included quizzes, reports and ideas for things to do. The list of activities reported in 1998 included stage

make-up, acrylic painting, stone carving and pewter working, animation, and silhouette cutting; the North Yorkshire and South Durham group saw Rossini's opera *La Cenerentola* at the Darlington Civic Theatre, while North Wiltshire benefited from a workshop by the travelling Playbox Theatre, and much, much, more!

In response to a suggestion from Kathleen Wareham, who was then National Chairman, and founder of NADFAS Tours, a trip to Paris for teenagers was organised. Shuna Cronin and Valerie Woodford planned an action-packed and ambitious eight-day trip to Paris in 1975, all for £54 per head. On 26 July, 37 children, three NADFAS helpers and the coach driver, set out for France. The trip was a huge success, aided by their guide M. Levy who addressed them as 'the little Fine Arts'. June remembers the hilarity caused at the ferry on return, when in her slow French she had unwittingly implied that all 37 children were hers! The profit on the trip was £99 17p, the largest sum of money that Young NADFAS had to date. The Young NADFAS holiday became an almost annual event, in 1976 it was in Amsterdam. Since then they

have taken place all over Britain, from West Sussex in 1977, Clwyd in 1981, Suffolk in 1991, the Orkneys in 1998, to Ayrshire in 2006. During the 2006 holiday, 24 children and five helpers were involved in a whole range of activities including collage-making, plasterworking while sitting beneath the fine Adam ceilings in Culzean Castle, a visit to a stonemason's yard where the children mixed their own lime mortar and learned to carve, and enjoying the freedom of the landscape, 'not just looking and seeing it, but listening to it, touching it, feeling it and becoming part of it'.[7] Such was the *camaraderie* and fun of these holidays that they were often followed up by Christmas reunions that cemented friendships and made lasting links across Societies.

The first Workshop was held in March 1976 at RIBA. This provided the opportunity for groups of three or four leaders to ask questions of the 'experts' including Nicolas Jones, Head of Public Affairs at the RIBA, Helen Lowenthal, Renée Marcousé, Anne White, and representatives from the Domestic Buildings Research Group, the Conference for Local History and Young

Opposite page
and right
A selection
of winning entries
from past Young
Arts competitions

Rescue. These Workshops became a much valued annual event. Renée Marcousé was a most enthusiastic and supportive adviser, with a wealth of experience in the field of children's education. She edited a special volume of the *Museums Journal* for the International Commission on Education and Cultural Activities (1973), and was author of *The Listening Game, Teaching in an Art Museum* (1961), and *Using Objects: Visual Learning and Visual Awareness in Museums and the Classroom* (1974). She continued as the Young NADFAS adviser until her death in 1981, when Anne White took over. The Workshops were replaced from the mid 1990s with training days.

In July 1976 the first Young NADFAS Committee was formed with June Fenwick as Chairman, Judith Nagle (West Sussex) as Secretary, and Sheila Chapman (Gerrards Cross). By November 1976 there were 29 Young NADFAS Groups. In 1978 Sheila became Chairman of Young NADFAS when she took over the reins from June Fenwick and she was elected to the NADFAS Executive. Sheila's first job was to form a sub-committee. Caroline Poyntz-Wright (Hart),

Judith Hammer (Sevenoaks), Jean Bagnell-Smith (West Wycombe) and Fiona Spring-Rice (Ashdown Forest) were recruited, and, after the first meeting, Pamela Makin (West Essex). They met in a small reading room of the University Women's Club in South Audley Street, London, thanks to the influence of Renée Marcousé who was a member. A report in *The Times* in December 1979 covered Young NADFAS under the title 'Safety valves for a child's Christmas', and noted that there were 41 groups, 'each group is as enterprising as its local organiser, and the National *Newsletter* describes dozens of tempting and unusual visits, some of which would not be possible for individual families'.[8]

In 1978 the first Young NADFAS National Day was held at the H.M. Tower of London. Sheila Chapman remembers that it involved a lot of worry, but it was a great success, with 147 members attending, and like the annual holiday became an important annual event in the Young NADFAS calendar. In 1979 the Day was held at Littlecote House in Berkshire and at Jacksons in Fulham to explore the plaster moulding workshop, with a visit to see their work *in situ* at Osterley Park. In 1980 the theme was London's Derelict Churches, and in 1981, the focus was Knebworth, the work of the stained glass manufacturers Goddard and Gibbs, and a visit to Middle Temple. Combined visits to the Commonwealth Institute and the National Portrait Gallery formed the 1982 National Day. In more recent years there have been events at Somerset House and the Tate, at Dulwich Picture Gallery, the Baltic in Gateshead, and Glasgow, and in 2007 the National Day was at the Fox Talbot Museum in Lacock. The days were always action-packed and stimulating.

Many Young NADFAS, and later Young Arts, events and activities have been made possible by the Patricia Fay Memorial Fund, in recognition of the Founder's support of encouraging the young to engage with the arts. In her first Chairman's Report of 1967/8 she stated that she 'hoped Member Societies will involve themselves in the education of children', echoing the suggestion at the 'foundation' meeting in June 1967, when she 'urged that young people should be educated about museums and country houses … They could be taught to help and care for these things … Lectures could be arranged for holidays and outings'. The idea of encouraging the young is further supported by the Trenchard Cox Scholarship, established in his name in 1998, to provide a place on an Art History Abroad summer course: a two-week tour of Venice, Florence and Rome in the company of enthusiastic tutors who will help bring the art of the Renaissance and the culture of Italy to life. The scholarship is open to all 16 to 18-year-olds, but is particularly intended to encourage students who do not have a scholarly interest in art history. It is awarded as a result of a competition which invites an imaginative, though not necessarily art historical, response. Applicants are asked to submit two 400-word reasoned descriptions; the first of a building, painting, sculpture or work of decorative art which they truly enjoy, the second of a building, painting, sculpture or work of decorative art which they loathe.

In 1985, Judith Waples, then NADFAS

Chairman, inaugurated the first Young NADFAS Chairman's Competition. There were at the time 50 Young NADFAS Groups in action across the country. Judith remembers talking to Roy Strong, who said 'Prizes, my dear, people always love prizes!', so she commissioned the silversmith Stuart Devlin to make a trophy to be awarded annually. Devlin was known to many Young NADFAS Groups as he had hosted visits by them to his London workshop. One of these outings was featured in the *Daily Telegraph*, and resulted in over 80 letters of interest in Young NADFAS. As the reporter noted:

*Not many silversmiths of Stuart Devlin's calibre are prepared to give up a couple of hours of their valuable time to show children round their workshop and showrooms but he feels this is an ideal way of introducing them to the craft.*

His representative had also spoken at

**Above**
Presentation of the
very first Young
NADFAS award in
November 1985.
The trophy, made by
Stuart Devlin, was
presented by then
National Chairman
Judy Waples

NADFAS events, so his was a familiar face. The circular design incorporates a series of harmoniously arranged ascending 'pipes' which represent children growing, a particularly appropriate stylised symbol of Young NADFAS. The first competition was entitled 'Down Your Way' and encouraged groups to discover people and places in their own neighbourhood. It was won by Itchen Valley Young NADFAS Group for their project on the Hospital of St Cross, Winchester. Judith presented the trophy to their organiser, Primrose Muir, at the January meeting of the Young NADFAS Council. The creation of the trophy raised the profile of Young NADFAS Organisers as in later years it was presented at the AGM. The 2006 competition was based on interior design and involved redesigning a room. An exciting day was spent at the Design Museum, London, with co-ordinated interior design based activities which provided all participants with a solid base for producing work to enter in the competition. The judges found the task of selecting the winners extremely difficult as there was such a variety of imaginative entries. They praised the fun, inspiration and polished execution of the designs.

## Coming of Age: The Twentieth Anniversary

To mark its 20th anniversary, Young NADFAS commissioned the singer, composer, musicologist and regular NADFAS lecturer, Peter Medhurst, to write and direct a special performance of an 'Elizabethan' masque, *A Twist in Time*. It was performed by members of Young NADFAS in the magnificent surroundings of the Old Palace, Hatfield on 28 October 1992. With 31 musicians from a Grade 1 trumpet to a Grade 7 cellist, 40 singers and some 45 dancers, the only group rehearsal was on the day itself. The costumes were designed by Jacky Wark of the Young NADFAS Committee and made by DFAS members from Hertfordshire. It was a suitably ambitious, and hugely successful, event to mark this important birthday. As one young participant reported 'It went quite well except for a few small mistakes – which were to be

expected since we had only a few hours to rehearse ... it was very enjoyable but very hard work'.[9] Reading the anniversary *Newsletter* one cannot help but be impressed by the range of innovative outings and events which Young NADFAS Groups attended. Over 80 new Young NADFAS members from Ayrshire enjoyed 'tasting' eight different crafts, where most of the equipment used was freely loaned or given to them by local companies and shops. There were also guided walks round London, and visits to museums. Children experienced medieval costume and food at Portchester Castle, while others took a blindfold tour round an arboretum, highlighting the use of senses other than sight. The Indonesian gong and metallophone captivated those at a gamelan workshop, and another group was allowed to rummage through the handbag and shoe storeroom at a theatre in Scarborough.

## Changing Times

In the foreword to the 'History of Young NADFAS', the question was asked, 'What will the story be of Young NADFAS 20 years from now? If it is to continue its success the changing interests and capabilities of young people will need to be watched'. It was, however, the shift in the age of the NADFAS membership as a whole that brought change to Young NADFAS, as much as differences in the interests of the young. As Pamela Cohn explained, with changing times 'Young NADFAS needed to change direction, since with ageing membership fewer Societies were able to maintain or run a Young NADFAS Group'.[10] Caroline Poyntz-Wright in the mid 1980s observed that:

*For so many senior NADFAS members young people are an enigma quite outside their experience; ... There is a general impression that Young NADFAS is irrelevant to the needs of the elderly members. Each Society should have an obligation to do something constructive for the future. It is vital to bring in new blood willing and able to serve on committees and take responsibility.*[11]

When one Young NADFAS Group closed the organiser stated 'Most younger mothers now work full or part-time and do not make up the membership of our senior Society which is much older, grandmothers rather than mothers'.[12]

Between 1972 when Young NADFAS had been founded and its Silver Jubilee in 1997, the world of the young had changed. In 1972, they listened to the Osmonds, heard the New Seekers teach the world to sing, and wore velvet, denim and corduroy. In 1997 the Osmonds had been replaced by the Spice Girls, the craze for Tamagotchi had been launched, and fashionable girls wore mini-rucksacks. The weight of change in society had become such that it was time to take action, to keep the principles behind Young NADFAS going. In response to issues arising from a working party devoted to Young NADFAS, a conference entitled 'A Way Forward for Young NADFAS' presented its findings and suggestions for future development. Under the banner 'Sow a seed now and you sow a seed for life' it was clear that the commitment to inspiring the young with a love of art was still as strong. Not only were the young the next generation of NADFAS members, but also the future decision makers of the country, whether property developers, local councillors or government ministers. As such it was felt that there was a need 'to make sure that they make informed decisions about the future of our national heritage'.[13] Although there were 2,800 children belonging to 65 Young NADFAS Groups, and an estimated 25,000 children had been at some time in their lives a member of Young NADFAS, the current methods of engaging the young were seen to be outdated, and increasingly ineffective. With the NADFAS audience getting older it was becoming difficult to recruit group organisers. While the National Curriculum now supported the teaching of history and art in a stimulating way, these departments rarely got the funds needed. In a similar way, although the majority of museums and art galleries now had education departments, they were the 'Cinderellas of the art world' and always the first to suffer the cuts necessary when overall budgets were reduced.

As a result, although the formation of new Young NADFAS Groups for the 8 to 18-year-old age group was encouraged, it was felt that support needed to be given to 'those Societies sowing equally important seeds by giving arts awards, sponsoring students and school projects'.[14] These groups were encouraged to nominate a Young Arts co-ordinator, to keep in touch with Area representatives and attend meetings. It was felt that if a DFAS could not support a Young NADFAS Group then it should be encouraged to support small projects. For example, £65 enabled a member of the Education staff of Dulwich Picture Gallery to spend a day in a school, while £8 would purchase a teacher's pack about a heritage site or a forthcoming exhibition.[15]

Therefore in 1998 'Arts for the Young', later to be known as 'Young Arts', was set up to enable Societies to support a local project where the young would benefit without having to run an actual Young NADFAS Group. For example, when North East Cheshire DFAS tried to set up a Young NADFAS Group to encourage members'

**Above**
Wirral Young Arts junior guides demonstrate their expertise in Merseyside's Lady Lever Art Gallery

children and grandchildren, it failed. The Society changed tactics, and decided to go into local schools with projects. Beaconsfield DFAS experienced a similar problem, 'although we have tried on more than one occasion to run a Young NADFAS Group' explained their chairman, 'this was never really viable for very long with the result that we have now changed our focus and are sponsoring practical art teachers in local schools'.[16]

Although, in 2007, there were only 21 Young Arts Groups, Societies support the involvement of young people in the Arts via some wonderful projects that suit the shift in the character of NADFAS membership. One that stands out, in the opinion of the then National Chairman, Nesta Waine, was the competition held by Mid Somerset DFAS for Young Offenders from the South West. It was controversial in so much as some members felt it was an inappropriate use of members' money, but any number of members attending must have been amazed at the standard of work.[17] In 2006 support for Young Arts activities rose again with 64% of Societies involved in arts events for young people. The total amount given in 2005/6 was £120,000 demonstrating an impressive commitment to Young Arts.

## Ideas into Action...
### ... Young Arts Projects
There is no set format for Young Arts Projects. Each can differ according to local circumstances, needs and facilities and also the funds available from the Society and other sources. A Society's involvement may be anything from sponsorship to hands-on organisation. Many are the result of partnerships with other local and national bodies. Experience has shown that even a small grant can make a big difference. Involvement in Young Arts has been called 'One of the most rewarding aspects of NADFAS'. This may be because there are just so many ways in which a NADFAS Society can take part. The wide range of activities include sponsorship of artists in residence in schools, museums and galleries; bursaries and awards to individual arts students and craft

apprenticeships; the organisation of arts lectures, exhibitions and competitions for schools and colleges; support for art projects in hospitals and hospices for children; arranging workshops in museums, galleries, cathedrals and historic houses; funding youth theatre or music and, especially for schools, providing resources for the purchase of art books and specialist art equipment and for visits to galleries and museums. More recently funds have been directed towards museum trails for children and, in collaboration with the Church Recorders, a relatively new venture has been launched, the creation of church trails along similar lines. The latter is an example of how different elements of NADFAS can be brought together in innovative ways. The following few examples can only hint at the diversity of approach, the enthusiasm of the participants and the sense of achievement gained from contributing to Young Arts.

### ... Artists in Residence
The constraints of the modern curriculum and the costs of 'buying-in' outside expertise mean that fewer schools have the opportunity to bring artists and craftsmen into the classroom. Even small amounts of money can facilitate the breath of fresh air and inspiration that these residences supply. By 1998 a register of artists and organisations in all arts disciplines who were interested in working with young people was available to many NADFAS Societies. Artists benefit from the challenging and stimulating experience, and raising awareness of their art form, while schools enhance the delivery of their art curriculum. There are many examples of how these ideas were turned into reality. South West London DFAS sponsored 'Ready, Steady, Build!' with an artist in residence to encourage three-dimensional responses to their local environment deriving from structures around Wandsworth. Harpenden DFAS enabled a potter to visit a local school once a week for ten weeks to help pupils enjoy working with clay. Basingstoke DFAS contributed £750 each to two local primary schools to provide for an artist in residence

for three days at each school. These grants stimulated matching funding by Basingstoke and Deane Councils.[18]

## ... Bursaries

Targeted funding to individuals can make dreams come true. Many aspiring students have been able to develop their potential through Young Arts bursaries enabling them to sign-on for courses that would be out of their reach financially. What better investment could a local NADFAS Society make in the future? Midhurst DFAS help finance Fine Arts students at West Dean College as part of the Sussex Area initiative. Sherborne DFAS Young Arts is well supported with funds being donated each year to the local primary schools or particular arts related projects. Other donations have for several years provided a bursary to Dorset Opera to enable a student to work with them as stage crew or chorus.[19] Sidmouth DFAS provide funding to help several students with foundation courses, leading to degree places.[20] Newick DFAS have made various contributions to Young Arts since 1994, including a NADFAS Award for Visual Arts students at Sussex Downs College set up in 2001.[21] Dukeries DFAS 'make an annual grant to a local school' and 'sponsored a student of sculpture who produced a lively work 'Spirit of Youth'. Evesham DFAS award 'two sixth form students at local secondary schools an annual £300 travel bursary.'[22]

## ... Art Exhibitions and Competitions

One of the most popular ways of supporting Young Arts is through the funding and organising of exhibitions and competitions. These attract both large numbers of participants and viewers, as well as local publicity. Shrewsbury DFAS helped to sponsor a touring exhibition from the Imperial War Museum, while North Lincolnshire DFAS (NLDFAS) organised an exhibition of Art at King Edward VI Grammar School, Louth, for AS and A2 level students. Kathryn Phillips's work won the NLDFAS Award of a scholarship.[23] A Young Arts Millennium Project combining the forces of West Surrey, Guildford Evening and Wey Valley Societies resulted in a major collaborative exhibition. Each one contributed £150, drawing in its turn a millennium grant from Surrey County Council, to provide display areas in Guildford House Gallery. They wrote to local schools offering to provide a lecturer to talk to children, and as a result Ann Clements spoke to pupils in two schools. Children drew figures which were then attached to panels creating their own work of art. Birmingham DFAS was working with a school that lies in the shadow of Winson Green prison. Only one of the 350 children was English, many of them coming from Eastern Europe with little or no knowledge of the language. Taking 'Identity' as the theme, this exciting two term project promoted the visual arts as a means of communicating. All the staff, parents and children were involved. The resulting display in a newly created art gallery reflected a sense of value and improved self-esteem. Not only did this help the children, but it also raised the Society's profile within the city. Elizabeth Dancey, their chairman, reports that 'In spite of meeting in Birmingham for 16 years, with 350 members and several voluntary groups, NADFAS is virtually unknown outside the membership'. Solihull DFAS make donations to local schools of up to £200 per year for projects concerning music, dance, theatre and practical art resulting in a decorative and permanent display. In 2004, Five Mole Valley Societies (Ashtead, Betchworth, Bookham, Dorking and Leatherhead) sponsored a schools exhibition of artistic talent from the area with 130 exhibits, supported and planned by Young Arts representatives. It drew 770 visitors over two days.[24] Such was its success that another Young Artists Exhibition was held in 2006, drawing nearly 1,000. Susan Sloan remarks in the history of her Society, Havering, that:

*One of the most rewarding aspects ... is the "Young Artist of the Year Competition". It was started in 2000 to encompass those taking GCSEs and A-levels. It has grown over the last two years and attracted over 100 entries last year ... the scheme has been extended to cover the*

**Above**

Mark Simpson's *Portrait of a Young Man*, one of the winning entries in Mid Somerset DFAS's controversial young offenders' art competition

*such a policy might be irrelevant but in fact it has proved to be very successful. The Society is fortunate in being close to the famous Gresham's School with the Auden Theatre being ideal for fostering these events. The first of these was a Drama Session led by Jenny Agutter of 'The Railway Children' fame.*

The project was initiated by the Society and was assisted by the School's Director of Art and Drama. The culmination was a public performance in the evening.[26] The Young NADFAS Opera programme in 1996 was Donizetti's *L'Elixir d'Amore*, when 67 North West Area members and friends joined the cast, director and pianist at Clonter Opera Farm in Cheshire exploring the process of producing an opera from music and drama to design and stage management. As one boy commented 'My sisters came too and now they want to be opera singers'.[27]

### ... Equipment

Sometimes it is the simple lack of tools and facilities that prevent the practical enjoyment of the arts. In this area a few pounds can make a difference, and several hundred can make possible a whole new area of activities. Horsham DFAS gave their local college a gas-fired kiln and computer extras including a flat bed scanner. Schools in Limpsfield, Rutland and Needwood have been given money to purchase art history books for their libraries, while Mid Essex DFAS provided disposable cameras to a local primary school. There are countless examples of Societies stepping in to supply equipment, responding to individual school needs quickly and effectively.

### ... Workshops & School Visits

How many of us remember the excitement of the school visit, the sheer novelty of escaping from the classroom, and broadening of the horizon? Visits make a huge difference. Rickmansworth DFAS supported a project called 'Making sculptures from recycled materials' with children collecting the materials themselves, working with schools from the most deprived areas.[28] The £1,500 raised by Edinburgh DFAS for the National Galleries of Scotland was swiftly put to use.

*primary school and 11-14 age groups.*[25]

A recent national initiative has been taking place entitled 'The Big Draw'. Designed to encourage drawing at all levels, events take place in museums and art galleries country-wide and the Greater London Area helped foot the bill of the 'Big Draw Day' at the British Museum.

### ... Youth Theatre

As the chairman of Glaven Valley DFAS explained:

*In view of the Society having so many elderly members it was important to encourage involvement with young people. Some thought*

They funded eight full days of workshops for children from primary classes and were specifically aimed at schools identified as non-users of the Galleries. These workshops included a guided discussion-based tour of selected paintings, a 'game' involving group discussion and decision-making, and then a practical art making activity.[29] The Society also funded a gallery trail for an exhibition, and gallery paintings provided the images and inspiration for an Apple Mac Photoshop programme to design book covers and publicity materials. Members of the Scottish Area Young Arts Groups were some young people who enjoyed this package. In 1998 Birmingham DFAS sponsored a children's holiday workshop in the city's Jewellery Quarter. North Lincolnshire DFAS organised a lecture by Paul Atterbury at Riverhead Theatre in Louth, in association with John Taylors, the local auctioneers and valuers. The £650 raised was used to send 72 children from Kidgate Primary School, Louth, to a whole day sculpture workshop at the Usher Art Gallery in Lincoln.[30] The day included a sculpture trail round Lincoln, drawing the statue of Tennyson, a look at the statuary in the Gallery and then choosing a topic and medium and making something themselves. Blackheath DFAS joined the Greenwich Education Department to commission a sculpture trail at a wildlife site in Eltham, winning prizes and attracting the attention of the national press. In 2006 one of the highlights was the Grampian Young Arts Teenage Group visit to the Peacock Visual Arts Centre in Aberdeen, for a workshop over two days in which resident print maker Michael Waight taught the participants the principles of lino printing using a selection of techniques and colours.

## ... Lectures

In 1988 Henley DFAS (HEDFAS), under the banner of Young NADFAS, launched a project which became known as 'Art in State Schools'. The aim was to stimulate children's interest in the arts generally. The project programmes were devised in order to awaken curiosity and open doors for all children, not just those with artistic ability. This project was made possible by a grant of £1,000 from the Patricia Fay Memorial Fund, a grant from Members of HEDFAS as well as funding from other local organisations and the District Council. The project initially provided six lectures per year to senior primary classes at a central venue, the local comprehensive school. There are now seven primary and two independent schools involved, meaning that approximately 500 children benefit from this project each year. Top class lecturers were used from the National and Tate Galleries, the V&A and Ashmolean Museums, the BBC and the NADFAS *Directory of Lecturers*. The Society paid for the coach transport for four local schools and also made two HEDFAS Art Prize awards of £100 each year.

While provision for the young has responded to changing times, the foundation philosophy of encouraging and supporting Groups remains unchanged, even though the name has moved from Young NADFAS to Young Arts Groups. Some of the more recent activities of these Groups testify to their liveliness. The Scottish Groups in Ayrshire, Angus, Grampian, Perth and Stirling are

**Above**

The Princess Royal attends an art exhibition organised by Abingdon DFAS of works by pupils at all the schools in the town

particularly active, with 137 families and 218 children involved. In 2006 an American Indian drumming class was organised in Fettercairn, a day at Her Majesty's Theatre, Aberdeen, and a 'noisy, messy and fun' felt workshop staged at the Inchbare Hall. The Hampshire Group serve 222 children, and the reports from the Test Valley Young NADFAS reveal an excitingly varied and stimulating programme of activities, including a workshop with the internationally acclaimed theatre company, STOMP, in Andover, a 'create your own coat of arms' session at Salisbury Cathedral, and close encounters with outdoor sculpture in Romsey. A pioneering new scheme operating at Merseyside's Lady Lever Art Gallery from 2006, and part funded by NADFAS, shows how members of Young Arts can make innovative contributions of both ideas and time to local culture. An enterprising member of Wirrall Young Arts, Paige Earlham, suggested that Merseyside should introduce a junior guides scheme to its museums in a bid to get teenagers more involved in the arts. Her idea was based on the popular and well-established 'docent' scheme in the United States that sees members of the public train as volunteer guides in museums and galleries. It was this scheme that Helen Lowenthal experienced while working in the States and 'brought home' as an example for the first NADFAS volunteer projects. Aided by a donation of £500 from the Patricia Fay Memorial Fund matched by Wirral DFAS 12 young people aged between 14 and 18 from local schools and Wirral Young Arts have been trained to act as guides in the Lady Lever Art Gallery. The idea behind the scheme is that it will speak to teenagers (an age group notoriously difficult to get into museums) on various levels. The success of the scheme will contribute to Liverpool's profile as European Capital of Culture in 2008.[31] The number and success of these activities prove that the early call by Anne White for use to be made of LOCAL resources continues to be met. The statement made by the National Chairman in 1976 in her annual report holds true today, 'Perhaps one of the most exciting and worthwhile parts of NADFAS is Young NADFAS'. These Groups continue to carry the torch of the original NADFAS mission 'to further the education of children by means of talks, visits to houses, museums and other places of interest'. Their leaders are dynamic and innovative, and are surely tending the seeds that will grow and flourish in the future. The 21 Groups that are active, with over 1,600 members, ensure that the next generation knows the name of NADFAS, what it stands for, and how it can contribute towards a life-long love of the arts.

NOTES
[1] Chiltern DFAS 40th Anniversary Recollections, NADFAS Archives.
[2] 'Museum Magic', The Times, 5 April 1965; 'Bringing the Old to the New', Glasgow Herald, 8 June 1965; Sheila Gittings, 'Other Mothers Lives', All About Children, 7 October 1965.
[3] June Fenwick, 'The History of Young NADFAS', 1987, p.1.
[4] Ibid.
[5] Ibid., p.14.
[6] Ibid., p.33.
[7] 'As Nature Intended', NADFAS Review, Winter 2006.
[8] Agnes Whittaker, 'Safety valves for a child's Christmas', The Times, 3 December 1979.
[9] Caroline Croft, 'The NADFAS Play at Hatfield Palace', NADFAS Archives.
[10] Pamela Cohn, Chairman's Report 1998-2000, NADFAS Archives.
[11] 'The History of Young NADFAS', p.28
[12] Sue Meehan, Leamington Spa Young NADFAS to Annabel Coghlan, Chairman Young NADFAS, March 1996, NADFAS Archives.
[13] 'A Way Forward for Young NADFAS', C4/97 for 18 March 1997, NADFAS Archives.
[14] Ibid.
[15] Ibid.
[16] Peter F. Vermeylen, Beaconsfield DFAS, October 2006.
[17] Nesta Waine, Chairman's Report 2004-2006, NADFAS Archives.
[18] Peter Redman, Basingstoke DFAS, 15 September 2006.
[19] Anne Brunker, Sherborne DFAS, July 2006.
[20] Sidmouth DFAS Newsletter, October 2006.
[21] Colin Walford, Newick DFAS, August 2006.
[22] Claire Charles, 'Fine romance with the arts', The Evesham Admag, n.d.
[23] Anne Else, North Lincolnshire DFAS, October 2006.
[24] Sheila Simkins, Dorking & Leatherhead DFAS.
[25] Susan Sloan, 'Havering DFAS, a brief history', 2002.
[26] Hilda Singleton, Glaven Valley DFAS, October 2006
[27] Young NADFAS, Images, 1997, vol.2, p.11.
[28] Jean Butler, Rickmansworth DFAS, July 2006.
[29] Marjorie Connell, Edinburgh DFAS, March 2007.
[30] Shan Shan To to North Lincolnshire DFAS, and article in Louth Leader, 13 October 2004.
[31] Danielle Green, 'Guiding Lights', NADFAS Review, Spring 2006, pp.16-18.

# 8

# The Art of Giving:
## NADFAS Digs Deep

*'... and the giving of aid to the preservation
of the artistic heritage...'*
Charitable Aims of NADFAS[1]

Over the years members' contributions to the Patricia Fay Memorial Fund and the receipt of two major legacies, from Mr Rex Britcher and Dr George Furlong in 1997, and Mrs Zena Walker in 2006, have enabled NADFAS nationally to further this aspect of its charitable aims, alongside the many local initiatives of Societies and Areas.

## The Patricia Fay Memorial Fund

After Patricia Fay's tragic early death in 1979, it was decided to set up a charitable fund in memory of her. There was much debate about where the money raised should go. One Society chairman who attended a National meeting at which the Fund was discussed, reported back to her group:

*One wanted to purchase an ornament, another have a course or bursary at West Dean College to study some form of craft or to teach or help. Perhaps a yearly lecture in the provinces NOT London. Then one who had really known her well said we must go OUTSIDE the museum, do something with PEOPLE that is what she would have wanted. The V&A had wanted us to*

*put a plaque on a showcase exhibiting the "object of the month". As someone said it would only need a change of government for that to disappear. Anyway it all remains open.[2]*

A Declaration of Trust was made in May 1981 to establish the Patricia Fay Memorial Fund. The Trustees agreed that the capital sum should be invested and the income only be 'applied to differing objects which the Trustees should from time to time consider to be particularly worthy of support'. From 1982 the Trustees made grants to the Voluntary Conservation Corps for their training courses, to the Church Recorders for reprinting their *Manual* and their residential seminar, and to Cathedral Camps, a registered charity which provided opportunities for members of Young NADFAS to help with the voluntary conservation of our national religious heritage. The total sum distributed in 1984 amounted to £2,750.

Initially funds were raised by allocating £1 from every membership fee to the Fund, and from 1980 (until 2004) an annual Patricia Fay Memorial event was organised to raise money. Christopher Chavasse, one of the Trustees of the Fund, who had been both a close friend of Patricia's and the first Hon. Legal Adviser to NADFAS, reported that 'Generous contributions flooded in, both from individuals and Member Societies, and by a year later the Treasurer [Nicky Foot] was able to report that the capital sum had amounted to approximately £16,000'. By October 1983 the market value had risen to £26,000. Major sources for the Patricia Fay Memorial Fund have changed over time, reflecting shifts in NADFAS activities and changes in the law. The Patricia Fay Days were at the beginning immensely popular annual events held around the country, each organised by a different Area. The first was held in conjunction with the Beverley Festival of Flowers, Arts and Crafts and lasted three days. In 1984 the Memorial Event was a private view of the V&A's *Rococo* exhibition in London, a path-breaking show that introduced the public to the art and design of Hogarth's Britain. The last was held in Worcester in 2004. The brief for each event was to raise at least £1,000 for the Patricia Fay Memorial Fund. However with increasing costs both of organising the event and of members travelling to it, it became difficult to attract sufficient support. As a result the 'Patricia Fay Days' were abandoned and a Memorial Lecture at the London AGMs took their place.

Societies are also encouraged to invest their 'spare cash' in the Fund, to make the money work, although it may be withdrawn on demand. Invested sums range from £200 to £10,000. Since 2004 the Fund has benefited from the Gift Aid Scheme through tax re-claimable on the affiliation fees paid by the members of Societies which are not charities in their own right, and up to October 2007 this had yielded over £160,000. This voluntary scheme has made a tremendous difference to the number of young people that NADFAS can support. This initiative was driven by a Trustee, Piers Ashworth, who sadly died before the true benefits became apparent. The Patricia Fay Memorial Fund continues to support the outward-looking aspect of NADFAS.

The Fund assists conservation students and young people interested in the arts. For the latter there are grants to Young NADFAS members which have enabled them to attend a whole range of stimulating courses, among them those held at the British Institute in Florence, the Prague Conservatoire, the Royal Opera House in London, and the National Theatre in Namibia. The Fund has also supported Young NADFAS events, Young Arts Workshops, an Art Competition to celebrate Ashridge DFAS's 40th anniversary and many other Young Arts exhibitions, both national and local.

The Patricia Fay Memorial Fund's other main area of support is for the training of conservation students, as well as those studying more broadly in the arts. For the former, the students now have to be enrolled at one of the leading relevant institutes, like West Dean College Sussex, the Textile Conservation Centre at Winchester, the Hamilton Kerr Institute in Cambridge, the Universities of Lincoln and Northumbria, or the Scottish Lime Centre, as well as the London based Courtauld Institute of Art and City & Guilds Art School. Past students supported by the Fund have also attended the Royal College of Art, Goldsmiths College, the Royal School of Needlework and the Frink School of Sculpture. There are currently eight colleges 'on the books' which allocate £2,500 to a student each year, as a contribution to their fees payable to the institution, or money for essential tools or books. Through the Patricia Fay Memorial Fund, Jemma Ooi was able to continue her two-year MA at the Royal College of Art, investigating textile design in relation to

**Above**
The brooch presented by Hamburg DFAS as a gift to the Museum für Kunst und Gewerbe

industry, working with Heals, the Italian silk manufacturer Manero, the National Opera Company and G.E. Plastics. The Fund also provided £1,000 to help Simon Keeley complete his three-year Historic Stone

Carving degree course at London's City and Guilds Art School. Another textile-based student that NADFAS has helped is Joelle Wickes who is doing her PhD research at the Textile Conservation Centre at Winchester, part of the University of Southampton. She is working on 'one of the biggest challenges facing upholstery conservators, foam-based furniture of the 20th century', like Aarnio's Globe Chair manufactured in 1968, now in

the V&A. Supporting this work not only assists the student, but also means that many iconic pieces of furniture will not be left to disintegrate for want of technical knowledge for their preservation. Shannon O'Neill, maker of the Australian ADFAS Badge presented to them by NADFAS in 2000, received a grant of £1,250 in 1997 towards a Young Silversmith Internship to extend her skills. A £2,500 Award from the PFMF has enabled Sally MacMillan to complete her final year of an MA in the Conservation of Fine Art at Northumbria University. The list of colleges supported is regularly reviewed and they work closely with NADFAS in giving feedback on the students' progress. In this way fruitful partnerships prosper.

Dr Thomas Cocke, when Chief Executive, established links with Cockpit Arts in London, and a grant of £2,500 was given by the Fund in 2006 to help this 'creative hub of individual and group studios of established designers' who work alongside emerging talent, to further their aims of building careers and developing their creativity.[3] One of those supported as part of the Cockpit Arts project is Thomas von Nordheim, a pattern cutter, fitter and tailor. He was awarded £2,500 in 2006 from the Patricia Fay Memorial Fund enabling him to rent a studio, giving him more space to pursue his dream of supplying period costume for film

**Above left**
The Tudor Tower at Liphook was famously saved from dereliction by a West Sussex DFAS raffle
**Left**
Taking the mission overseas: Costa Del Sol DFAS helped raise funds to restore the historic English cemetery in Malaga

and television productions.[4]

An exciting new development for the Patricia Fay Memorial Fund is assistance for the training of apprentices in the applied arts and crafts, via support for employers prepared to take on and train a new apprentice or trainee. Bursaries of up to £5,000 for each of three apprentices will be available for the first year of training. This initiative comes at a time of widespread concern amongst professional, trade and academic organisations about the current state of apprenticeship within the fine and applied arts and crafts. The main problem is that the vast majority of fine and applied artists or craftsmen are sole-traders with no employees, and therefore few of them can afford to pay a second salary to an apprentice, especially whilst taking time away from their own gainful employment to train a junior.[5] The burdens of insurance, health and safety and employment law are further disincentives for such people. In supporting this scheme NADFAS shows that it has its finger on the pulse on one of the most pressing issues within contemporary arts and crafts. Once skills have been allowed to die, it will be far harder to revive them. Timely help now will not only save the loss of generations of knowledge, but also encourage creativity for the future. NADFAS is also a major partner in a new initiative being developed by the Art Workers' Guild to put together funders, employers and potential apprentices or trainees in the applied arts and crafts via a newly designed website. It will contain a comprehensive list of funding organisations like NADFAS, educational institutions specialising in the applied arts, and potential employers willing to take apprentices. Such a scheme has been long promised by the Arts Council but has never materialised. The early supporters of NADFAS like Helen Lowenthal, Trenchard Cox and Hugh Casson would be delighted that their exhortations to the Association to support the arts and crafts of the present, as well as of the past, are being so earnestly taken to heart by NADFAS in the twenty-first century. In 2006-7 the Patricia Fay Memorial Fund

**Above**
Bourne Hall is still standing thanks in great part to the efforts of Epsom DFAS

distributed between £40,000 and £50,000, making it NADFAS's key grant-giving body.

## The Britcher Furlong Bequest

Rex Britcher and Dr George Furlong were active and enthusiastic members of NADFAS, they had been friends of Patricia Fay and members of the Royal Borough of Kensington and Chelsea DFAS. In 1997 they left a generous bequest of £100,000 'for the benefit of members', a phrase which initially proved difficult to define. However, this bequest has now assisted Societies with particular needs, and will, on occasion, underwrite Society or Area projects against loss, although the fund has never had to pay out on this front yet! Help given includes money towards the purchase of a radio microphone at Derwent Evening DFAS, to develop websites for both Chiltern and Liverpool Societies and support the launch of Devizes DFAS. The Britcher Furlong Bequest also made possible the upgrading of IT equipment for NADFAS House. The resulting improved speed and efficiency of communication was of immense value to everyone. Any Society or Area can apply, and a new Society is now eligible, subject to certain criteria, for a one-off £500 grant to help a recruitment drive or in the purchase of essential equipment.

## The NADFAS Zena Walker Scholarship

In 2006 a Scholarship was launched, thanks to a legacy of £120,000 left to the Association by Zena Walker, another friend of Patricia Fay and one of the early activists in NADFAS, who helped set up four Societies in Yorkshire. She acknowledged that after her husband's death 'NADFAS was my life'. A former student at art college in Leeds, a gifted designer, who worked, alongside Hardy Amies, as a camouflage painter for the Army during the war, it is fitting that her generous bequest is used to support a postgraduate student in the arts. Katya Belaia is the first recipient of the £4,000 per annum grant for the duration of her three-year postgraduate course on the conservation of easel paintings at the Courtauld Institute of Art. Katya is a graduate of Goldsmiths' College, University of London, with a BA in Fine Art and History of Art, who recently completed an apprenticeship in the conservation of historic and artistic works in Lisbon. Through these funds Patricia Fay, Rex Britcher and George Furlong and Zena Walker are permanently remembered by all who benefit from their determination to do something practical to support the arts, and in NADFAS House where meeting rooms have been named after them.

## Local Initiatives: Support from Societies

While these three funds are administered centrally there are many other local initiatives which reveal an astonishing range of projects that the member groups of

NADFAS have supported through fund-raising. Member Societies can also apply to the Association and channel central funds into suitable local causes. What emerges from the diversity of projects is a consistency in enthusiasm, efficient organisation and effectiveness. Many projects are innovative, all deserve greater recognition, and cumulatively they add up to a significant impact on the preservation and promotion of our cultural heritage.

## Thinking Big: Buildings and Open Spaces

Societies take their own decisions in coming to the aid of local causes. One of the earliest DFAS initiatives concerned the Tudor Tower at Liphook in Hampshire. This fine, now

Grade II listed, gatehouse built in 1575, was all that was left of a fine Tudor Mansion, which had been knocked down in the nineteenth century to build a country house. The Tower had fallen into serious decay, and the hospital in whose grounds it lay could not afford the funds for its repair. Rising to the challenge a member of the NADFAS Executive Committee, who lived nearby, took action by organising a raffle of antiques by West Sussex DFAS. It raised enough money for the necessary remedial work, the Tower was saved from dereliction and rescued from obscurity. Sir Trenchard Cox, the President of NADFAS, was impressed by this successful, and first, NADFAS 'Rescue Operation' and refers to it in his report to the NADFAS Council in 1971 as proof of the diverse and very effective activities of the Association.[6] The impact of these projects lives on. Since the hospital was decommissioned in 1986 the area has been subject to several plans for development. The existence of the Tower, although still on the English Heritage 'At Risk' register, has meant that any plans now incorporate its retention and enhancement, together with the surrounding walled garden.

There were other early projects afoot to help preserve buildings of local and historical importance. As Helen Lowenthal remarked, 'preservation was not a political matter, but rather the case of "spotting the villains!"'.[7] Thanet DFAS sent money to rescue the eighteenth century theatre in Margate from closure in 1971. It is both the second oldest theatre in operation, and the oldest unrestored theatre in the country. Established by Royal Patent in 1786, it has a spectacular auditorium dating to 1874. The future of this historical and architectural gem is currently back in the news, as its future is now in the hands of Thanet Council, which plans to hand it over to the Theatre Trust to keep it as a place for live performance. More recently, West Suffolk DFAS raised £8,000 for the Theatre Royal in Bury St Edmunds Appeal. William Wilkins, who went on to design the National Gallery in London, was the architect of the theatre which opened in 1819. Its fate hung in the balance in the 1960s and locals

**Above and left**
The newly re-opened Bury St Edmunds' Theatre Royal, whose fate once hung in the balance, was helped by a grant from the Patricia Fay Memorial Fund, not to mention tireless campaigning by local NADFAS Societies

raised over £37,000 to rescue it from closure and in 1975 the building was handed over to the National Trust. In 2006, helped by a grant from the Patricia Fay Memorial Fund, which permitted more ambitious planning than their own resources would have allowed, a special event was organised by local NADFAS Societies to raise awareness of the theatre's historical importance with the aim of attracting donations to the Restoration Appeal. Six local Societies (West Suffolk, Bury St Edmunds, Sudbury, South Suffolk, Newmarket and Diss) worked together to great effect.[8]

True to the NADFAS mission energies are not just concentrated on the old. Epsom DFAS (EDFAS) took action in 1992 when the local Bourne Hall came under threat of closure. Set in a Victorian park, the Hall comes as a surprise as it is a large cylindrical building built to a revolutionary design in the 1960s. Local Societies, including EDFAS, supported the action group, and as a result of their efforts, the building is still open to the public, thanks in part to NADFAS. The Costa del Sol Society helped raise the profile of and funds for the English Cemetery in Malaga. It was created in 1831 by the British Consul as part of the elegant nineteenth century suburb. As the city has grown it is now a rare haven of peace and tranquility hemmed in by high rise apartment blocks. The work of the Society has done much to rescue this rarity from disappearing, and carries the NADFAS mission overseas.[9]

## Adding to Collections

NADFAS groups all over the world have raised money to buy important additions to public collections both national and local. NADFAS has regularly given money to the V&A in recognition of its support of the Association. In 1974, NADFAS sent £50 towards the purchase of the Lord and Lady Clapham dolls, dated to c.1690-1700, now stars of the British Galleries displays, and rare evidence for the history of dress. In January 1976, £230 was sent to the Donatello Fund, to help purchase the so-called 'Chellini Roundel', a mid 15th century circular bronze, bearing an image of the Virgin and Child. It was made by the great Renaissance sculptor Donatello (1386-1466) to give to his doctor Giovanni Chellini in lieu of payment for the treatment he was receiving for a serious illness. The roundel, brought into the V&A by a dealer in the mid 1960s, was recognised by the Director Sir John Pope-Hennessy, and a public appeal was made in 1976 to prevent it being exported to the United States. It remains one of the Museum's most prized possessions. It is important to recognise the significance of these, what now appear small, sums of money. In 1975 the annual purchase grant for the whole of the British Museum with its twelve departments was £167,000.[10] On a more mundane level, at the same time petrol was 20p a gallon!

For many years individual Societies have made donations to The Art Fund (formerly the National Art Collections Fund). If these gifts are not made in response to a specific appeal, they are aggregated each year and put towards a single acquisition, which the National Chairman is invited to choose from a shortlist, in the name of NADFAS. Donations have averaged over £3,000 per annum and museums and galleries all over the country have benefited as a result. In recognition of this long relationship and in celebration of NADFAS's 40th anniversary, The Art Fund has purchased an important collection of pattern books, special order books and individual watercolour designs for Royal Worcester Porcelain which have been presented to the Worcester Porcelain Museum

where Heritage Volunteers from Malvern Hills and Worcester will be helping with their conservation.

A rather unusual gift was made by Hamburg DFAS to their 'local', although internationally important, Museum für Kunst und Gewerbe, in 1991. A gold and silver brooch in the shape of a sheaf of flowers, and made in Paris in the 1940s was bought and presented in 1992, on the occasion of the fifth birthday of the Society, as a fine example of 'Resistance' jewellery. The evident appreciation with which this gift was received has led to a further donation by the Society of a seventeenth-century silver snuff box to the Altona Museum in 1997. In 2003 Southport and Formby DFAS presented the Walker Art Gallery with new picture frames

**Above**
Southport and Formby DFAS vice chairman Sheila Edward presents the Walker Art Gallery with new frames for two of its key paintings

**Right**
The four swans from the gallows sign in Waltham Cross that were restored thanks to donations from East Hertfordshire DFAS

**Above right**
Frame restoration of *Shakespeare's Bianca* in Worthing Art Gallery was enabled by Arun DFAS

for *The Birth of the Virgin* by Pietro Perugino and Raphael's *Votive Picture,* two important Italian renaissance paintings in a key provincial collection.

Sheffield DFAS has over the years helped to add to the City's internationally famous metalwork collection by contributing to the purchase of a Mappin & Webb electroplated tea service of 1950, a 1797 silver teapot and stand by John Young, another local maker, and a set of four 1894 knives. The Museum's own fundraising was helped when the Society

sponsored the reproduction of Sir William Rothenstein's painting of *Sheffield Buffer Girls* as a greetings card celebrating the city's pre-eminence in the cutlery industry. A further donation was made to permit the acquisition of a Rockingham teapot – again of great local interest, as the factory was only a few miles from the city.[11]

## Cash for Conservation

Conservation is time-consuming and costly work. Thanks to funds raised by NADFAS groups many objects that would be languishing in backroom stores, in poor condition, are on display for all to enjoy. Only three years after its foundation in 1968, Hertfordshire DFAS (later Harpenden Area DFAS) was able to raise money to help restore

the medieval wall paintings at St Leonard's Church in Flamstead, one of the best examples of such work in the county.[12] East Hertfordshire DFAS raised £200 for conserving the four original swans from the gallows sign in Waltham Cross. One was in fragments, another badly fractured, and all were infested with woodworm. The cost of the restoration was met by the Society's donation. In 1994 they were returned to the Lowewood Museum where they are on show to the public. Arun DFAS paid for the restoration of a large gilt frame for an oil painting of *Shakespeare's Bianca, the Patroness of Heavenly Harmony*, by the Pre-Raphaelite painter William Holman Hunt (1827-1910), which is still advertised as one of the highlights in Worthing Art Gallery. Some projects lead to long term relationships. The Watts Gallery at Compton has benefited greatly from the support of local NADFAS Societies over many years. In 1986, Shalford

**Below**
The Chellini Roundel remains in the V&A thanks to donations from organisations such as NADFAS, which also helped save the Lord and Lady Clapham dolls (right) for the Museum's collection

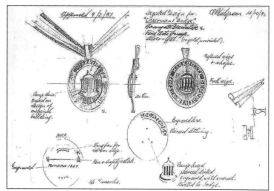

DFAS raised more than £200 to pay for the restoration of G.F. Watts's painting, *The Seamstress*, 'after decades in the dark', making possible the display of the 'complete quartet' of pictures that the artist had painted in 1847 showing aspects of the life of the Victorian poor.[13] The curator commented that 'In the economic gloom of the 1980s, the sufferings of the poor have aroused a new interest in the paintings', which before then could only be seen by going down into the storeroom. The Gallery itself was in 'a very precarious financial position'.[14] The Wey Valley Society stepped in nine years later to help finance the restoration of another work by the artist, titled *Uldra*. It had been acquired for £17,645 and is one of Watts's most mysterious and beautiful pictures. The curator, Richard Jeffries, was most grateful to the 'NADFAS angels and saviours'. In 2001, Wey Valley came to the rescue again. An album of the young artist's work appeared at auction and the Society appealed to the West Surrey Area to assist in raising money for its purchase for the Gallery. An afternoon tea was arranged that raised £2,000 which helped secure the album for the collection. NADFAS Societies in the Area continue to support this Gallery, which is one of the few purpose built picture galleries in Britain housing a single artist's work. Today, the Watts Gallery still retains the ethos upon which it was founded, that great art should be accessible to all, and so helps to restore Watts's former reputation. It is 'a national gallery in the heart of a village'. The effectiveness of Societies joining together with a common aim proves Patricia Fay's point made in 1968, that:

*By pooling our resources we can tackle any number of projects which you might like to suggest and which are denied to a single Society. … Above all we can help others to share the enormous pleasures which we are fortunate to enjoy.*[15]

## Investing in the Future

From the early days NADFAS 'looked to the future by giving encouragement to the contemporary arts as well as enjoying things of the past'. As firmly stated by the National Chairman in 1972, 'If people aren't encouraged to buy from them our craftsmen and women won't be able to reach their full potential'.[16] Helen Lowenthal reminded readers of the 1985 NADFAS *Newsletter* 'In this chilly financial world, support for the creative arts was ever more urgent, it was much simpler twenty years ago'. Support of contemporary arts and crafts is not just achieved by raising awareness via lectures, but by active commissioning and stepping from the passive to the active mode. 'Whenever I go to NADFAS meetings in London', wrote one Society chairman in the

**Pictured**
A selection of badges specially commissioned for National Association and local Society officers from local jewellers

1980s, 'we are urged to encourage the arts, to buy something from local craftsmen'.[17] Both the National Association and several local Societies have commissioned special badges for their officers, which are regular reminders of the skills of young metalworkers and jewellers. Societies have discovered that the commissioning process can be almost as exciting and rewarding as the receipt and wearing of the final piece. Ann Parkinson presented NADFAS with a special badge for the National Chairman and, as a retiring gift, also gave silver enamelled badges for Past National Chairmen and Lady Vice Presidents. They were commissioned from Bob Martin, a silversmith based in Canterbury. The Harrogate group chose a chairman's badge as a means to celebrate their 20th anniversary in 1988.[18] Having given three pieces of modern jewellery to Lotherton Hall to mark their 10th anniversary, it seemed fitting to commission, rather than to buy an antique piece.

Silversmiths were invited to submit proposals, and C.J. Philipson's was chosen, with his suggestion of a silver gilt badge based on the classical temple designed in 1806, as depicted in a lithograph of 1829. The temple, which was removed in 1842 to build the town's Royal Pump Room, covered the sulphur well. As Mary Furniss, former chairman of the Society, explained 'The design of the badge seemed to embody the mineral wells which brought prosperity to Harrogate and classical architecture symbolising the arts'. The idea of a chairman's badge for the Nidd Valley Society was proposed by their vice president, who felt that it would be a worthy symbol to mark their 25th

anniversary in 2006. The resulting silver badge, made by silversmith Mary Dean, which can also be worn as a pendant, has an upper part bearing the logos and lettering with the lower section showing the water of the River Nidd, in green enamel, flowing under Knaresborough Bridge.[19] The simple interlinked letters of the Gade Valley badge are reminiscent of Victorian style, yet it is totally original in appearance. Gravesend Society's chairman wears a chain with simple pie-crust edged cartouche in silver with gilded letters. A later president gave a matching chain so the badge could be worn

as a pendant.[20] A dramatic brooch of office was commissioned by NADFAS for the Australian Association of Decorative and Fine Arts Societies to commemorate its foundation. The large sterling silver acanthus leaf is not cast, but hammered from flat sheet and worked in repoussé, making it light to wear, with details picked out in chasing. It is a most striking piece of contemporary jewellery by one of Britain's newly

established young silversmiths, Shannon O'Neill, who had, in 1997, received an award from the Patricia Fay Memorial Fund. The badge was presented in 2000, as a symbol of friendship and alliance.

There have been many other innovative ideas using various media. In 1988 the Harrow Society commissioned a display cabinet for their local museum to house its collection of Whitefriars Glass. The decorative motifs include a reference to Whitefriars and the NADFAS acanthus leaf. Until its closure the firm had its works in the Harrow area, making this a particularly appropriate gift from the local Society. The Kent Area part-financed a project to create a new nave altar frontal for Canterbury Cathedral. Work began in June 2005, with twelve different embroiderers working a total of 1,500 hours to complete the frontal. The design is inspired by the Compass Rose, the symbol of worldwide spread of the Anglican faith, with Canterbury at its centre. The acanthus leaf symbol of NADFAS is subtly included in several areas of the design.[21]

## Supporting Training

One of the great investments in the future being made by NADFAS Societies is the support of training for young students. Arun DFAS, together with the other Societies in the Sussex Area, supports a student at West Dean College, where the subjects studied have included stonework, musical instruments and clocks.[22] Havering Society launched a bursary to help a student on her three-year course at the University of Hertford in Hatfield, and the members have enjoyed seeing 'evidence of her obvious talent and will continue to watch her progress with interest'.[23] South Mercia Area makes an annual award of £2,000 to Ryecotewood, a well-known furniture college, which includes a scholarship of £1,500 to a student chosen by the College, with £500 to finance two special lectures. This Area makes an additional grant of £500 to a student of its own choice which in 2006, was awarded to the young metalworker, Bryony Knox, who used her £500 to spend a week with the renowned Norfolk-based silversmith, Rod Kelly, to learn flat chasing and repoussé work. Her quirky copper and silver pieces are beginning to appear in major exhibitions and galleries. One of the most innovative and creative projects that NADFAS has launched recently is the North East Area award of a bursary to a young metalwork student. Discussion with the tutors of the B.A. Hons Jewellery and Metalwork course at Sheffield Hallam University resulted in the involvement of the Area in the second year module 'Designing for Clients'.[24] The Area offered to fund the silver for the manufacture of the winning student's design, which then went on public display in the renowned metalwork collection of Sheffield's Millennium Galleries. Rose Lees' design for 'a photographer specialising in flowers, often single blooms,

**Above left** Jenny Adin poses with the nave altar frontal she designed for Canterbury Cathedral in a project part-financed by Kent Area
**Right** Rose Lees' award-winning vase design was made possible thanks to North East Area's Silver Bursary in association with Sheffield Hallam University

who favours a modern functional aesthetic in everyday objects and has a collection of antique watering cans', was certainly a challenge to the imagination. However, her response was clearly a winner. Her flat sheet worked silver vase presents the bloom through a window of silver, like a slide, but with the image bursting through. Course leader, Chris Knight, felt the competition stimulated both the artistic and business skills of his students; Curator Dorian Church was delighted with the addition to the collection, and Rose's career as one of Britain's leading silversmiths of the future may well have been launched. Such was the success of this Silver Bursary that it has been repeated and by 2008 four products of this creative partnership will be on public display.

NOTES
[1] NADFAS Website, October 2007.
[2] Helen Fielden, Teme Valley DFAS, 23 March 1980. Private Collection.
[3] Trish Lorenz, 'In Full Flight', *NADFAS Review*, Summer 2006, p.20.
[4] Buff Reid, 'The Future Today', *NADFAS Review*, Spring 2007, p.21.
[5] 'Craft Apprenticeship Initiative', The Art Workers Guild Trustees Ltd, January 2007.
[6] NADFAS *Newsletter*, 1 January 1971.
[7] Helen Lowenthal, 'Report on NADFAS', 29 March 1984, Chiltern DFAS Archives.
[8] 'Local Heroes', *NADFAS Review*, Summer 2006, p.25.
[9] Joan Tomson, 'The English Cemetery in Malaga', Costa del Sol DFAS Newsletter, Summer 2005, no.23.
[10] Sir John Wolfenden, 'Arts and the People', NADFAS Conference, 1975, NADFAS Archives.
[11] Caroline Hopps, Sheffield DFAS, August 2007.
[12] Lynne Edmunds, 'Branching out for the Arts', *Daily Telegraph*, 15 December 1972.
[13] Ibid.
[14] Ibid.
[15] Chairman's Report, 1967/8, Patricia Fay, NADFAS Archives.
[16] Edmunds, op. cit.
[17] Fielden, op. cit.
[18] Mary Furniss, 'The History of the Chairman's Badge of Office', Harrogate DFAS Newsletter, November 2004.
[19] Elizabeth J. Scott, Nidd Valley DFAS, October 2006.
[20] Gill Pearson, Gravesend and District DFAS, October 2006.
[21] 'Local Heroes', op. cit. p.26.
[22] Patricia Neild, Arun DFAS, July 2006.
[23] Susan Sloan, 'Havering DFAS. A Brief History', 2004.
[24] Barbara Hickman, 'Glittering Prize', *NADFAS Review*, Summer 2005, p.15.

# 9
# Travelling the World:
## NADFAS on Tour

*'...something more exciting and adventuresome should be attempted.'*
Kathleen Wareham on North Kent DFAS's tour plans, 1969

The 'Tours Division' evolved as a natural consequence of the curiosity inspired by NADFAS lectures. Audiences wanted to go and see for themselves the artistic treasures of Renaissance Italy and Medieval France, not only in British museums and country houses, but also in their geographical, historic and cultural context. This desire to see was coupled with new possibilities for travel. The early 1970s were a time of growth in the holiday industry, with the appearance of new jet planes, and affordable air transport. The postwar introduction of an international system of airline regulation was another important factor. These developments coincided with a significant increase in the standard of living in Britain.

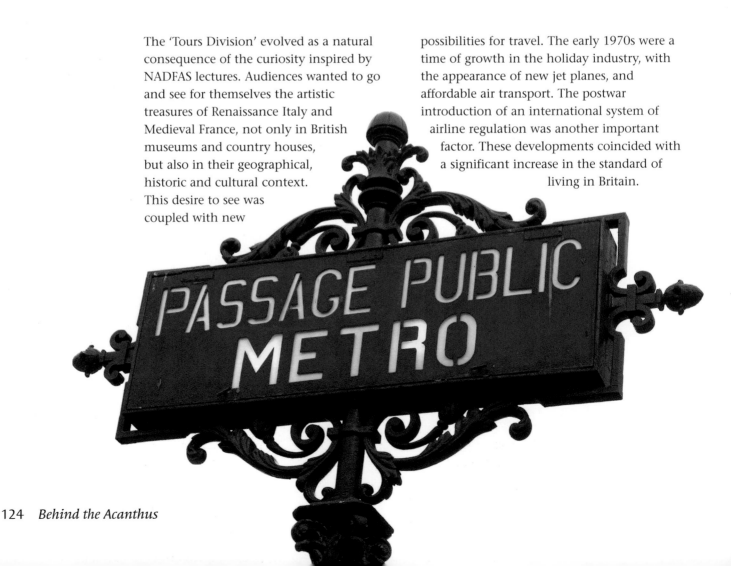

**Above**
When North Kent DFAS
headed to Paris for a week
in 1969, enthusiasm for
overseas exploration took
hold within NADFAS

Although package holidays had first emerged in the 1850s thanks to Thomas Cook, and were to become 'one of the most remarkable social phenomena of the second half of the twentieth century', there were in the early 1970s still no reasonably priced organised tours that specialised in art and culture.[1] Within NADFAS there was a hunger to learn more, and the provision of specially devised holidays for members met with huge demand.

Overseas tours for NADFAS members began in a small and unexpected way in 1969 when Kathleen Wareham and Shuna Cronin took members from their own North Kent DFAS to Paris for a week. Kathleen Wareham recalled that members of her Society rejected the idea of going to Blenheim, 'on the grounds that most members would have been there already, and that something more exciting and adventuresome should be attempted'.[2]

Having decided upon Paris, a programme was set up to include some of its museums, galleries and historic houses but with a difference – a host of private invitations were organised through Shuna's contacts. 'Members went by coach to Lympne airport, caught a plane to Beauvais where another coach was waiting to take them to their Paris hotel ... The whole trip cost £24'.[3] This was the time of currency control and V-forms. The programme included a wonderful party in the Paris flat of the chairman of one of the great fashion houses, to see his spectacular collection of miniatures. Rosemary Lenanton, one of the fortunate few on this maiden visit, also recalls visiting an apartment where the corridors were lined with Picasso paintings.

When Patricia Fay heard of these tours she suggested to Kathleen Wareham that as they were such an excellent idea, why didn't she 'offer the itineraries to all the other

Societies around the country'.[4] At an Executive Committee meeting Shuna Cronin was introduced by Kathleen and all agreed that notices of North Kent DFAS's trips should be circulated to member Societies. The response was overwhelming. The Paris trip was repeated in May, July and October, and

in August 1971 Shuna was asked to become National Tours organiser.[5] On the advice of Patricia's husband, a barrister, that year the 'Tours Division' became a limited company, thus protecting Societies, chairmen and NADFAS. It was called Shuna Cronin Associates, in recognition of the major role that Shuna played.

Meanwhile Shuna was busy organising monthly visits for her own Society and planning further overseas trips including ones to the Chateaux of the Loire, and two to Paris, followed by Delft, Amsterdam and The Hague. As if this were not enough she was also arranging a programme of trips to London for art connoisseurs from Paris, a reciprocal venture after their help with the Paris visits in the first year.

Kathleen Wareham and Shuna Cronin

made a dynamic partnership. Kathleen had travelled extensively as part of her international lecturing experience, had a passion for skiing, and had trained as a pilot after reading medicine at university.[6] She was to become NADFAS National Chairman from 1974 to 1976. Shuna, a much travelled and long-standing friend joined Kathleen's North Kent Group with the object of running visits and projects. They became the ideal leaders for members wishing to increase their knowledge of art by travelling both at home and abroad.

Other Societies were beginning to spread their wings, too. Helen Ouin, of West Sussex DFAS, remembers that in 1970 'Professor Bertram gave the Society a series of lectures on Renaissance Art and Sculpture which sparked off the idea we should visit Italy armed with a list of what we should see'.[7] A group of eighteen members, led by Margaret Thorp, set forth on their first overseas expedition. She remembers that 'when NADFAS heard of our plans they told us that they were on the verge of starting their own tours, organised by Shuna Cronin, and suggested that she should break her journey from South Africa to join us in Italy where she was a great asset'.

In 1972, the four-day trip to Paris was repeated, and another four-day trip to Bruges, Ghent and Brussels was advertised. The very special nature of these trips is evoked by the itinerary for the afternoon of the second day in Brussels. It began with a visit to the home of Monsieur and Madame Roger Stallaerts, who acted as guides; then went on to Chateau de la Hulpe where the group were shown round by Le Chevalier Charles Selliers Jr. and, lastly, to Chateau de Sterrebeek, home of Madame Ernest de Selliers de Moranville, who with her children acted as guide and entertained the group to tea. These tours did not just focus on the art and culture of the past, on the last day in Belgium the group enjoyed the sculptures of Eduardo Chillada and Beverly Pepper, and the 'canvasses of the American School of Andy Warhol, Roy Lichtenstein and Frank Stella'. The continental tours were complemented by

**Left**

Shuna Cronin, a pioneer of NADFAS tours. Shuna Cronin Associates, a precursor to Tour NADFAS, was named in recognition of her key role in the Association's overseas excursions home tours, introduced in 1972, the first focusing on the 'Stately Homes of Yorkshire' including in five days, Harrogate, the Minster and Treasurer's House in York, Ripley Castle and Fountains Abbey, with Chatsworth *en route*. Five years later country weekend and mid-week home tours were added to the programme. By 1974 overseas tours had spread to Vienna; Moscow and Leningrad; Holland (taking in Amsterdam, Haarlem and The Hague) and a fifteen-day visit to Barbados under the auspices of the Barbados National Trust. The memories of the lecturer Eve King, who accompanied many of the early tours, bring the pioneer spirit of these ventures to life. These were the days before continental travel was a regular pursuit, and the concept of tourism very new. She remembers taking a NADFAS group to Leningrad in 1974 where the rooms in the hotel were bugged. During their first trip to Rome and Florence, alternative plans had to be made to accommodate the flash 48 hour strike of government workers. Shuna repeatedly advised the ladies not to drink water from the tap, but they didn't listen and 19 went down with salmonella![8]

The seven-day trip to Vienna was accompanied by the lecturer Nancy Armstrong and included, according to the brochure, an 'evening at the Opera when long dresses will be worn'. The following year all the European trips were accompanied by NADFAS lecturers, Eve King for Florence, Pisa and Sienna; Wellesley Clinton for Vienna, and Mary Stoyle for the Chateaux of the Loire. As the early brochures for these trips advertised, they were 'rather special programmes for NADFAS people by NADFAS people'.

In 1975 the Tours Division organised the first Young NADFAS overseas visit to Paris. A characteristically action-packed itinerary had been planned, assisted by their guide Monsieur Levy who captivated the youngsters 'with his accent, sense of humour and his strong sense of direction when lunchtime came'.[9] Three senior members accompanied the group – June Fenwick, Valerie Woodford and Pamela Turner. It turned out to be a hot few days – 'degrees mounting; mosquitos biting'. Sunday was spent at the Carnavalet Museum and at the Tuilleries; Monday at the Louvre and Notre Dame; Tuesday on the Seine, with a tour of the Basilica of Sacre Coeur and Montmartre; Wednesday at the Jeu de Paume and Versailles; Thursday at the zoo followed by the Gobelins factory; and Friday was the day the 'leaders' had all been dreading, 'letting 38 youngsters free for an hour and then collecting them for lunch'. The organisers need not have feared as 'at the appointed time, all the little Young NADFAS badges began to appear with their wearers loaded with all sorts of unsuitable purchases for such heat'. To this day, recalls Valerie Woodford, 'I wondered how some of those cheeses survived getting home to mum and dad'. On the journey to Malmaison on their last day a van collided with their coach and 'the children thoroughly enjoyed the colourful argument that took place'. The leaders had developed a comradeship which comes from hard work and a common cause, even on the day when they resorted to whisky in their tea for strength! The following year the Tours Division devised an equally memorable trip to Amsterdam for members of Young NADFAS.

In the NADFAS Chairman's report for that year Kathleen Wareham thanked Shuna, who 'plans, manages and takes these tours with unabating cheerfulness and energy. That they always go out full must be most gratifying to her'. In the same year budget tours were introduced to Paris (four days for £49.85), and Amsterdam (five days with Peter Cannon-Brookes as their lecturer), and John Cushion accompanied a 21-day tour of America. The latter complemented the 'National' American Days that took place that year, highlighting American culture in Britain. The American tour started in Boston and ended with a cruise up the Mississippi in a paddle steamer. Perhaps the most ambitious trip was advertised the same year, to China, taking in Peking, Hangchow, Nanking, Shanghai, the Ming Tombs and the Great Wall, stopping off *en route* in Moscow. In 1977 the intrepid NADFAS travellers went to Mexico, the 15-day tour cost £760.

## Expansion

Kathleen and Shuna worked together for seven years until the popularity of the tours meant that the operation had grown too large for them. So in 1977 a notice was put in *NADFAS News* asking for volunteers to be trained as organisers. Following that, six members were trained and the expansion of worldwide tours began. Each tour took with them a lecturer but all the administration was undertaken by a volunteer organiser, under the control of Kathleen and Shuna, and a percentage of the income was handed over to NADFAS, which was vital to the Association's survival. Pamela Cowen, National Chairman 1978-80, reported that 'without the money received from the then voluntarily run home and foreign tours, £2,500 in one year, NADFAS could not have existed. A charge of 2 1/2 p in every pound was added to members' bills for these tours'.[10]

In 1982 NADFAS Tours was granted an ATOL (Air Travel Organisers Licensing) number by the Civil Aviation Authority (CAA). This scheme was set up to protect consumers in the event of their tour operator ceasing to trade. Acquisition of this number not only enabled the purchasing of 'Part-Charter' priced seats on scheduled flights, but also gave added financial protection for every member who travelled on one of the tours. These developments reflect the growth of the travel industry generally, and increasing popularity of NADFAS tours, all of which were fully booked with waiting lists.

To celebrate the 15th Anniversary of the Tours Division a trip to Venice on the Orient Express was organised. Sir Trenchard Cox, the President of NADFAS, who went along was full of praise:

*No journey, I think, has given me greater pleasure than the trip to Venice, as the guest of*

**Above**

To celebrate the 15th anniversary of the Tours Division of NADFAS, members enjoyed a trip to Venice on the Orient Express

how images are made, people appreciate the ideas being expressed and the intentions and skills of the image makers. Here was another example of NADFAS showing that it was open to new ideas, celebrating the present as well as the past, the *avant garde* as well as the antique.

An idea of the expansion in the number and ambition of the tours offered can be gained from glancing at the 1984 brochure which included trips to Leningrad, Verona, Mantua and Vicenza, Kashmir, France, Petra, Tunisia, the Nile, Rome, the Loire, Vienna, Paris, Copenhagen, Madrid and Toledo, Holland, Dresden, Meissen and Bruges, Ghent and Antwerp. Several were repeated in the same year due to demand.

## NADFAS Tours Limited

In 1986 Kathleen and Shuna felt that it was time to retire. Shuna wanted more time to see family in South Africa and Kathleen only stayed on a short while after her departure. Christopher Chavasse paid tribute to them both in the Autumn/Winter NADFAS *Newsletter* of 1986:

*In return for being allowed the exclusive use of NADFAS name and style, Kathleen and Shuna between them put in all the necessary capital and knowledge, and undertook to concentrate on providing the type of tours that NADFAS members wanted. Throughout the years it ran, NADFAS Tours provided thousands of pounds for central funds from the small percentage added for the Association, and because all worked voluntarily.*

Kathleen recalls that through endless backroom work, city connections, kindnesses and help from Embassies, she and Shuna became on first name terms with most of the curators throughout Europe, Russia, Thailand, Japan, China and Mexico. Because they were voluntary workers within NADFAS, interest was created wherever they went.[12] When Kathleen and Shuna gave up,

*their active involvement in a concern which had grown far more time consuming than had ever originally been imagined, the Executive had to give serious thought to the problem and to face up to the certain loss, if nothing were done, of not only a substantial source of income, but also*

*the members of NADFAS Tours, ... the arrangements made for our journey had the cachet of expertise; everything possible was done for our comfort and enlightenment. As an experienced tourist I appreciate the privilege – a rare one – of travelling without fuss!*

Another element of the birthday celebration was a Photographic Competition which met with a resoundingly 'enthusiastic, although administratively shattering' response. 785 slides were submitted, and a selection chosen by Kenneth MacGregor of the BBC. These were shown in the V&A lecture theatre, with Roy Strong announcing the winner.[11] The idea for this competition reflected the recent emergence of photography as a field for museums and galleries, with a new gallery at the V&A and the opening of The National Museum of Photography, Film & Television in Bradford. Colin Ford, then head of the new museum, held the view that by understanding

*a much valued service to members generally.*[13]

At this point NADFAS Tours Limited was formed with, for the first time, a paid manager and secretary. A Board of Directors, drawn from the National Executive and the Tour Organisers, was the body which ensured that NADFAS Tours Limited was correctly run. An office was set up in Beckenham, and 80% of the profits were annually covenanted to NADFAS. This additional source of finance was a tremendous help in funding the future development of NADFAS, although it was always a worry that the Association depended so heavily on the tours for income.

Over the years, quite naturally, the Company grew to around 27 voluntary organisers working for NADFAS Tours from all parts of the United Kingdom. All were keen members of their local Societies, mostly experienced travellers and linguists. Organisers were not salaried but travelled free with their groups and were paid expenses and a small daily allowance. It was a unique Company in this respect, with a dedicated band of volunteers always with the best interests of the members at heart. Margaret Webb (formerly Tolhurst), who was one of these volunteers, remembers that 'We were sometimes referred to as shepherdesses, and to some extent that is exactly what we were in the best possible way'.[14] About three or four times a year there was a general meeting to discuss ideas and problems and to exchange information among themselves. Each volunteer was taken on a tour with an experienced organiser as part of the training programme. A management team dealt with the day to day planning and they in turn were responsible to the Board.

Of course, some difficulties were experienced, particularly overseas where political uncertainties occurred and places suddenly became no-go areas. Popular destinations would close without warning. The first Gulf War (1980-88), when Iraq invaded Iran, left the British and Italians the only people staying on in India, whilst the Americans and everyone else departed immediately it started. The British on the other hand had to fly home via Russia instead

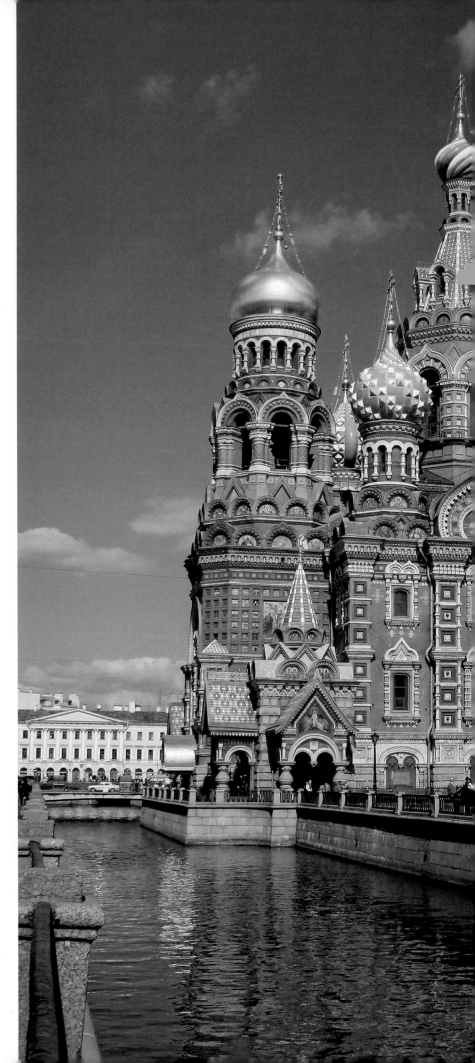

of the Gulf! Later, the organisers were challenged by overseas guides who felt that NADFAS lecturers were taking their jobs away; approval had to be obtained from the EEC to enable NADFAS to bring their own lecturers. It took a year to obtain the approval and tour leaders would carry a translation of the document in the language of the country in which they happened to be working.

In 1987 Home Tours, managed by Margaret Purkis, formally took over the running of Forthcoming Events including the annual Sir Trenchard Cox Lecture and Patricia Fay Memorial Events, and NADFAS Tours, also reported a very successful year with a gross income of approximately £65,000. After payment of £57,000 to the CAA as security for the NADFAS ATOL Bond, the surplus was used to promote the work of the Association as an educational charity and to assist voluntary work.[15] The tours brochure was brought up to date during Shirley Hewett's National Chairmanship. She had been on the board of the Tours company since its early days, and appreciated the need to respond to the pressures of an increasingly competitive marketplace.[16] In 1992 the first International Conference of NADFAS was held in Brussels, and Tours were introduced to overseas Societies both in mainland Europe and Australia.

Probably the most ambitious event was the Swan Hellenic Cruise in May-June 1993, arranged to celebrate the Silver Jubilee of NADFAS. The entire ship, The *Orpheus*, was chartered by NADFAS Tours for £500,000. As Nancy Hodgson, then National Chairman, recalls, 'It could not afford to be a failure' and of course it was not, the ship was over-subscribed and £50,000 was donated to the Jubilee Appeal.[17] Members from all parts of the UK travelled to take part in this cruise which had the added bonus of NADFAS lecturers on board to speak and lead guided tours ashore.

There were two joint NADFAS/Historic

**Left** In the 1970s, tours to St Petersburg – then Leningrad – saw members run the gauntlet of bugged hotel rooms!

Houses Association tours to the USA. The first, in 1994, to the Amish Country and Philadelphia; the second, in 1995, to New England taking in Boston, Salem, Newport, Rhode Island and New Haven, Connecticut. Both were organised by NADFAS Tours and helped cement a working partnership with another heritage orientated group.

## Contracting Out

Between 1994 and 1996 NADFAS Tours increased the number of trips available, although some had to be cancelled not only due to lack of support, but also because of the political situation in the Middle East and elsewhere. More and more legislation was introduced, much due to EEC regulation, and the Tours Board had to implement this. As the National Chairman, Anthea Johnston, reported 'NADFAS Tours did not make much profit in those years', but 'nevertheless contributed much to the pleasure and interest' of the members. By this time, of course, NADFAS Tours found itself in a different and narrowing market with many more travel agents specialising in decorative and fine art tours.[18] After 25 years of operation NADFAS Tours was now only attracting a small percentage of the membership and was no longer cost effective, therefore a change in direction was needed.[19] In 1998 the NADFAS Executive decided that the previously in-house organised programme of art history tours should be contracted out to a specialist operator. Cox & Kings' Travel Limited was chosen, the 'world's longest established tour operator', having been founded by Richard Cox in 1758. This ended the old system of tours run by a group of volunteers in conjunction with lecturers. As the Tours office had moved from Beckenham to NADFAS House in London in September 1997, the change was even more marked. Chairmanship of the 'new style' Tours passed into the capable hands of Pat Turner, a former Chairman of the NADFAS Education Committee, and currently National Vice Chairman of the Association. Cox & Kings' marketed the travel programme under the Tour NADFAS name and every

booking earned a commission for NADFAS.

In 2005 the Tours contract with Cox and Kings' was extended for another year but the travel market was changing once again – budget airlines and the growth of the internet, meant that new locations were becoming accessible and people were now able to book cheap flights and find and book their own hotels relatively easily. Whilst there remained a role for tour operators to play (indeed bonded operators are still recommended for group tours), it was felt that perhaps it was time to consult the membership as to what they wanted NADFAS to provide.

The message was loud and clear. They were looking not only for different locations, but also holidays to suit all budgets. From a commercial angle it was sensible to widen the choice of advertisers in *NADFAS Review* and it was felt that there might be opportunities to earn not just commission, but also to encourage sponsorship of National Events.

In 2006, after a great deal of research, NADFAS began negotiations with several travel companies, including Swan Hellenic

was not endorsing any one travel company, but that the Tour NADFAS logo could be used to convey to members that specific travel companies were making a commission payment to NADFAS.

After successful test marketing, the first six Preferred Partners were signed up in 2007: Hebridean International Cruises, Kirker Holidays, Mundy Cruising, Saga, Tailored Travel and Travel Editions. It was also decided to allow a limited amount of advertising from non travel partners, who continue to support NADFAS with a range of generic advertisements.

This combination is already proving successful. The very welcome commission income, which was threatened particularly by the cessation (albeit temporary) of the Swan Hellenic cruises, is being restored. Members have also already experienced the benefit of sponsorship for some of the National Events, and NADFAS looks forward to developing this programme further.

NOTES
[1] History of ABTA, website 11.7.07.
[2] 'North Kent DFAS, A Short History 1968-1993', 1993, p.4.
[3] Ibid.
[4] Ibid., p.5.
[5] Ibid.
[6] Diana Campbell, 'She has plenty to say, and people all over the world want to hear it' [on Kathleen Wareham], *Kentish Times*, 27 December 1968.
[7] Helen Ouin, West Sussex DFAS, reminiscences, 18 July 2006.
[8] Telephone interview, August 2007.
[9] Report on the Paris trip by Valerie Woodford, 1975, NADFAS Archives.
[10] Chairman's Report, 1978-80, Pamela Cowen, NADFAS Archives.
[11] *NADFAS News*, October 1983.
[12] North Kent DFAS, op. cit., p.101.
[13] Christopher Chavasse, *NADFAS News*, Autumn 1986.
[14] Margaret Webb, 'A Short History of NADFAS Tours', 2007.
[15] Chairman's Report, 1986-1988, Penelope Chitty, NADFAS Archives.
[16] Chairman's Report, 1988-1990, Shirley Hewett, NADFAS Archives.
[17] Chairman's Report, 1992-1994, Nancy Hodgson, NADFAS Archives.
[18] Margaret Webb, op. cit.
[19] Chairman's Report, 1998-2000, Pamela Cohn, NADFAS Archives.
[20] Swan Hellenic, under new ownership, will be re-introducing a cruise programme in 2008.

whose cruise programme had proved so popular with the membership over the years. Sadly the Swan Hellenic brand was put up for sale and its future seemed uncertain.[20] Fortunately NADFAS had taken the advice of the then Hon Treasurer, Roy Brooks, who had warned that the Association should not count on income from tours for core expenditure. As a result the affiliation fee was raised to help overcome this dependence.

Although a difficult, and in many quarters, an unpopular decision, it was proved right when the income from Swan Hellenic came to an end. After the Cox & Kings' contract was terminated in mid summer, subsequent editions of *NADFAS Review* carried advertising from selected travel companies, with the view that some of them would eventually become commission partners. It was made very clear that NADFAS

**Above** Pioneering spirit: Rutland DFAS in Jordan
**Left** Egerton DFAS members pose in front of the Taj Mahal during a tour of India

# 10 Finding a Home:
## *Bricks and Mortar*

*'Nothing worthwhile is achieved without difficulties'*
Sheila Marshall, *Development of a Dream*, 1982, p.5

One of the earliest problems for NADFAS was the need for a central point of contact, and an office. In the beginning Helen Lowenthal had made her home in Elizabeth Street available for meetings, but the Committee soon outgrew the space. Close association with the Victoria & Albert Museum resulted in the offer of the use of the Director's Committee Room for meetings, although the problem of an office remained. Up to November 1968, the Chairman and Vice Chairman shared the burden of dealing with the growing pile of paperwork. Then, much to everyone's relief, Nadine Mitchell was appointed part-time secretary, paid at a rate of 5s. per hour, raised to 7s. 6d in July 1969. The accumulating paperwork, and lack of a permanent office was, however, causing communication problems. In April 1970 NADFAS rented a room in Nadine's house, which in 1975 cost £2.50 week, and increased the following year to £3.[1] It is astonishing how much was achieved under such make-shift circumstances, but sheer hard work made up for the lack of money. As

the National Chairman reported in 1974, 'It … seemed possible that one day we might have to leave Nadine Mitchell's home and find an office in London, the cost of which would be prohibitive'. Nadine's unexpected death in 1978 was a shock to everyone, and forced the problem of space to the top of the agenda. Finding a more permanent home was now an urgent priority.[2]

### 625 Grand Buildings, Trafalgar Square

The first official NADFAS office was in Grand Buildings, Trafalgar Square. It had been spotted by the husband of the then Chairman, Pamela Cowen, and was for rent at a price that could just be afforded. As Pamela noted, 'Although only the size of a rather large cupboard it was an office and in central London, and being a charity NADFAS only had to pay half the usual rates to Westminster Council'. The majestic Grand Buildings had begun life as the Grand Hotel, built in 1844 and an important architectural element in London's largest square. With the

National Gallery and National Portrait Gallery nearby it was suitably at the centre of London's cultural and artistic life. On 14 March 1979 NADFAS moved in. As Sheila Marshall related, the unloading of a large bookcase, a vast solid oak filing cabinet and tea chests all stuffed with papers, was no mean task. She and Helen Lowenthal agreed to act as trustees for guaranteeing the lease. Nannette Foster was officially appointed Honorary Secretary to work with the part-time paid secretary. The Chairman wrote letters by hand, and they were:

*typed up, using carbon paper if copies were needed. The only method of producing copies of anything was to type on wax stencils and put them into our old-fashioned duplicator which needed kicking every twenty minutes or so to make it function.[3]*

Sheila Chapman remembers that the office was on the top floor, and was told that it proved an excellent vantage point to see the wedding procession of Prince Charles and Diana (although she had to rent a television as she was with Young NADFAS in a youth hostel at Edding, near Wrexham at the time!).

## 38 Ebury Street

In 1981, with 126 Societies formed, it soon became necessary to move to larger premises in Ebury Street, an elegant tree-lined street, close to Victoria Station and Helen Lowenthal's house. The office at number 38 was found by Nicky Foot, the Honorary Treasurer. The building, which was owned by Grosvenor Estates, was at the time being let to charitable organisations and, as a consequence, the rent was much lower than the 'going rate', which was an enormous help to NADFAS. The Historic Houses Association, with whom NADFAS had such good links, had the top floor. After the 'broom cupboard' in Grand Buildings the office provided much needed space, having two rooms with a little passage between into which the door from the hall opened. NADFAS was allowed to use the Boardroom on the first floor for all the important meetings, such as those of the Executive, Volunteers and Church Recorders. All the furniture and equipment was given by members of the Executive, apart from items moved from Grand Buildings. In 1982, Rowena Mitchell joined as secretary, leaving in 1986, by which time the space problem cropped up again. The National Chairman, Penelope Chitty, undertook to research the feasibility of NADFAS either buying or renting larger premises. However, Lindley Maitland's ingenious re-arrangement of the furniture and the acquisition of new streamlined desks, on her arrival that year as the new Secretary and Administrator, partially solved the problem. Lindley's memories of Ebury Street are of the noisy traffic outside, and the wonderful sunshine which flooded into the office.

**Below**
The current home of NADFAS on Guilford Street, in the heart of Bloomsbury

Heather Staffurth vividly recalls working there when she joined the Directory Committee in 1987[4]. She had not known the confinement of the office in the Grand Buildings, and to her this 'new' space seemed limited, to others it was an immense improvement. The Directory shared one desk, the knees under one side, drawers down the other, with all the other volunteers. The main office was one room, approximately 12 by 15 feet, and shared with Lindley Maitland and Jill Hardie-Bick, the Finance Director and book-keeper. The adjoining room, approximately 7 by 9 feet, had the door removed for better access and was used for storage, filing cabinets, electric kettle and mugs. You were lucky if there was a spare chair to sit on, the tops of the filing cabinets were used standing up as they provided a good surface for writing. 'We had a lot of fun and managed to be quite efficient in spite of the conditions'.[5] Judith Waples, who was then Chairman of the Directory, remembers that she and others worked at home to save the expense of travelling to Ebury Street, and to reduce the amount of overcrowding.

## 8A Lower Grosvenor Place

Within ten years it was becoming very obvious that the office accommodation in Ebury Street was much too cramped. NADFAS was growing with 250 Societies now, but the Chairman had no desk or even space to work in, and the volume of work undertaken by the Administrator, her small staff, and the Sub-Committee Chairmen was fast becoming overwhelming, especially for the volunteers. Matters were set in motion to look for more suitable office space, which finally resulted in the move to an office in Lower Grosvenor Place. Opposition had first to be overcome from the membership because of the costs involved, finance had to be found, and much shoe leather expended in viewing properties before a suitable place was located but, in 1991, NADFAS found its third official home. Lindley Maitland remembers that 62 packing cases were required to ship the contents of the Ebury Street office to Lower Grosvenor Street. Jenny Stephenson's husband managed

to organise the re-decoration of the office, which would otherwise have been expensive and complicated. They moved into the premises in January, during a long period of snow, and no central heating! The extra space was much needed and enabled the numbers of staff to expand. NADFAS was growing, as Lindley states, not in huge leaps, but in a steady evolutionary way. One of her many memories of this site was the fire practice, which involved ascending to the roof, which in summer afforded some good views of neighbouring garden parties.

However, while the main NADFAS office was in Lower Grosvenor Street, it was impossible to house the Church Recorders, or the Tours Division under the same roof. Sheila Chapman and Angela Goedike remember that at first the Recorders were rather like 'gypsies' camping out in different places. They soon outgrew Jane Wright's home in Beaconsfield. In December 1989, in exchange for inspecting the 420 Parish Records and Registers for the Diocese of London, the Recorders were allowed to use

one of their empty premises in Regency Street, off Vauxhall Bridge Road in Pimlico. When this site was redeveloped in 1992 the London Diocese found the Recorders another 'home', a flat at 13a North Audley Street next door to the redundant St Mark's Church. The two-room premises had a bathroom complete with piano and the bath was boarded over to provide workspace. In 1994 the Church Recorders were to 'move in' with NADFAS in Guilford Street.[6]

### The Purchase of 8 Guilford Street

In 1992, having had six different homes in the first 24 years of its life, the need for a less migratory existence became all important. Now with 260 Societies, increasing by around ten a year, it was agreed that the Silver Jubilee of NADFAS should be used to launch an appeal to raise funds to acquire a permanent home for the Association. The debate as to its location was a closely argued one with some members wishing to remain in the capital but others feeling just as strongly that advantage should be taken of lower property and staff costs in the provinces. Advice was sought from other organisations which had had to make a similar choice and the additional cost and inconvenience of cross country journeys for members attending meetings was closely examined. Eventually it was accepted that in the prevailing climate the most accessible and convenient place, from every corner of the United Kingdom and Mainland Europe, was central London, but this question continues to be raised from time to time and the Trustees keep the situation under review. So the search began. It was after Heather Staffurth had broken her ankle while bicycling round in search of suitable premises that the then National Chairman, Jennifer Stephenson, was deputed to take over the task. One of the buildings she looked at was 8 Guilford Street, which Heather had thought unsuitable due to some subsidence. The price was ridiculously low, owing to the recession, the subsidence could be dealt with, and there was plenty of room for all the NADFAS disciplines to come together under one roof

**Above**
Jill Hardie-Bick (left) and Rowena Mitchell at the Ebury Street office
**Right (top)**
The move from Ebury Street to Lower Grosvenor Street
**Right (bottom)**
From left to right: Nancy Hodgson, Lindley Maitland and Jenny Stephenson at the Lower Grosvenor Street premises

(Church Recorders and NADFAS Tours were then in Pimlico and Beckenham).[7] This was of vital importance so that the Committees of Council could work more closely together.

In 1994 the Jubilee Appeal enabled the Association to purchase 8 Guilford Street, London, in the heart of Bloomsbury, now named NADFAS House. £50,000 was raised from the Jubilee Cruise, and £1,000 from the

competition to name the Jubilee Rose, developed by Harkness and christened 'Renaissance'. After two surveys, including reports from structural engineers, a final purchase price of £385,000 was agreed (it had first been offered at £600,000).[8]

*It was due to the negotiating skills of the National Treasurer, Valerie Anderson, and the National Chairman, Anthea Johnston, that*

*agreement was reached with the vendors, and a dream was about to become a reality.*[9]

When it was announced that the contracts had been exchanged, large amounts of money were sent in by Areas, Societies and individuals. This was very comforting as there were no reserves and a shortfall. There were contributions to NADFAS House of pictures, lighting, furniture and many more essential items which at the time were unaffordable. These physical manifestations of support were all the more valued because there had been dissension among the Societies about the purchase of the house, relating to recurring worries about the role of the central office in NADFAS affairs. In August 1994 NADFAS moved in, including the Church Recorders. NADFAS Tours followed in September 1997. The building was at first shared with other tenants, on the second floor The Patients Association and on the third (now the Chairman's Office), the graphic designer, Peter Constable, was installed. The Patients Association did not stay long, but Peter remained there until 2000 and his services were used by NADFAS.

8 Guilford Street has a suitably interesting history for the home of an Association dedicated to the support of our cultural and architectural heritage. Plans for building a

handsome residential street linking Russell Square to Grays Inn Road were first made in 1790. By 1800 the first tenants were moving in, mostly solicitors, attorneys, and barristers working in the nearby Inns of Court, as well as surgeons, and governors of the Foundling Hospital. Number 8 was one of the 'first grade' houses in the Street, distinguished by its spacious entrance hall, principal rooms on the first floor, with two bedroom floors and a servants' attic (where Promotions and Marketing are now based, it is a steep climb up to the top!). In the nineteenth century the Street was 'home' at various times to the poet Algernon Swinburn (at number 25), the famous collector of decorative and fine art Ralph Bernal (at number 33), the architects William Mitford Teulon (at number 42) and Matthew Digby Wyatt (at number 54) who played an important role in the organisation of the 1851 Great Exhibition. The celebrated cabinet-maker George Seddon occupied number 75 Guilford Street. NADFAS House lies within a short walking distance of the British Museum, and Gordon Square where the Bloomsbury Group met. University College London is a stone's throw away, where in 1868 the London Ladies' Educational Association was born. From the mid-nineteenth century it would have hummed with traffic making its way to busy Kings Cross and St Pancras railway stations, completed in 1852 and 1864 respectively. These main communication links mean that NADFAS House is easy to get to and centrally situated. The Bloomsbury Quarter continues to be a hive of activity and its arts charities, museums, galleries, libraries and academic institutions work together through 'Cultural Bloomsbury', in promoting the area as a wonderful place to work and visit. Members of NADFAS House staff attend the bi-monthly breakfasts which help to develop partnerships between the various organisations.

It was at this time that the NADFAS Patron, Lady Salisbury, retired after five years. After various tentative enquiries, the Administrator, Lindley Maitland, and the National Chairman, Anthea Johnston, were invited to Kensington Palace to meet the

**Above**
NADFAS made its home in the Guilford Street office in 1994
**Above right**
The Duchess of Gloucester gives the building her 'seal of approval'

Assistant Private Secretary to HRH The Duchess of Gloucester. They were informed that HRH was willing to become Patron of NADFAS, and two weeks later the Duchess came to a Council Meeting. She met the members of the NADFAS Council and the staff and toured the building. The visit provided a symbolic seal of approval of the new premises, and a resumption of royal patronage for the Association.[10]

In 2004 NADFAS was faced with the problem of making the building compliant with the impending legislation under the Disability Discrimination Act 2005 (DDA), as well as the requirement for a larger room to obviate the need to rent outside space for meetings of the Advisory Council and other big gatherings. After protracted negotiations, and several different proposals, it was decided to reconfigure the ground floor to create a self-contained conference suite. The outcome was a spacious meeting room, with air conditioning and up-to-date audio-visual equipment, complete with an adjacent area for serving refreshments and modern cloakroom facilities. The re-ordering was completed by moving the reception area and relocating some members of staff to other floors of the building. Life at NADFAS House was disrupted for many months, but the staff coped magnificently with all the upheaval and the results have proved their worth in providing a really comfortable and efficient space for meetings which does not interfere with work going on in other parts of the building. The newly refurbished NADFAS House has become a busy hub for many members involved with the Association.

The main meeting room, the Patricia Fay Room, can now host Lecturer Selection Sessions in a suitably professional environment and there is sufficient space to permit the interaction between participants and group discussions which are so essential to the success of Training Days. The new suite provides an excellent backdrop as NADFAS increasingly develops partnerships with like-minded organisations and involves external experts in volunteer meetings. With two further meeting rooms on the lower ground floor, the Britcher Furlong Room and the Zena Walker Room, NADFAS House now provides a welcoming space for members and an efficient administrative centre. The renovation has also enabled NADFAS to generate income by hiring out the meeting rooms to other organisations. It is proving attractive to 'outsiders' and to increasing numbers of members with, on average, 45-50 using the House weekly, for whom greater familiarity with the site fosters a better understanding of what goes on within the administration and a sense of 'ownership'.

The upper floors are the 'engine room' of NADFAS and here the Staff provide the administration and support so essential for the smooth running of an Association with around 90,000 members, and, a far cry from earlier days, the National Chairman together with volunteers have proper working space and no longer have to 'perch' or use the tops of filing cabinets as desks! A number of dedicated departments handle the day-to-day running of the organisation and staff are always available to answer the telephone calls, e-mails and letters of individual members, Society and Area chairmen and their committees. The first point of contact is often the Communications, Societies & Membership Department which helps potential members to find their nearest Society, answers queries on all aspects of running a Society or an Area, and also works closely with the New Societies Team. It produces a regular *Societies Bulletin* designed to ensure that essential information reaches Society chairmen and their committees. It collaborates with the Training Team to give the necessary information and skills to new Society and Area chairmen and new Trustees, and to organise similar courses in their Areas for committee members. The Volunteering Department brings together the administration of Church Recorders, Heritage Volunteers and Young Arts. It provides a link between the management team of each discipline and the various Society groups, is a source of the many publications and documents needed for this work, and can give access to outside experts when required and support and advice to the group leaders. Publishing the *Directory of Lecturers*, seeking and assessing new lecturers, monitoring standards and running the Annual Directory Meeting, as well as providing wide-ranging advice for Programme and Study Day Secretaries are some of the main tasks of the Education Department, another key building block in the structure of NADFAS. The Promotions & Marketing Department publishes the quarterly *NADFAS Review*, actively promotes the Organisation through the media and through external partnerships, and runs NADFAS Enterprises Limited which handles all the Association's merchandising.

**Right and below**
Since the refurbishment of NADFAS House in 2006, the Association now enjoys a bright, airy and welcoming space for members, not to mention an efficient administrative centre

The Finance Department's responsibilities move from the collection of affiliation fees, arranging insurance, and running training courses for Society and Area treasurers, to producing the Annual Accounts for members' scrutiny. The management of the building, the front of house welcome at reception, and the well-being and comfort of the staff, volunteers and visitors who work within it, are all the responsibility of the House Department. The 21st century communication needs of members, Societies, Areas and NADFAS House are met through an increasingly sophisticated IT system and website. Finally, each one of these essential divisions of NADFAS comes under the supervision of the Chief Executive whose own responsibility for the prudent and efficient management of the whole Association is to the Trustee Board.

While there has always been a certain wariness of a London base, symbolic of what in 1998 the National Chairman, Judith Thomas, described as the feeling that 'London wielded too much power', the efficient service and improved communication at 8 Guilford Street has helped dispel some of these concerns. The current Chief Executive, David Bell, hopes NADFAS House will increasingly become a focal point where the Association and like-minded organisations can meet to further common aims within the world of Arts and Heritage. NADFAS House represents in bricks and mortar the solid foundations upon which NADFAS stands, with the flexibility for future growth and development.

NOTES
[1] Ex.Co. Minutes, 9 May 1975, NADFAS Archives.
[2] Ex.Co. Minutes, Jan 1979, NADFAS Archives.
[3] Chairman's Report, Pamela Cowen, 1978-80, NADFAS Archives.
[4] Heather Staffurth, 'Headquarters Office of NADFAS, 38 Ebury Street' 9 August 2006, NADFAS Archives.
[5] Ibid.
[6] Angela Goedicke, September 2007.
[7] Jennifer Stephenson, 3 September 2006, NADFAS Archives.
[8] Ibid.
[9] Chairman's Report, Anthea Johnston, 1994-96, NADFAS Archives.
[10] Ibid.

# 11

# Unity and Diversity:
## *The Challenges of Success*

*'Unity and Co-operation through Communication'*
June Fenwick quoting Patricia Fay's own motto, Minutes of AGM 28 April 1980

The success of NADFAS presented its own problems: how to cope with an increasing administrative burden as the number of Societies and 'divisions' like the Volunteers, Church Recorders and Young NADFAS grew, how to keep everyone informed, and how to provide plenty of opportunities for individual members to feel part of the larger Association and its aims. These three problems converge around one of the continuous themes within NADFAS, the relationship of the individual Societies to the National body. As early as June 1969, Patricia Fay noted at an Executive Committee meeting that she was particularly concerned that 'there was not enough rapport between NADFAS and the Member Societies'.[1] In one of the earliest promotional leaflets for NADFAS published in 1968, Patricia stated very clearly that 'The Association's main concern is not so much to develop centrally but to devolve activity onto the groups'.[2] A letter from one Society chairman to Sheila Marshall in 1970 hammered home the view held by some of the Societies:

*The large proportion of members of most Societies is I am sure, mainly interested in lectures and study groups held locally ... the enormous success of our Societies has been due principally to the fact that we can offer locally lectures of a high standard which before were available only in London and possibly the larger provincial towns. Only a very small proportion of members, in our case less than ten per cent, and always the same few, attend events arranged by NADFAS in London.*[3]

She continued, 'many members of other NADFAS Societies are not really aware, not even interested in the functions or aims of NADFAS'. In the June 1971 *NADFAS Newsletter*, the Cinque Ports Society reported that it was their policy 'to help LOCAL art and preservation', but 'a "whip-round" at the February meeting' raised £13 for the St Paul's Cathedral Fund. The decision made in 1971 that the appellation 'Decorative & Fine Arts Society' be given to all future Societies, was an affirmation in the belief of unity over diversity, although in a few cases it led to the withdrawal of Societies from the Association, as they preferred to keep their own titles. Two years later Kathleen Wareham, as NADFAS Vice Chairman, reiterated to the Executive Committee, that 'Better liaison with Member Societies and in particular the main mass of ordinary Members' was needed. She stated that:

*The National must act as a guiding service-providing body – in short, a forceful GOVERNING body. More emphasis needs to be given in finding out what Societies need … In this way the idea of "them" and "us" will be broken down and it will be appreciated that it is only "all of us" and that the National works solely for the interest of the Societies.*[4]

Looking back over forty years of NADFAS one can see the wheel turn full circle, perhaps as a result of the confidence that maturity of years brings. When in the early 1970s Patricia and the Executive Committee decided to enforce unity via the adoption of the appellation, 'Decorative and Fine Arts Society', for all member groups, they were worried about weakening the power of the Association. Now the Association has grown in numbers, strength and alliance, it has been decided to relax this rule, requiring only a 'strapline' recognition that they are 'A Member Society of NADFAS' on all printed matter relating to the Society.

Lindley Maitland joined NADFAS in 1986 as its first manager, a sign of its continuing growth. She had been taken to a NADFAS lecture by her parents, who were members of Wrekin DFAS, and had been inspired by Margaret Rule's lecture. She went on to become a member of South West London DFAS. Little did she know that her wry thought that she would like to become the NADFAS Secretary, would become reality, but not immediately. She wrote to NADFAS offering her services, only to be turned down. However two years later she responded to the advertisement placed by the Association and became its first Secretary and Administrator.

Her experience at the Royal Commonwealth Society and St Thomas's Hospital stood her in good stead, and soon she had taken on the duties of the Honorary Secretary at NADFAS. Her job continued to expand, first as a secretary, typing for the *Directory* and the Chairman, then as Administrator, working alongside Jill Hardie-Bick who was the part-time Finance Administrator. During her years with the Association, the number of Societies doubled to over 300, the Australian Association was formed, NADFAS moved offices twice and she masterminded the first three out-of-town AGMs.

The relationship between the 'centre' and the Societies periodically moves to front stage at crucial times in the NADFAS story. It surfaced during the debate about whether NADFAS should become a charity in the early 1970s; in the 1980s before the introduction of the Areas; in the mid 1990s in response to restructuring and the 'Plan for NADFAS' (the Compass Report), which referred to 'Societies indicating increasing satisfaction with the Area format and agreeing that a strengthened Area structure was required, but that this should be kept as simple as possible'. The Report recommended the employment of paid professionals, and the purchase of NADFAS House. The tension between NADFAS House and Societies was again a hot topic in the late 1990s in response to the Planning Review 'set up to take a long and hard look at the organisation, examining its strengths and weaknesses both at the present time and in the future'.[5] This resulted in the appointment of the first Chief Executive, Jeremy Warren, in 1999 to be in charge of the day-to-day management of the Association, and the separation of the management from the governance of the charity. This had far reaching effects, not least of which was the realisation that NADFAS was an unincorporated association which meant that the Trustees, all the members of the Council, had unlimited

**Right**
The original NADFAS pin, 1988, designed by silversmith and jeweller Lexi Dick, whose work features in major British collections

liability in the event of legal action. NADFAS was not an entity in itself and so could not be sued, only the Trustees as individuals. A governance working party recommended that NADFAS should become a company limited by guarantee, with a Trustee Board.[6] This led to lively and lengthy Board meetings with all members wanting to speak on every subject.[7]

There was much unrest. There seemed to be evidence that the bureaucracy was increasing at an alarming rate, particularly with the appointment of a Chief Executive. However little consideration seemed to be given to the workload of the volunteers in the senior management of the Association, nor to the complexity of the financial and legal restraints under which NADFAS had, along with other charities, to operate. As the National Chairman at the time explained 'it was cheering that major consultation with Societies on the change to a company limited by guarantee was overwhelmingly approved'. The first ever Annual Review was published and was greeted by many ordinary members as a 'breath of fresh air' in terms of accountability.[8] This amity however was brought to a grinding halt by the publication of the Forward Plan on which the Chief Executive had worked extremely hard. Efforts to emphasise that this plan only referred to the work of NADFAS itself were unavailing. The Statement of Purpose caused particular offence as 'giving' was put before 'learning' and a fair amount of abuse was hurled at the concept that NADFAS might be 'the leading provider of giving and learning opportunities in the UK heritage sector' despite the fact that tens of thousands of members were already 'giving' of their time, talents and money in many different ways, a point which it was important to emphasise in an age when, as is the case today, the Charity Commission was putting greater emphasis on the need for charities to demonstrate their public benefit. In a letter to the National Chairman, Jean Read, Christopher Chavasse, who had formulated the founding rules of NADFAS, wrote:

*The first thing we must always remember is that NADFAS is not a Head Office and the Societies are not the branches. The individual Societies are completely autonomous and have their own separate constitutions. They have of their own volition decided to become affiliated to NADFAS because of the great advantage that this brings, but they are entirely free to break the affiliation if they wish.*[9]

However, as he later states, NADFAS has:

*if you like, been the victim of its own success, so much so that although it continues to attract ever increasing numbers of highly skilled volunteer officers, it can no longer go on growing without skilled professional administration.*

There were some, of course, who disagreed with him. He went on to identify the main division in NADFAS, between those Societies who preferred to keep the Societies to themselves and their friends, and others who could see the advantage of opening things to other like-minded people. It was an issue that took NADFAS back to its founding days when Patricia had worried that the Chiltern Antiques Group would not take kindly to the idea of a National Association aimed at providing a public service. This major step of course led the way to charitable status, enhancing the reputation of NADFAS in the public eye, making possible close connections with other national bodies such as the National Trust, English Heritage and the National Art Collections Fund (now The Art Fund), the relationship with the V&A and the privilege of Royal patronage.

To everyone's relief the memorandum and articles of the new company limited by guarantee were approved by the 2001 AGM, despite the meeting itself being fraught. It was held in Westminster Central Hall as the usual venue, Kensington Town Hall, was out of action. It was huge, the microphones were faulty and there was a vocal and cross minority. However, harmony prevailed and the ground was laid for the birth of a 'new NADFAS' at the following year's AGM.

Although the recently appointed Chief Executive resigned to go to a prestigious appointment as Assistant Director and Head of Collections at the Wallace Collection, under the leadership of Dr Thomas Cocke, who replaced him, preparations were made

**Above**
Sir Trenchard Cox, who inspired a new annual lecture
**Above right**
Zena Walker, who took over the chairmanship of the New Societies Sub-Committee

for the pivotal AGM at Scarborough in 2002. The event was advertised as 'the moment when NADFAS becomes a grown-up body, harnessing the energy and enthusiasms of its many thousands of volunteers with the discipline of a professional organisation'. The weather was perfect, a cloudless blue sky, and the membership in good heart. The meeting saw the end of the old Unincorporated Association and the creation of the new Company Limited by Guarantee under the direction of the Trustee Board, (which took the place of the old Executive Committee) and an Advisory Council of Area Chairmen, Chairmen of Volunteer Committees and representatives of the lecturers. It was an historic moment.

The fruits of Jeremy Warren's Forward Plan were a 'raft of things', which Thomas Cocke took further and developed, and which were aimed at drawing centre and Societies together including making staff at NADFAS House more visible to members by putting their photos and job descriptions in the magazine, and reconfiguring certain posts; overhauling the system for selecting

and monitoring lecturers, improving and re-launching NADFAS *News*, as well as tackling a backlog in setting up Societies and encouraging the establishment of new ones where they did not previously exist.

The restructuring of the NADFAS finances was also taking place at this time. In 2001 the Hon. Treasurer, Roy Brooks, devised a comprehensive reporting and budgeting system. He was mindful of the need for NADFAS to establish sound financial intelligence on which to base future plans. This was especially relevant to discussing the proposal for the then unincorporated association to incorporate as a company limited by guarantee. He is still remembered by today's Trustee Board as the Hon. Treasurer who warned that the organisation could not continue to rely on surpluses from NADFAS Tours to cover annual operating costs as the travel industry would prove to be too volatile. The result was an unwelcome increase in the affiliation fee but subsequent developments have clearly demonstrated the inherent risks. Strong feelings about the level of members' contributions have been a fact of NADFAS life since the beginning. In 1968 the original membership subscription was set at 1/- (5p), 2/6 (12p) had been recommended but was thought 'too much'. In 1970 a rise to 3/- (15p) caused 'controversy', and in 1976 a proposal to increase the fee to 50p was 'outvoted by senior members' but a little while later the figure of 75p was said to be necessary 'to survive'.[10]

In 2003, shortly after the incorporation of NADFAS as a company limited by guarantee, Trustees decided that it was time to engage a full time Finance Director and Company Secretary to further strengthen the financial structure of the Association. The Hon. Treasurer's function was at that time very hands on and the engagement of David Bell that year enabled the further development of a professional department and would allow subsequent Hon. Treasurers to adopt an essential governance and strategic focus. This development coincided with the wide-ranging debate with members for the establishment of the 'Focus Forward' strategy. The deliberations were facilitated by the inclusion of financial forecasts looking forward over four years. It was recognised that this was the first time NADFAS had in place an agreed long-term strategy alongside a coherent financial plan. Following the retirement of Thomas Cocke earlier in the year, David was appointed Chief Executive in November 2006 and leads a team of professional staff and volunteers all of whom are committed to the core ideals and current strategies of the charity.

## The Council and the Committees

Turning back to the early days, there were various strategies employed to address the problems caused by expansion, which was a very real concern. The first was to create a Council. By the time 20 Societies had formed it was decided to institute a Council, composed of the chairman of each member Society who in turn appointed an Executive Committee to run the day-to-day affairs of the Association.[11] By 1975 the Council consisted of 'a formidable body of 68 women who are Madam Chairmen of our members'

Societies'.[12] As the outgoing Chairman reported in 1974:

*There is no doubt the work of the Officers and Executive Committee has quadrupled over the last two years – we have had many successes and few failures – we are now confirmed as a national organisation – and there is no turning back from the opportunities that lie ahead.*

Administratively, one of the ways to cope was to create sub-committees, the first for Policy was set up in 1969. In the same year Pamela Rowan from the Chiltern Antiques Group joined the Executive team to help with the setting up of new Societies. She had an assistant and agreed to deal with all letters requesting help with forming a Society, she offered to meet the founding committee and advise on initial procedure. Records of all correspondence were to be held centrally. This became the first New Societies Sub-Committee recognised in 1972, which was later led by Lally Robinson, then Zena Walker, who expanded the members to eight and divided it into Northern and Southern regional teams. Other sub-committees followed.

As Thomas Cocke, Chief Executive 2001-06, was to state, when he took over:

*I inherited a complex mixture of volunteer committees. While Jean Read had successfully reduced their number, we still had separate ones for New Societies, Events Planning, Patricia Fay Memorial Fund, Britcher Furlong Bequest, quite apart from those for Church Recorders, Heritage Volunteers and Young Arts.*

Thomas saw his task as 'loosening up the structure so the volunteers were free to deploy their talents out in the field leaving the administration at NADFAS House to the paid staff'. He came up with the concept of Teams, meeting two to three times a year, 'to provide strategic guidance to the various activities' which could include non-NADFAS members with professional expertise. For Education and New Societies rather different arrangements were appropriate since they were involved with NADFAS House on a weekly basis. For these the concept of Advisers was introduced. For Finance tighter controls were introduced, such as quarterly management accounts and more user-friendly presentation so that the movement of funds in and out was much more transparent. As part of this wider strategy of improved communication the different *Handbooks* for the various NADFAS activities were drawn together in a single new-style *NADFAS Handbook*, with all the essential information collected between its covers. It has been designed to accommodate development and change.

The fundamental changes to NADFAS in 2001 and 2002, with the demise of the old unincorporated Association and formation of the new Company Limited by Guarantee, were very carefully thought through and it was realised that it was essential to maintain a formal link with the Area Chairmen and enable their input to the newly elected Trustee Board's discussions. The Memorandum and Articles of Association, therefore, provided for the establishment of an Advisory Council, which would meet three times a year, and consist of all Area Chairmen, the Chairmen of the three volunteer disciplines, the Head of Training, Chairman of the New Societies Committee, and representatives from the Education Department and of the Lecturers, elected from among their number. There is a two-way movement of information in that the Trustee Board may ask the Advisory Council to consider proposals and vice versa, and the Area Chairmen facilitate the consultation with their Societies. Although the ultimate responsibility lies with the Trustee Board, itself elected by the member Societies, all its decisions are thoroughly informed by the opinions of the Societies through their Area Chairmen and all other aspects of NADFAS life through their representatives on the Advisory Council. The Advisory Council is chaired by the National Vice Chairman and a number of Trustees are invited to each meeting as observers, giving them an opportunity to network with its members. The Area Chairmen also have a Forum three times a year where they exchange ideas and concerns in a less formal setting. This new structure has greatly improved communication between NADFAS House and

**Right**
Sir John Pope-Hennessy, one of the first NADFAS Vice Presidents, in his office at the V&A

members and has further strengthened the feeling of teamwork within the Association.

Trustees themselves play an active part outside the formal Board meetings, in sub-committees and working parties, through attending Area Meetings, and in sharing the representational role of the National Chairman at special events and celebrations. These are further important opportunities for Trustees to keep in touch with the opinions and feelings of Societies and to make themselves better known to the membership.

## Areas

An obvious way of connecting Societies to each other, and to the Executive Committee, was through the concept of Areas, whereby Societies in adjacent places could meet together, exchange information and relay their ideas back to London. This idea took a surprisingly long time to take hold. As early as May 1969 Sheila Marshall had been in touch with Hull & East Riding AFAS with the idea of forming a North Eastern Area. She envisaged regional committees in the North

East, North West, South West and South East, and possibly London. The idea was not popular. In January 1973 another attempt was made to establish regional committees, when Kathleen Wareham proposed a meeting of chairmen from the South East. By December the message came back that it was too early to form Areas yet. A memorandum from the National Chairman compiled from letters from Societies reported that 'they did not want too much centralisation and still resisted the idea of areas or regions'.[13] However by the following year regional workshops were set up in the North and South, and by 1980 Area meeting guidelines had been drawn up, and Area Representatives appointed. The first Area meetings were held in London, the South West and East Anglia. In 1981 the first Area Sub-Committee was formed followed by an Area Representatives meeting, and an Area Day. By 1984 Area Representatives attended Council meetings.

The good sense of establishing NADFAS Areas was driven home by Sylvia Horwood-Smart, one of the early Area Representatives, who wrote in the 1982 *NADFAS Newsletter*:

*In a time of change and growth the importance of communication and of understanding between Societies and the Executive of NADFAS cannot be overemphasised. It is vital that NADFAS continues to embrace widely differing memberships and the Executive must be as alive to the needs of the Rural West or Industrial North as to those of the Home Counties. This can only be achieved through the work of the Area Meetings and the Area Representatives elected to them.*

The development of the Areas was slow, but sure, although the early get-togethers met with mixed responses from individual Societies. A report by one Society chairman who went to meet the North Powys, Malvern and Wrekin Societies reflects the nature of the mutual misunderstanding about the purpose of these sessions:

*I thought it was a meeting to express our views on different aspects of NADFAS and our problems with Head Office but we were all so blunt that afterwards, I felt obliged to write to the poor lady who came from London and apologise. She obviously thought us all most peculiar and unusual and was particularly surprised that we didn't want to travel miles for National functions.*[14]

By the late 1980s the number of Society chairmen who constituted the Council was so large as to make its workings unwieldy and, inevitably, somewhat of a rubber stamp in nature. It was, after considerable discussion, resolved to make the Area structure more formal with the Area Chairman, or National Area Representative, being elected by the member Societies in each Area to sit on the Council on their behalf, Not unexpectedly, there was disquiet, with some Societies feeling disenfranchised, and much debate as to whether those elected were representatives or delegates. It had the effect, however, of freeing each Society chairman from attending frequent meetings in London and reducing the numbers on the Council, and now the Advisory Council, to manageable proportions.

Areas, as do Societies, vary greatly in character with great distances between Societies in Scotland, the North of England and the Southwest and a densely packed membership in some southern Areas, leading occasionally to the need to create two Areas out of one. There is a common pattern of Spring and Autumn meetings, but beyond that the number of study days and visits, grant making and other aid to our heritage, as well as social events, is developed according to local demand.

Today the Areas are one of the most effective ways of communicating between the 'centre' and the Societies. Over the last six years the use of structured consultations via the twice yearly Area Meetings has been a vital part of bringing NADFAS House and Societies closer together. Such issues as lecture fees, Tour NADFAS, and changes to the Memorandum & Articles of Association have been effectively debated, increasing the importance of the Area Meetings as a means of communication.[15]

Area Meetings are vital not only to take messages out, but also to allow the Trustees, senior volunteers and staff who attend them to hear, at first hand, the issues that matter most to Societies. One important debate concerned the strategic direction for NADFAS. Following discussion at the Spring Area Meetings in 2004 and by the Advisory Council and Trustee Board, a paper entitled 'Focus Forward' was written by Thomas Cocke. This document set out the Board's agreed strategic direction for the following three years and included specific goals. It was

opportunities to meet socially'.[17] This would be another means of connecting members with Societies other than their own, and sharing the NADFAS aims. There was much debate about how this could be done, 'it was felt that one major event per year, with accommodation for a large number of Members' was the best idea. The idea of a lecture dedicated to Helen Lowenthal was put forward, but Helen herself demurred. Various

**Above**

Members celebrate a National Day at Lyme Park, Cheshire, in 1975. Included in the picture are: Shuna Cronin (second from left); Kathleen Wareham (fourth from right); and Nadine Mitchell (second from right)

concerned 'not with building empires or dreaming castles in the air, but with stating a coherent policy for developing NADFAS'.[16] Once accepted it was not left on a shelf to gather dust but is reviewed and amended by the Trustees annually, and still sets the agenda for the future course of NADFAS.

## National Events

In June 1969 Patricia Fay suggested 'that it would be a good thing if there were more

other suggestions were made, John Pope-Hennessy was asked to approach Sir Kenneth Clark to see if he would be willing to give a lecture, he had been knighted that year for his inspirational television series *Civilisation* first broadcast in 1966. A sherry party at the Soane Museum was mooted with a talk by the Curator, the eminent architectural historian, Sir John Summerson. An evening party at the Courtauld with the Director Anthony Blunt was another option, or a

period ball at Woburn, but it was noted that 'costume was not popular with husbands'. Someone else offered to ask Laurence Olivier to talk on the Theatre, that year he appeared in three classic British films, *Oh What a Lovely War*, *The Battle of Britain* and *David Copperfield*. The first 'National' event was in fact a private view of the *Samuel Pepys* exhibition at the National Portrait Gallery. Such was its popularity a second event was organised at the Goldsmiths' Hall the same year. The combined film, buffet supper, exhibition view and craftsman demonstration was a huge success and members from 'Societies from as far away as Harrogate and Hull' attended.[18] In 1971 there was a concert of eighteenth-century music at Osterley House to celebrate the third birthday of NADFAS, and in 1972 a private view of the Neo-classical Art exhibition with two visits to the sensational *Tutankhamun* exhibition at the British Museum. These special national

events became a regular feature of the NADFAS calendar.

Kathleen Wareham suggested a NADFAS conference would be another good way of drawing the membership together around a common cause, and that it 'should be held in a different city every two years with ideas from various Societies. Participation is the key word for all National bodies'.[19] It was not until the fifth birthday of NADFAS that the first conference was held in 1973 at the V&A, the ground-breaking *Arts and the People* event. It drew in members from all over the country, attracted internationally distinguished speakers, and helped raise the Association's profile as a serious force in the world of arts and culture. The conferences became an important element within NADFAS, helping it participate in the rapidly evolving world of arts and heritage. The next conference was staged in 1979 on *Heritage Co-ordination*, and in 1981 *Action in the '80s*,

# Domestic bliss

For Charles Rennie Mackintosh architecture was as 'artistic' a discipline as painting or sculpture, a view demonstrated in his designs for what was to become the celebrated and supremely beautiful House for an Art Lover. By Professor James Cosgrove.

"You ask how are you to judge architecture. Just as you judge painting or sculpture — form, colour, proportion, all visible qualities — and the one great invisible quality in all art, soul."
From 'Architecture', a talk given in February 1893 by Charles Rennie Mackintosh

Nineteen hundred was perhaps one of the most creative, prolific and optimistic years in the short architectural oeuvre of Charles Rennie Mackintosh. Newly married to the artist Margaret MacDonald, Charles had just built Windy Hill – his first 'white house', completed the first phase of what has proved to be his masterpiece, Glasgow School of Art, and designed and installed an entire room based on his startling designs for Glasgow restaurateur Catherine Cranston in the eighth Secessionist Exhibition in Vienna where he and Margaret were feted and formed friendships with several leading Viennese artists and designers.

In December 1900 Alexander Koch, a German publisher, launched a competition seeking solutions to "questions confronting modern architecture" in the form of a grand mansion house suitable for a wealthy client, an art lover, to offer lavish entertainment in. The competition attracted 36 entrants including Leopold Bauer from Vienna, Baillie Scott from England, and Charles Rennie Mackintosh from Glasgow, with a contribution from Margaret MacDonald, a significant decorative artist in her own right. The judges, disappointed that the challenge had not been met, did not award a first prize but placed Baillie Scott in second place with Bauer, Oscar Marmorek and Paul Zeroch being awarded third prizes. The entry by 'Der Vogel' ('The Bird'), Mackintosh's pseudonym for the competition, was disqualified because the architect had not submitted the prescribed number of interior perspectives. However, the submission won him a purchase prize, his entry to be

Left: Austere and brooding – the house's oak-lined main hall. Top: Leafy detail from a Music Room table.

**Above**
*NADFAS Review* in its current incarnation meets Sir Trenchard Cox's ideal of 'a prestigious publication, more like a magazine which could be sold outside member Societies'

followed by a Symposium in 1984 to celebrate the 15th anniversary of the Association and in 1992 the first European Conference was held in Brussels.

In 1988 the first AGM to be held outside London was staged in Harrogate, and owed much 'to the persuasive powers of the town's Decorative and Fine Arts Group … [who] wanted to do something different for their 20th birthday and the provinces'.[20] In April 1988 representatives of the nation's 226 Societies descended on the spa town. The success of the AGM, and the symbolic importance of holding the Association's most important annual meeting outside the capital, led to further provincially based AGMs, taking members all over the country: in 1991 Buxton, in 1998 Bath, in 2002 Scarborough, in 2004 Eastbourne, in 2006 Cardiff, and Liverpool in 2008. With their associated visits, these meetings allow the NADFAS Area to show off their local culture

and heritage. These visits and the social events also mean that members who might not normally travel too far away from their county have the opportunity to meet one another, the Trustees, members of the Advisory Council, and some of the staff from NADFAS House.

Another new venture was launched in 1974 with National Days, the first organised around Italian culture. Events were held across the country at prestigious historical venues that held collections of Italian fine and decorative art, at Hever Castle, Woburn Abbey, Lyme Park and Castle Howard. In the following years National Days followed first a French (at Waddesdon, Goodwood, Bowes Museum, Lady Lever Art Gallery and Audley End) then an American theme. In 1975 a new annual national event was introduced, the Trenchard Cox lecture, to honour the President. Roy Strong gave the inaugural lecture on 'The English Country House. *Ave et*

*Vale'*, which was followed by a reception in the Raphael Cartoon Gallery at the V&A. It was attended by 300. As one Society chairman announced to her members, 'Trenchard Cox … He's not dead but Mrs Atkinson thought … [the annual lecture] would be a nice idea to remember him by'. In 1976 the Trenchard Cox Lecture was given by Hugh Casson, who was followed each year by a distinguished speaker, including Geoffrey Elton on the Tudors at the National Portrait Gallery in 1978, and Alan Bowness on 'Moore & Hepworth' at Leeds City Art Gallery in 1983, affirming that NADFAS was neither totally pre-occupied with the past, nor exclusively London based. Each year the number of national events increased, matching the growing number of NADFAS members. In 1976 two private views were arranged of the Constable exhibition, and American Days were held at Chatsworth, Capesthorne, Beaulieu, Hatfield, Windsor, Stowe and Firle, with a private view of the *1776* American Exhibition at Greenwich. The death of Patricia Fay in 1979 resulted in a new annual national event, dedicated to the memory of the founder and now held in conjunction with the AGM. The first, in November 1980, was a lecture by Eve King and a private view of the Van Dyke exhibition at the Tate Gallery. These events were not always lectures, in 1985 a dinner at the House of Commons was arranged which was a great success. As the author of one article explained 'The National Days … are a marvellous idea because they give different Societies a chance to meet and exchange ideas and always in fine surroundings'.[21]

In 1996 the annual NADFAS lecture was introduced, and launched with a talk by the Secretary of State for National Heritage, the Rt. Hon. Virginia Bottomley. These 'one off' events were supplemented from 1971 with Study of Style Days, open to NADFAS members from Societies all over the country. They were advertised in the *Newsletter*, as 'a course of eight lectures giving background information in recognition of style and period from Greco-Roman to High Renaissance, ending with a tutorial by Helen Lowenthal at the V&A'. It cost £4.50 for the course, and was extended in October for a further eight courses from High Baroque to the Nineteenth Century. These courses were so popular that these national study days were repeated and built upon. The first aim of the Education Committee, set up in 1988, was to arrange a number of NADFAS Study Courses based on events and exhibitions that were part of the NADFAS 20th Anniversary Celebrations. Like the Study of Style Course they offered members the opportunity of extending their knowledge with other like-minded NADFAS members from across the country. On such courses not only are new things learnt, but new friendships made, connections created and ideas exchanged. They play an important part in maintaining a 'joined-up' Association. The majority of study events are no longer organised nationally but, in keeping with the strategy of devolving activities away from NADFAS House, they are now arranged by ACEs (Area Co-ordinators for Education), enabling many members to study a wide range of subjects in greater depth at different venues around the country.

The management of this cumulative growth in activity was largely borne by a small band of hard-working volunteers. The weight of work that fell on the first part-time paid secretary, Nadine Mitchell, was huge. It was only in 1986, with the appointment of Lindley Maitland (until 1999) that a full-time Secretary and Administrator was employed. On their shoulders lay an immense responsibility and countless National Chairmen have expressed their gratitude for their hard work and dedication.

One of the more complicated issues that they had to deal with was VAT. In October 1976 it was realised that NADFAS was liable for VAT at 8%, and would be owing £2000 to £2500 in arrears. The Executive Committee was told that Margaret Flory, the Treasurer, had been 'working 18 months with Customs and Excise to see if exemption could be given on educational charity grounds'. In November it was reported that 'VAT all hinged on whether NADFAS was charitable or not'. A year later a further 12 hours had been spent at the Treasurer's house going through the books. In January 1978 Sheila Marshall received a letter to confirm that 'NADFAS no longer has to be registered for VAT retrospectively'. There must have been a huge sigh of relief.[22] Another important financial matter the Hon. Treasurer had to deal with was insurance. It was not until Nicky Foot inaugurated a blanket insurance policy in

**Above**
Pamela Makin, the first Editor of *NADFAS News* (which later became *NADFAS Review*), presenting a media award

1978 that Societies were protected. She was also the first Treasurer to present a properly forecasted budget, which 'helped members appreciate the way the money was spent'.[23]

One of the very important ways in which NADFAS has supported Societies and Areas is in the provision of training and this has expanded enormously in recent years. In the early days, all new Society chairmen were invited to an induction session in London. These events concentrated on imparting facts about the Association and space and time did not permit much interaction between participants. It became apparent that members were often reluctant to serve as chairmen or on committees because they felt unsure about the responsibilities or that they lacked knowledge of NADFAS as a whole.

In 1996, Pat Turner became Head of Training and began to put matters on a more professional footing. The days became broader in scope and included input from

those taking part. New Chairmen's Days and, later, New Treasurers' Days arranged independently by the Finance Department, are always held at NADFAS House but it was felt that similar opportunities could be offered to other committee members, covering a wider range of skills. Realising that travel to London was proving a deterrent to those living at a distance, it was decided to try moving some training out to the Areas. As one participant reported 'marvellous not to have to go all the way to London'. Days focusing on Society Administration, for any committee member, and on 'Planning a Programme', particularly aimed at Programme and Study Day Secretaries, were devised and, after some initial hesitation, these proved very popular. One lady wrote after attending a session: 'Has made my appointment as programme secretary less daunting'. This was precisely their intention.

The demand was such that in 2003, when Libby Hipwell took over as Head of Training, a further three experienced members were added to the strength, and each Area was asked to appoint an Area Trainer to its team. Each year two Training Days are held in an Area and these enable not only established committee members to take part, but can also encourage those who are uncertain whether they wish to be involved in the running of their Societies. While imparting information about NADFAS is important, a great advantage of these more relaxed days is the opportunity it gives for networking between committee members of different Societies. As one former Society chairman said, 'there is rarely a new problem in NADFAS, merely one you haven't encountered before!'. Another plus point of these Area Training Days has been the involvement of different members of the NADFAS House Staff who have brought their particular expertise to the meeting and, in turn, had an opportunity to learn of Society concerns first-hand. In turn, Society members 'understand better how it all works' and the role of the London-based administration.[24] The support gained from shared ideas and solutions is very valuable and this concept has now been developed

This page and opposite
A selection of some of
the more popular
goods sold through the
NADFAS gift catalogue

rapidly expanding membership. The first 'occasional newsletter' appeared in January 1968, informing members of the first five Societies of the inaugural meeting at the V&A in May. It was a single photocopied sheet. The National Chairman in her December 1968 report claimed that 'a great many of our problems would disappear overnight if every member Society representative read the *Newsletter* and minutes and passed the information into the appropriate channel'. Kathleen Wareham's idea, presented at the December 1968 Executive Committee, of a 'magazine with articles, photographs, advertisements etc at a cost of 2s 6d [was] felt to be too ambitious at the time'.[27] In 1970 the growth in the number of Societies who needed to be kept informed justified the first printed newsletter. It bore the distinctive anthemion border heading, organised by Lally Robinson. By the following March Kathleen Wareham had the task of producing a twice yearly publication. In 1984 Pamela Makin was responsible for revamping the *NADFAS Newsletter*. In true NADFAS style there was little fear of no response to requests for comment. One irate gentleman was appalled by the innumerable faults in punctuation, spelling, vocabulary and sentence structure displayed, saying, 'Never have I

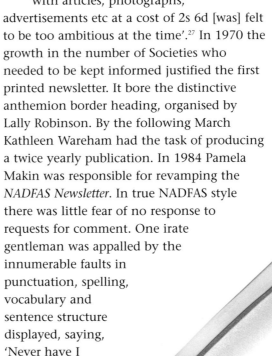

even further in the training of new chairmen with the addition to the programme of a second day entitled 'Running a Successful Society'. This day is very informal and run for the most part by the participants themselves. As well as advice on running an efficient meeting or an AGM, on public speaking and solving the common problems of a chairman, there is the opportunity for a vigorous exchange of ideas which draws on the widely differing backgrounds of today's Society chairmen. 'Good to meet other NADFAS people' wrote one participant, 'for ideas and general swapping of information'.[25]

Training does not, of course, stop at Society level and new Area Chairmen and Treasurers and Trustees also benefit from this now firmly embedded feature of NADFAS life, and the trainers themselves must keep abreast of all the latest developments.

*In the end though, even if the presentation moves from overhead projector to powerpoint, training is all about helping and encouraging members to fulfil Patricia Fay's inspired vision through listening, lively debate and perhaps, just as importantly, laughter!*[26]

## Keeping in Touch:
## From Newsletter to Review

As NADFAS grew it became essential to be able to communicate effectively with the

come across such a succession of gross blunders as have been perpetrated within the compass of these few pages'.[28]

In her restrained and polite reply Pamela detailed the immense amount of work involved in producing the *Newsletter*, 'administered on an entirely voluntary basis'. It entailed many hours of work. Apart from planning, it has to be laid out for artwork and typesetting; collated; researched for accuracy; typed; and presented to the printers. Distribution requires checking of labels, totals, packaging etc. If one is part of a commercial magazine all these matters are handled by individual departments. The Editor is left with the academic areas of policy, writing leaders, and final proofing, often assisted by a Sub-Editor. In our case all the tasks devolve onto the Editor:

*My prime task is to see the Newsletter is kept alive as a means of communication between every level of the Association. This would not happen if I became too demanding, and over-critical. The Newsletter is produced on a very low financial budget, which is achieved by using small local printers. Costs escalate with every issue, despite economies.*

The Autumn 1984 *Newsletter* had in fact taken an 'historical step forward'. For the first time there were twelve pages, and 'News from Societies', which at that time was printed on a tinted centrespread, was to become an integral part of the issue. Another first was the offering of advertising on the back cover. The print run exceeded 34,000.[29]

The following year NADFAS Enterprises Limited (NEL) was set up, its main activity being the publication of *NADFAS News*. In 1988 Pamela Makin retired as editor. During her nine years she had gradually enlarged and improved it from a simple four-page news sheet to her final issue, the splendid 20th anniversary number with 20 pages and a coloured cover. Pamela presented a new Media Award, for the best contribution to *NADFAS News*. By 1997 advances in modern technology had made it possible for some Societies, Areas and Committees of Council to produce their own newsletters and magazines, and with the agreement of the donor, the criteria of the Award was broadened. More recently the importance and value of Society website designs has been acknowledged, and granted a separate prize.

Prior to her departure as Editor, Pamela had undertaken research into a Forward Plan for the production of the *Newsletter*. She suggested that the editor's role needed to be:

*broken into four parts, an Editor to retain final responsibility to printers, contributors and overall management and link with the Association; an Art Editor to advise on layout etc; an Advertising Agent or Manager, and a Production and Distibution person.*

In effect a management team. The *Newsletter* policy must be to widen the membership horizons – create more feeling of belonging to an Association which is participating in the Fine Arts World. Forthcoming Events, or whatever they become, must be sold with articles, pictures and information to the members. 'Communication … should be at the top of the thinking of every chairman'.[30]

Margaret Garbett took over the reins as the new editor until 1997. Under her direction there were major developments reflecting the continuing increase in membership, in 1990 direct mailing of *NADFAS News* was introduced. Though resisted in some quarters, this was a great relief to most Society chairmen who had previously received bulk deliveries which

they then had to lug to lectures for distribution, with the possible additional inconvenience of having had to go to the sorting office to collect the heavy boxes if they were out when the post delivery van called! Colour advertising followed in 1993. The Autumn 1995 edition was the first to be desktop published, and by that year circulation had grown to 72,000.[31] By then NEL produced not only the *News*, but also the book *Inside Churches* and the *Directory of Lecturers*.

In 2001 a feasability study was carried out to investigate turning *NADFAS News* into a quarterly magazine. A questionnaire was sent to one Society in each Area asking them to comment on the various sections. Increased costs were always something the membership was very keen to avoid, although better quality does not necessarily equate with spending more money. This theory was to be put to the test.

At this time the magazine industry was also going through huge technical changes and the old ways of reproduction were being phased out and being replaced by new cheaper digital technology. With competitive tendering, and the belief of existing advertisers that more regular appearances of the magazine would attract more custom, the first *NADFAS Review* was given the green light to proceed in 2003. The new *Review* did not meet with universal approval and for quite a time members reported that they did not want four issues a year. 'A waste of money and paper' were frequent criticisms, and for some time questions were raised at the AGM about the changes. Gradually members were won over as they saw the benefit of having a more regular magazine. Stories and courses that were often out of date by the time the old bi-annual publication came out suddenly became relevant, and as increased revenue was generated, it was possible to invite more and higher profile journalists to contribute. In short the magazine got better

**Above**
NADFAS's striking table frontal, designed by Rosalie Williams, greets AGM attendees each year
**Left**
Veronica Shaw redesigned the NADFAS stick pin in 2004 with a stylised treatment of the Association's logo

and better, and more members started not only to read it, but also await its arrival with excitement. One lady commented that when the *Review* hit the doormat she had to compete with her husband to read it first.

As to increased costs, the membership now contributes less of their affiliation fee to the new quarterly *Review* than they did to the old bi-annual publication. The fiercest critics have been replaced with a membership that is generally very pleased with the improved quality and content, thanks largely to the current editorial and design team. It is now possible to feature many more volunteer projects that are completed at Society, Area and National level, as well as sharing some of the Societies' visits and anniversaries. The complaint now is that more Societies want to appear in the publication, and are disappointed when their news cannot be included due to pressure on space.

So what about the future? Could we see the *Review* produced for the members to download, or perhaps extend some features so they become podcasts? One thing is certain, this aspect of NADFAS has a history

of innovation, and changes in modern publishing will be embraced as long as the benefits can be justified to the membership. The new *NADFAS Review* in fact came close to Trenchard Cox's idea aired in 1978, that it 'should be a prestigious publication with contributions from experts, more like a magazine, which could be sold outside member Societies, rather than our *Newsletter* which is purely for home consumption'.[32]

NADFAS Enterprises Limited (NEL) did at times provoke strong feelings. It was essential for the Association in sheltering it from VAT and also providing protection in the event of any failure of the trading activities. NADFAS benefited from any profits made by NEL, in the same way as it did from NADFAS Tours Limited.[33] In 1995 NEL began selling products following a request from NADFAS Volunteers for aprons and tote bags, to which were added postcards, enamel collectors' boxes, and the acanthus leaf coffee spoon. They 'all make attractive gifts for friends and relatives and help publicise NADFAS and its charitable activities'.[34] However, when Societies were asked through their Areas if they wanted to increase the variety of goods sold and to make NEL more commercial, the vote was extremely close and the Council decided not to proceed with further development and continued to sell goods that applied particularly to NADFAS, including the diary, publications like *Inside Churches*, aprons, bags and Christmas cards.[35] As part of the review of NADFAS in 2004, a Promotions and Marketing team as part of NEL was created with a Director and 'experts from within and outside the membership'.[36]

## The Website

The introduction of the New Media Award in 1997 recognised the importance of new technology in NADFAS's internal and external communications. While early attempts came to nothing, the first NADFAS website was eventually designed in-house in 2002. It was deliberately kept simple, with no money to waste on extras, and because it had been self-designed it was securely under NADFAS's control. As Thomas Cocke was to comment when discussing plans for an upgraded site, it was more important to have someone who knew NADFAS than to have a 'technical geek as webmaster'.[37] How right he has proved to be. The new site was based on many meetings with Volunteer Heads at NADFAS House, Area Representatives, and a small consumer panel. The designer was chosen not only for his skills and track record, but also because he had been a member of what was then Young NADFAS and therefore knew the character of the Association.[38] The fresh version is brighter and more inviting, while still in keeping with the NADFAS 'Corporate Image'. It is easier to navigate and can now accommodate much more information. Password protected areas of the website mean that members, Society committees, Area Teams and Trustees can conveniently access and download key documents and working papers for forthcoming meetings, making great savings in both time and costs. The new site was launched early in 2007, and has already had hundreds of visits from all over the world, including America, Brazil, China and Italy. As a result, NADFAS is reaching parts of the globe that it has never reached before.

## Corporate Identity

The need for what we would now call 'corporate identity' was recognised very early on in the development of NADFAS. At the February 1968 Executive Committee meeting 'The Vice Chairman passed around for approval various printed stationery which carried a special NADFAS Design'. This was the anthemion pattern border.

*It was agreed that this was most attractively done, apart from the envelope which was better plain. It was proposed that a letter conveying the grateful thanks of the Association be sent to Mr Davis of the British Printing Corporation, who had undertaken the work.*

Ten months later Patricia Fay 'felt that it was important to promote NADFAS' and suggested 'that the guides and members doing conservation should be wearing NADFAS badges'. 'It was felt that a symbol was needed which could be incorporated into notepaper-headings by all member Societies.'[39] Lally Robinson agreed to sound out Graham Davis, who had designed the NADFAS letter-heading, in the matter. Nothing was to come of this, and the acanthus 'motif' was only to emerge from the anthemion border in the later 1980s. When Shirley Hewett, the National Chairman, began researching ideas for a new logo in 1988 she was horrified to discover that the:

*border used by NADFAS since the beginning was an ordinary border to be found in any Stationers' Directory and could therefore be used by anyone, presenting problems of copyright for the Association. Much consultation followed with various designers; finally it was decided to use the theme of our new stick pin.[40]*

This had been designed by and commissioned from the established silversmith and jeweller, Lexi Dick, whose work is now in major British Collections, including the Downing Street Service, part of the National Silver Collection. Her pin, a cast acanthus leaf, had gone on sale for the first time at the AGM in Harrogate in 1988. There was 'a certain amount of opposition to changing the logo from the original founders of NADFAS who were upset at the change to the image of the Association'.[41] The acanthus symbol underwent another change in 1990, when it was stylised, which again provoked adverse comment. In 2004, Veronica Shaw interpreted the revised motif in a new stick-pin with blue enamel added that harmonised with the logo. The 40th birthday of NADFAS in 2008 will see the introduction of a new stick-pin, designed by the silversmiths, Padgham and Putland. Their elegant and simple style will ensure a balance between tradition and modernity which is the *leitmotiv* of the NADFAS story.

The acanthus is a powerful symbol, and it has weathered many changes in design, during its association with NADFAS. It is a symbol that reflects longevity and creativity, a recurring motif within the arts and architecture of western civilisation, and of NADFAS. Since 1990 the acanthus leaf motif has welcomed all those attending the AGM and Annual Directory Meeting at Kensington Town Hall, in the form of a handsome table frontal. A competition for the design, launched in 1988, originally focused on a wall hanging, but it was soon realised that this was impractical. The competition was won by Rosalie Williams, a member of Newick DFAS, with her interpretation of the acanthus leaf, a strong modern design, easily visible from a distance. She worked the centre leaf, and oversaw the early stages of the frontal's creation by the volunteers Margaret Beard, Maureen Brill, Jill Crampton, Michaela Jenkerson-Kenshole, Pamela Makin and Judith Waples, who collectively spent two years and 140 hours of hard work making it. The 12-foot long frontal is not only an impressive way of promoting NADFAS in a vivid symbol of unity, but also perhaps an inspiration to member Societies to celebrate and promote the symbols of their own identity, whether copying, emulating or entirely original.

NOTES

[1] Ex.Co. Minutes, June 1969, NADFAS Archives.
[2] Published in *The Antique Finder*, 1968/69, see Ex.Co Minutes, 9 December 1968, NADFAS Archives.
[3] Private Collection.
[4] 'Some suggestions for consideration of the Executive Committee', Kathleen Wareham, 4 January 1973, p.1. Private Collection.
[5] Chairman's Report, Pamela Cohn, 1998-2000, NADFAS Archives.
[6] Chairman's Report, Jean Read, 2000-02, NADFAS Archives.
[7] Chairman's Report, Sheila Jones, 2002-04, NADFAS Archives.
[8] Jeremy Warren, correspondence, November 2007.
[9] Christopher Chavasse to Jean Read, National Chairman, April 2001. Private Collection.
[10] Sheila Marshall, *Development of a Dream*, 1982.
[11] Chairman's Report, Patricia Fay 1967/68, NADFAS Archives.
[12] Patricia Fay, 'Historic Houses of Europe Conference' in Oxford, 9 July 1975, NADFAS Archives.
[13] Ex.Co Minutes, 24 Feb 1975, NADFAS Archives.
[14] Teme Valley DFAS, chairman's report, 18 April 1984. Private Collection.
[15] Thomas Cocke, Chief Executive 2001-06, Retrospect, NADFAS Archives.
[16] Thomas Cocke, Focus Forward: NADFAS 2005-07 (with grateful acknowledgement to Bert Spiekman for the title), 2004.
[17] Ex.Co. Minutes, 9 June 1969, point 43, NADFAS Archives.
[18] *NADFAS Newsletter*, January 1971.
[19] 'Some suggestions' Wareham, 1973, op. cit.
[20] *Yorkshire Post*, 26 April 1988.
[21] Selina Sinker, 'Discovering NADFAS', *Hunting Group Review*, August 1983, p.8.
[22] Ex.Co. Minutes, 9 October 1976, 5 November 1976, 21 November 1977 & 19 January 1978.
[23] Chairman's Report, Pamela Cowen 1978-80, NADFAS Archives.
[24] Pat Turner, November 1996.
[25] Comment Sheet, 23 February 2001.
[26] Libby Hipwell, August 2007.
[27] Ex.Co. Minutes, 9 December 1968, under 'NADFAS Promotion', NADFAS Archives.
[28] Pamela Makin, *Newsletter* Editor, on the revamped NADFAS News, Autumn/Winter 1983, NADFAS Archives.
[29] Pamela Makin, Editor, NADFAS *News* Autumn/Winter 1984, p.1.
[30] Forward Planning Document, 10 June 1987 compiled by Pamela Makin, FP 4/87 for 8.7.87, NADFAS Archives.
[31] NADFAS Annual Report for 1995-6, p.7.
[32] Trenchard Cox, from 'suggestions raised from the Next Ten Years Conference, V&A Museum 16 March 1978', NADFAS Archives.
[33] Chairman's Report, Nancy Hodgson, 1992-94, NADFAS Archives.
[34] Strategy Paper, N33/94, NADFAS Archives.
[35] Chairman's Report, Anthea Johnston, 1994-96, NADFAS Archives.
[36] Chairman's Report, Nesta Waine, 2004-06, NADFAS Archives.
[37] Cocke, Retrospect, op. cit.
[38] *NADFAS Review*, Spring 2007.
[39] Ex.Co. Minutes, 9 December 1968, NADFAS Archives.
[40] Chairman's Report, Shirley Hewett, 1986-88, NADFAS Archives.
[41] Ibid.

# 12

# Forty Years On:

# *... and Looking Ahead*

*'We know we are allowed to enjoy ourselves
– our constitution exhorts us to do so'*
Report on Henley DFAS 30th Anniversary, 2007[1]

**Opposite**
Artists such as
Damien Hirst,
whose *Arginine*
is pictured
opposite, set the
tone for the new
art movement
of the 1990s

1968 saw not only the official birth of
NADFAS but also Alan Bennett's West End
debut with his play *Forty Years On*. The play,
drawing on a song written in 1872 and sung
by generations of Harrow schoolboys, asks
'How will it seem to you, forty years on?'.
The same question can be asked of NADFAS.
How has NADFAS adapted to changes in the
economy, society and culture over the last
forty years? What has the infant of the
sixties, the child of the seventies, the
teenager of the eighties, become in the
new Millennium?

The sixties and the decade after 1997
both saw Britain under Labour leadership,
with Harold Wilson and Tony Blair, the same
name 'Labour', but with very different
agendas. The Space Race had been put to one
side, and the Berlin Wall had come down.
The baby boom of the 1960s has been
replaced by a falling birth rate. The technical
colleges that became universities are now
feeling the pinch, and escalating fees restrict
access to higher education. Mia Farrow, Liza
Minelli and Glenda Jackson have been

challenged by Julia Roberts, Helena Bonham
Carter, and Gwyneth Paltrow, although Judi
Dench, Maggie Smith and Helen Mirren, are
still among the Nation's favourites. The
Flower Power children have paid off their
mortgages, and youth culture now looks to
environmentalism and entrepreneurship.
While Op Art was the latest trend in the
1960s, the 1990s saw the arrival of the Young
British Artists, first brought to public view at
Saatchi's 1992 show, and consolidated in
1997 with the Royal Academy's *Sensation*
exhibition, starring the shock tactics of
Damien Hirst's stuffed shark, Tracey Emin's
*My Bed* and Marcus Harvey's homage to the
1960s with *Myra*. Some are still reeling. Those
who watched the first series of *Going for a
Song* in 1965 would surely never have
imagined that a programme on antiques
would win an award for the most popular
daytime television show in 2002. Yet the
winner, *Bargain Hunt*, represents a completely
different world to that of its direct forebear.
The fashions of the 1960s and 1970s have
returned, as popular 'retro-style', similar, but

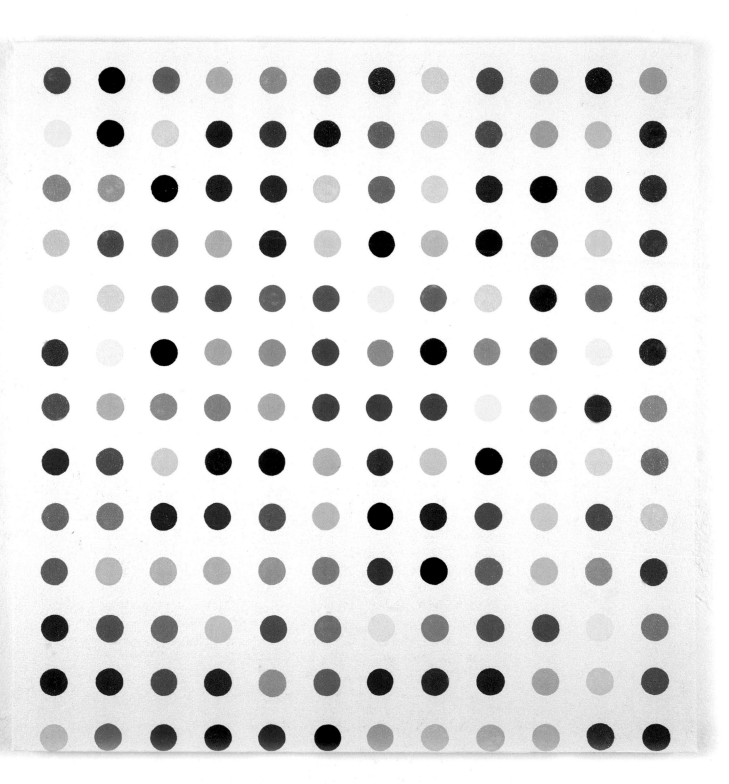

not the same as the originals which they copy. Now NADFAS Societies can hear lectures on the 1950s and 1960s. The 1990s saw the departure of our first female Prime Minister, Margaret Thatcher, after 11 years in office, and the arrival of women in important positions of power, Betty Boothroyd elected the first female speaker of the House of Commons, in 1994 the Church of England ordained women priests, Stella Rimington became the first female to head MI5, and in the 1997 general election the number of female members of Parliament was doubled to 120. In the home the 'Hoover' has been replaced by the 'Dyson', the microwave has challenged the place of the cooker, and the mobile phone and computer have become 'necessities' rather than luxuries. While the capitation (now affiliation) fee has risen from 50p in 1978 to over £10 today, so has the price of every other membership fee, service and commodity.

NADFAS, like the economy, saw growth and rapid globalisation in the 1980s, it not only survived the recession but flourished. In 1981, 14 new Societies were launched, the maximum annual increase in the history of NADFAS, in 1983 and 1985 this figure was reached again, and in 1989 a record number of Societies, 20, were formed in a single year. This has yet to be equalled! The 1990s saw a stabilisation and, from 2000, a more modest growth. In 1991 the 250th Society was founded, Pantiles, and in 2001 the 325th

**Above and right**
The Apple Mac and Dyson are the new domestic icons of the day

Society, Kingston-upon-Thames. New Societies are still opening and last year there were nearly 340 in the UK with 10 in Mainland Europe and three in New Zealand, with a fourth in gestation, whilst our sister Association in Australia, AADFAS, had 30 Societies and is still growing. NADFAS may have come to its maturity but it is certainly not ready for a mid-life crisis. Its current membership of around 90,000 is the envy of many other organisations and nearly half the Societies have waiting lists of varying lengths. There has been no real decline, only the occasional closure of Societies, spread over its forty years, which is surely indicative of good health. In a period which has seen what was called 'an explosion in the arts', NADFAS has maintained its position, by virtue of its experience. These:

*years have seen the growth of museums and galleries, the formation of education departments in nearly every museum, the Open University, a rash of art magazines and books, and courses of art lectures 'ad infinitum'. There are now many other avenues for study of the arts.*[2]

Since Anne White made these observations in the mid 1980s this trend of growing popularisation and access to the arts has continued. There are more organisations, more courses, more books, more programmes, more opportunities to engage with the arts than ever before. The question asked then, which is still relevant today, is whether NADFAS is happy to stick with the tried and tested formula, or does it to want to move ahead, to re-establish the reputation it gained in the 1960s and 1970s for pioneering? Ideas for the foundation of a University of NADFAS, and liaison with the Open University, were discussed but never pursued.

Another major change in society, as well as NADFAS, has been the rising age of the population, and, in

consequence, of its membership. With improvements in health care and advances in medicine people are not only living longer, but are active longer. Many have grown up with NADFAS, and are still manning committees and coming to lectures in their 70s, 80s and 90s. The young married mothers, who were the target group for the NADFAS of the 1960s and 1970s, are now grandmothers. They have daughters who go out to work, and whose lives leave little space for evening, let alone daytime lectures, courses and commitments. As the former chairman of Mendip DFAS, Ian Deane, observed looking back over 25 years of his Society:

*whilst many used to join NADFAS in their 30s and 40s, this is now quite rare. Despite our success, which suggests strongly that what we do fills a need, we are an ageing organisation. NADFAS has become something to look forward to when we are retired and have more*

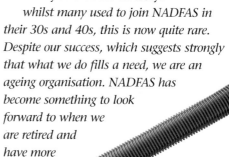

*time – like a prize to be collected when we pass "go" at 60 or 65.*[3]

Advances in technology and communication also open up opportunities for NADFAS. The indefatigable Anne White asked in 1986: 'Do you have a sub-Committee looking into TV and Video?', and reflected 'If one wants any proof of how a Video film can put across in 12 minutes something difficult to explain in an hour you only have to look at the Video film of Young NADFAS ... that is ... pioneering work'. DVDs have replaced videos, and increasingly lecturers and Societies are adapting to the digital age. We have to adapt, or be left behind. Now many Societies have websites, and also communicate with lecturers, NADFAS House and other members by e-mail.

Sadly many of the 'old guard' are no longer with us, Helen Lowenthal died in 1993, and Sir Trenchard Cox and Lally Robinson in 1995, but their spirit lives on. They all rose to a challenge, were forward-thinking, and knew that the NADFAS that they had helped to build was a sturdy edifice. None were afraid to stand up for their causes. Helen was famously declared *persona non grata* in perpetuity at the V&A after challenging the closure of the Slide Library in 1980. This feistiness is all part of the NADFAS story. The appointment of Timothy Clifford as President of NADFAS after Sir Trenchard Cox's death was 'a controversial choice in some areas and one of ... [the] Vice Presidents, Sir Roy Strong, resigned in protest'.[4] While some have felt that 'it was much more fun when everything was on a small scale', Patricia Fay's ambition was that it should continue to grow, because strength in numbers meant an increased presence, providing power to get things done, to be heard, to have an impact, to really carry out the aims of the Association. While the Constitution of NADFAS has been amended over time, its principles have not.

## Life Begins at 40

The 40th birthday of NADFAS is a time to celebrate its many achievements and encourage more people to join us. It is a time to re-connect with our past, re-affirm old friendships and make new ones. While many things have changed in the world the NADFAS story is one of continuity. The clarity of the NADFAS mission has not been dimmed over time, but has gained strength through experience. The Association is always looking for new ways of interpreting the founding principles, which remain solidly at its core.

When Ann Parkinson reminded the Association that the work done by preceding Chairmen and NADFAS itself, 'needed to be recognised not only by our own members, but by the outside world and in particular ... the Art World', she would have been surprised that 30 years later the same call for recognition is still being made.[5] With over a thousand churches recorded, countless houses, museums and galleries benefiting from volunteer NADFAS help, numerous young people being supported either through Young Arts projects or direct grants, and hundreds of heritage venues and causes supported via the 90,000-strong membership, NADFAS remains the demure Cinderella of the arts world, working away in the background. Nesta Waine reported that one of her main tasks as Chairman in 2002-04 had been to raise the profile of the organisation and promote NADFAS to the outside world. The current National Chairman, Susan Sellers, confirms that this is a continuing theme for the Trustee Board, which is constantly exploring different ways to promote NADFAS. This may be through making new partnerships, or seeking greater recognition, locally, regionally or nationally, from organisations with which it has been working over the years. NADFAS no longer needs to be grateful to be included in the list of the country's key heritage bodies. It is there because it has a recognised, significant and established role to play. It is perhaps because NADFAS gets on with its work in such a quiet and effective manner that it remains under-appreciated, it is not by nature attention-seeking. As Roy Strong commented at the First Five Years Conference in 1973: 'If you happen to ... produce sculpture by hacking nine pianos to pieces and putting them in some pile of concrete ... you will be on television like a shot'.[6] Yet in the early days NADFAS did get good coverage. In 1976 'all the major national papers have carried stories on NADFAS activities and four radio stations have broadcast interviews'.[7] Our 40th birthday is a time to trumpet our achievements once again.

The healthy growth of NADFAS is due to its slow but sure evolution, rather than to any revolutionary developments. Without losing its primary aims it has adapted to a

nourished those who have joined it. It is through this family that knowledge, support and aims are shared. As in all families from time to time there are squabbles, reconciliations, forgiveness and the need for tolerance. However NADFAS is united by a common cause, firm friendships are made which stand the test of time. Many organisations say that people are their main asset; this is certainly true of NADFAS which, without the commitment and enthusiasm of

**Above**
One of the 'old guard', Helen Lowenthall died in 1993, but her spirit lives on in today's NADFAS
**Above right**
The CityArts initiative is extending the benefits of NADFAS to a young, professional audience

changing social, economic and cultural environment. In the beginning the Association had 'just a few male members'.[8] Today, reflecting earlier retirement, and the growth of evening Societies, 'hitherto somewhat passive observers, husbands are becoming fully involved'.[9] The benefits are reciprocal, with an increased membership and range of professional skills. Those who joined in the 1960s and 1970s still enjoy the pattern of regular lectures, enhanced by Study Days, visits and tours. The subjects might have diversified and increased, but the passion, enthusiasm and commitment are the same. When asked for memories of NADFAS many have given them with great affection, and a recurring word has been 'family'. 'Everyone' remarked the National Chairman in 1976, 'seems happy to be part of the family', and they still are.[10] The NADFAS family has welcomed, nurtured and

so many in Societies, Areas or at a national level, just could not work. Thousands of members work as volunteers either as Church Recorders, Heritage Volunteers or with Young Arts, but also – crucially – as committee members, running their own Societies. Many of those who work nationally for NADFAS began as members, organisers and helpers in their own Societies, so they know the stresses and strains, as well as the pleasures and benefits of the Association. It is worth noting that since the establishment of 'new' NADFAS, a Company Limited by Guarantee, a healthy number of members have offered themselves for election as Trustees. This is by no means always the case in the charity world and reinforces the impression of a sense of ownership and involvement that many members feel, and which is one of the enduring strengths of NADFAS. Another affirmation of these bonds is the popularity

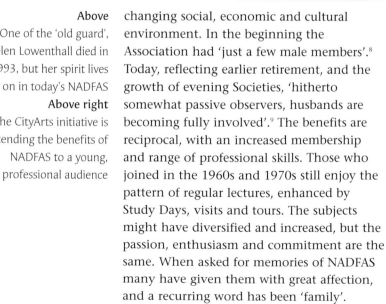

of the National Events that go from strength to strength, with members travelling from all over the country, even the world, to attend. The other words that frequently spring out of letters from members are 'enriched' and 'enlarged'. NADFAS in its unique way has helped thousands connect with the larger world of art. Mary Bourne, in *The Lady*, stated: 'I think it is no exaggeration to say that it really has enriched lives, established friendships and educated or re-educated many of us in our own great art heritage as well as that of other countries'.[11] Eira Hibbert explained that she 'must be one of the oldest members' of the Association, and is 'delighted to have had my life enriched by NADFAS'.[12] A recently retired Trustee charmingly describes NADFAS as a 'delight in her life' a phrase that seems to chime a chord with many members. Within each Society there is friendship and fun, something that Patricia Fay saw as an essential element of what NADFAS is. 'It always ought to be fun' she said.[13]

NADFAS serves an ever growing family in many ways, with members from different stages of life. Those who joined in their 30s and 40s are now in their 70s and 80s. Children are still welcome and catered for in Young NADFAS Groups and through Young Arts projects, young people become aware of the Association through competitions, exhibitions, events, visits and school projects, and later on grants and bursaries.

Associate Membership began in the 1980s solely to provide insurance cover and some contact with the main Association for Church Recorders and VCC members (Heritage Volunteers) who were unable or did not wish to join a Society and, in 1994, there was a constitutional change to make this a formal category of membership. In 2000 it became known as National Membership and is now open to people on Society waiting lists, and members of the public and other institutions with an interest in NADFAS. Lecturers who are not members of a Society and those who attend CityArts events automatically become National Members and therefore receive the quarterly *NADFAS*

*Review* which keeps them abreast of all the Association's news, including national study courses and events in which they are eligible to participate.

CityArts is a recent NADFAS initiative which gives people aged 25 to 45 the opportunity to widen their knowledge of the arts in an informal setting. Held three times a year, the evenings provide engrossing and stimulating lectures on a variety of topics. Speakers have included Ken Shuttleworth and Roger Ridsill-Smith, respectively architect and engineer of the Millennium Bridge in London, and art critic Andrew Graham-Dixon. This aspect of NADFAS life is one where new partnerships can be developed and it has been most rewarding for the Association to work with Gerrard Limited, a leading UK private client wealth manager, who sponsored CityArts from its launch in 2003 until May 2005, and European Connoisseurs Travel, one of NADFAS's travel sponsors, who have supported the current series of lectures.

Perhaps the way forward is to diversify further, with activities organised to cater for

**Above**

Forty years on, Twiggy, like NADFAS, is still going strong

other specific age groups, meeting at different times and in different places, possibly with variations on the 'traditional' monthly lecture format. NADFAS is part of the life-cycle. Perhaps, too, it is part of the evolutionary process to lose some Societies, while others prosper and new ones start up. Whatever the case, it is certain that NADFAS as an organisation will not rest on its acanthus leaves. NADFAS is once more going out as it did in the 1960s and 1970s, recruiting and spreading the word. If you have a good story, like a good product, then you need to go out and sell it. Growth is as important now as it was in the 1970s when an article in the *Newsletter* stated 'Growth creates greater public awareness and makes the Association's national influence stronger and more powerful'.[14] Further expansion cannot be taken for granted and concerted efforts are still needed to encourage new Societies in areas where NADFAS remains unrepresented. Despite its excellence NADFAS sometimes appears to be a secret that is rather too well kept.

Nevertheless NADFAS has become one of the nation's great institutions. As Martin Drury, who went on to become Director General of the National Trust, stated ' … there are countless people who would include Patricia's brainchild in their own shortlist of British institutions from which they derive a particular sense of pride, inspiration and comfort'.

Perhaps the last word should go to the current National Chairman who said:

*We have a great story to tell not just of the past but for the future as well. NADFAS has continued to thrive against the backdrop of enormous social change. Possibly this is because what does not change is the essence of the human mind – our thirst for knowledge, the urge we have to understand the world about us and our enduring need for friendship. Where can we find something that responds to all these needs? NADFAS. We listen to superb lectures that stimulate our minds and expand our knowledge. We derive great pleasure not only from sharing our enjoyment of all this with each other, but also by encouraging and supporting young people*

*to discover and explore the world of art and the many opportunities we have to contribute to society by helping to protect and preserve our heritage. Patricia Fay's vision therefore is as relevant today as it was 40 years ago. The bedrock of NADFAS remains the individual Societies each of whom is dependent for their continuing good health on regularly passing on the baton of committee membership. This is essential not only to provide the regular Society activities, but also to support and encourage its volunteers who reach out and work within their own communities. It is our hope that having read this story members will feel pride, not only in their own Societies, but also in belonging to the wider family that is NADFAS which, in its own distinctive way, remains such a significant force for good in the art world.*

NOTES

[1] The Report compiled by Ann Ducker and Hilary Beck-Burridge, sent by Geraldine Crippen, makes the point that one of the Henley DFAS (HEDFAS) members had a hand in drafting the new NADFAS Constitution, which included 'enjoyment' of the visual arts, wording taken from the HEDFAS Constitution.
[2] Anne White, Paper given to NADFAS 3 July 1986, Private Collection.
[3] Susan Sellers and Ian Deane, 'The Way Ahead – Message from the Chairmen', Mendip DFAS Newsletter, 2006, p.4.
[4] Chairman's Report, Judith Thomas 1996-98, NADFAS Archives.
[5] Chairman's Report, Ann Parkinson 1972-74, NADFAS Archives.
[6] Special Newsletter, November 1973, reporting on the First Five Years Conference.
[7] Chairman's Report, 1976, NADFAS Archives.
[8] Veronica Papworth in the *Sunday Express*, 31 March 1968.
[9] Ann Templar, Godalming DFAS, in NADFAS *Newsletter*, Autumn/Winter 1983.
[10] Chairman's Report, 1976, NADFAS Archives.
[11] Mary Bourne, review of *Development of a Dream*, *The Lady* corrected proof, 8 May 1984.
[12] Eira Hibbert, who from West Wycombe DFAS went on to become a founder member of Lymington, Exeter & Truro Societies, October 2006.
[13] Elliott Viney, 'The beginning of it all', in Chiltern DFAS Newsletter, no.26, Spring 1980, p.6.
[14] NADFAS *Newsletter*, January 1979.

# Societies

| Area | Society | No | Venue |
|---|---|---|---|
| **BEDS & HERTS** | | | |
| | ASHRIDGE DFAS | 8 | Potten End, Hertfordshire |
| | BISHOP'S STORTFORD DFAS | 69 | Bishop's Stortford, Hertfordshire |
| | BUSHEY DFAS | 211 | Bushey, Hertfordshire |
| | CHORLEYWOOD DFAS | 169 | Chorleywood, Hertfordshire |
| | EAST HERTFORDSHIRE DFAS | 12 | Broxbourne, Hertfordshire |
| | ENFIELD DFAS | 13 | Enfield, Middlesex |
| | GADE VALLEY DFAS | 29 | Potten End, Hertfordshire |
| | HARPENDEN AREA DFAS | 10 | Luton, Hertfordshire |
| | HARPENDEN EVENING DFAS | 241 | Harpenden, Hertfordshire |
| | HARROW DFAS | 25 | Harrow, Middlesex |
| | HERTSMERE DFAS | 51 | St Alban's, Hertfordshire |
| | MOOR PARK DFAS | 7 | Ruislip, Middlesex |
| | NORTH BEDFORDSHIRE DFAS | 195 | Kempston, Bedfordshire |
| | NORTH HERTFORDSHIRE DFAS | 139 | Letchworth, Hertfordshire |
| | RICKMANSWORTH DFAS | 62 | Sarratt, Rickmansworth, Hertfordshire |
| | TRING PARK DFAS | 277 | Berkhampstead, Hertfordshire |
| | WELWYN GARDEN DFAS | 106 | Welwyn Garden City, Hertfordshire |
| | WOBURN AREA DFAS | 78 | Woburn, Bedfordshire |
| **EAST ANGLIA** | | | |
| | BURY ST EDMUNDS DFAS | 248 | Great Whelnetham, Suffolk |
| | CAM DFAS | 304 | Cambridge |
| | CAMBRIDGE DFAS | 33 | Cambridge |
| | DEBEN DFAS | 184 | Woodbridge, Suffolk |
| | DISS DFAS | 230 | Diss, Norfolk |
| | EAST SUFFOLK DFAS | 103 | Aldeburgh, Suffolk |
| | ELY DFAS | 161 | Ely, Cambridgeshire |
| | GLAVEN VALLEY DFAS | 210 | Cley-next-the-Sea, Norfolk |
| | GRANTA DFAS | 172 | Cambridge |
| | HUNTINGDON DFAS | 155 | St Ives, Cambridgeshire |
| | IPSWICH DFAS | 253 | Ipswich, Suffolk |
| | KING'S LYNN DFAS | 221 | West Winch, Norfolk |
| | NEWMARKET DFAS | 75 | Kirtling, Suffolk |
| | NORTH WEST NORFOLK DFAS | 335 | Sedgeford, Norfolk |
| | NORWICH DFAS | 141 | Norwich, Norfolk |
| | ORWELL DFAS | 309 | Ipswich, Suffolk |
| | PETERBOROUGH DFAS | 70 | Fletton, Peterborough, Cambridgeshire |
| | SOUTH SUFFOLK DFAS | 154 | Sudbury, Suffolk |
| | SOUTHWOLD & BLYTH VALLEY DFAS | 197 | Southwold, Suffolk |
| | SUDBURY DFAS | 243 | Sudbury, Suffolk |
| | WENSUM DFAS | 203 | Norwich, Norfolk |
| | WEST SUFFOLK DFAS | 40 | Stowmarket, Suffolk |
| **EAST MIDLANDS** | | | |
| | DERBY DFAS | 279 | Derby |
| | DOVE VALLEY DFAS | 87 | Ashbourne, Derbyshire |
| | DUKERIES DFAS | 114 | Worksop, Nottinghamshire |
| | GAINSBOROUGH & DISTRICT DFAS | 83 | Gainsborough, Lincolnshire |
| | GRANTHAM & DISTRICT DFAS | 314 | Grantham, Lincolnshire |
| | HARBOROUGH DFAS | 290 | Market Harborough, Leicestershire |
| | HOLLAND & KESTEVEN DFAS | 24 | Osbournby, Lincolnshire |
| | LEICESTER DFAS | 152 | Leicester |
| | NORTH LINCOLNSHIRE DFAS | 285 | Grimsby, Lincolnshire |
| | NORTHAMPTONSHIRE DFAS | 129 | Northampton |
| | NOTTINGHAMSHIRE DFAS | 66 | Nottingham |
| | OAKHAM DFAS | 312 | Oakham, Leicestershire |
| | OUNDLE DFAS | 316 | Barnwell, Northamptonshire |
| | RUSHCLIFFE DFAS | 149 | West Bridgford, Nottinghamshire |
| | RUTLAND DFAS | 194 | Corby, Northamptonshire |
| | SPARKENHOE ARTS SOCIETY | 338 | Market Bosworth, Leicestershire |
| | STAMFORD DFAS | 240 | Stamford, Lincolnshire |
| **EAST SURREY** | | | |
| | ASHTEAD DFAS | 125 | Ashtead, Surrey |
| | BETCHWORTH DFAS | 287 | Betchworth, Surrey |
| | BOOKHAM DFAS | 329 | Great Bookham, Surrey |
| | CHEAM DFAS | 167 | Cheam, Surrey |
| | CHIPSTEAD DFAS | 198 | Banstead, Surrey |
| | COBHAM & OXSHOTT DFAS | 298 | Oxshott, Surrey |

|  |  |  |  |
|---|---|---|---|
|  | DORKING DFAS | 131 | Dorking, Surrey |
|  | EPSOM DFAS | 213 | Epsom, Surrey |
|  | HORSLEY DFAS | 262 | East Horsley, Surrey |
|  | LEATHERHEAD DFAS | 297 | Leatherhead, Surrey |
|  | LIMPSFIELD DFAS | 64 | Limpsfield, Surrey |
|  | LOVELACE DFAS | 337 | East Horsley, Surrey |
|  | REIGATE DFAS | 166 | Reigate, Surrey |
|  | WALTON ON THE HILL DFAS | 57 | Walton on the Hill, Surrey |
| **ESSEX** |  |  |  |
|  | BANCROFT'S DFAS | 101 | Woodford Green, Essex |
|  | BLACKWATER DFAS | 128 | Wickham Bishops, Essex |
|  | BRENTWOOD & DISTRICT DFAS | 116 | Ingatestone, Essex |
|  | COLCHESTER DFAS | 115 | Colchester, Essex |
|  | FELSTED DFAS | 91 | Felsted, Essex |
|  | HARLOW DFAS | 214 | Old Harlow, Essex |
|  | HAVERING DFAS | 43 | Upminster, Essex |
|  | MID ESSEX DFAS | 38 | Little Baddow, Essex |
|  | NORTH EAST ESSEX DFAS | 269 | Colchester, Essex |
|  | SAFFRON WALDEN DFAS | 95 | Saffron Walden, Essex |
|  | THAMES ESTUARY DFAS | 200 | Rochford, Essex |
|  | WEST ESSEX DFAS | 27 | Theydon Bois, Essex |
| **GREATER LONDON** |  |  |  |
|  | BECKENHAM DFAS | 100 | Beckenham, Kent |
|  | BLACKHEATH DFAS | 110 | Blackheath, London |
|  | CLAREMONT DFAS | 72 | Stoke d'Abernon, Surrey |
|  | CROYDON DFAS | 37 | Sanderstead, Surrey |
|  | DULWICH DFAS | 44 | Dulwich, London |
|  | EALING DFAS | 307 | Ealing, London |
|  | GREENWICH DFAS | 305 | Greenwich, London |
|  | HAMPSTEAD HEATH DFAS | 247 | Hampstead, London |
|  | HIGHGATE DFAS | 63 | Highgate, London |
|  | HILLINGDON DFAS | 310 | Ruislip, Middlesex |
|  | KENSINGTON & CHELSEA DFAS | 52 | Kensington, London |
|  | KINGSTON UPON THAMES DFAS | 325 | Kingston upon Thames. Surrey |
|  | NORTH KENT DFAS | 15 | Orpington, Kent |
|  | NORTH KENT EVENING DFAS | 153 | Bromley, Kent |
|  | NORTH LONDON DFAS | 14 | Hampstead, London |
|  | REGENTS PARK DFAS | 86 | St John's Wood, London |
|  | RICHMOND & DISTRICT DFAS | 80 | Richmond, Surrey |
|  | SANDERSTEAD DFAS | 111 | Sanderstead, Surrey |
|  | SOUTH WEST LONDON DFAS | 32 | Putney, London |
|  | WESTMINSTER DFAS | 132 | Westminster, London |
|  | WIMBLEDON DFAS | 177 | Wimbledon, London |
| **HAMPSHIRE** |  |  |  |
|  | ALRESFORD DFAS | 193 | Itchen Abbas, Hampshire |
|  | ALTON DFAS | 303 | Alton, Hampshire |
|  | BASINGSTOKE DFAS | 259 | Sherfield-on-Lodden, Hampshire |
|  | GRAYSHOTT DFAS | 165 | Grayshott, Hampshire |
|  | HART DFAS | 11 | Fleet, Hampshire |
|  | ISLE OF WIGHT DFAS | 138 | Ryde, Isle of Wight |
|  | MEON VALLEY DFAS | 90 | Meonstoke, Hampshire |
|  | NEW FOREST DFAS | 42 | Brockenhurst, Hampshire |
|  | NEW FOREST EVENING DFAS | 85 | Brockenhurst, Hampshire |
|  | NEW MILTON DFAS | 235 | New Milton, Hampshire |
|  | PETERSFIELD DFAS | 127 | Petersfield, Hampshire |
|  | PORTSDOWN DFAS | 157 | Bedhampton, Hampshire |
|  | PORTSEA ISLAND DFAS | 251 | Portsea Island, Hampshire |
|  | ROMSEY DFAS | 134 | Romsey, Hampshire |
|  | SARISBURY GREEN DFAS | 225 | Sarisbury Green, Hampshire |
|  | SOLENT DFAS | 148 | Titchfield, Hampshire |
|  | SOUTHAMPTON DFAS | 330 | Southampton, Hampshire |
|  | TEST VALLEY DFAS | 31 | Wey Hill, Hampshire |
|  | VECTIS (ISLE OF WIGHT) DFAS | 256 | Newport, Isle of Wight |
|  | WEST SOLENT DFAS | 60 | Milford-on-Sea, Hampshire |
|  | WINCHESTER DFAS | 99 | Winchester, Hampshire |

**KENT**

| | | |
|---|---|---|
| ASHFORD DFAS | 156 | Aldington, Kent |
| CANTERBURY DFAS | 45 | Thanington, Canterbury, Kent |
| DOVER & DEAL DFAS | 96 | Sandwich, Kent |
| EGERTON DFAS | 323 | Egerton, Kent |
| FAVERSHAM DFAS | 135 | Faversham, Kent |
| FOLKESTONE DFAS | 93 | Folkestone, Kent |
| GRAVESEND & DISTRICT DFAS | 266 | Gravesend, Kent |
| HIGH WEALD DFAS | 295 | Benenden, Kent |
| KNOLE DFAS | 183 | Sevenoaks, Kent |
| MALLING DFAS | 216 | Ryarsh, Kent |
| MEDWAY DFAS | 308 | Gillingham, Kent |
| MID KENT DFAS | 98 | Sutton Valence, Kent |
| PANTILES DFAS | 250 | Royal Tunbridge Wells, Kent |
| ROYAL TUNBRIDGE WELLS DFAS | 107 | Royal Tunbridge Wells, Kent |
| SANDWICH EVENING DFAS | 207 | Sandwich, Kent |
| SEVENOAKS DFAS | 41 | Sevenoaks, Kent |
| SOUTH CANTERBURY DFAS | 219 | Canterbury, Kent |
| TENTERDEN DFAS | 244 | Tenterden, Kent |
| THANET DFAS | 6 | Broadstairs, Kent |
| TONBRIDGE DFAS | 126 | Tonbridge, Kent |

**MAINLAND EUROPE**

| | | |
|---|---|---|
| ANTWERP (BELGIUM) DFAS | 919 | Belgium |
| BERLIN (GERMANY) DFAS | 928 | Germany |
| BRUSSELS (BELGIUM) DFAS | 903 | Belgium |
| COSTA DEL SOL (SPAIN) DFAS | 911 | Fuengirola, Malaga, Spain |
| DE LA FRONTERA DFAS | 942 | San Roque, Spain |
| THE HAGUE (NETHERLANDS) DFAS | 918 | The Netherlands |
| HAMBURG (GERMANY) DFAS | 909 | Germany |
| NERJA (SPAIN) DFAS | 939 | Nerja, Malaga, Spain |
| OSNABRUCK (GERMANY) DFAS | 932 | Germany |
| PARIS (FRANCE) DFAS | 925 | France |

**NORTH EAST**

| | | |
|---|---|---|
| BEVERLEY DFAS | 67 | Willerby, E. Yorkshire |
| DERWENT (EVENING) DFAS | 226 | Wykeham, N, Yorkshire |
| DRIFFIELD WOLDS DFAS | 199 | Driffield, E. Yorkshire |
| HALIFAX DFAS | 319 | Halifax, W. Yorkshire |
| HALLAMSHIRE DFAS | 252 | Sheffield, S. Yorkshire |
| HAMBLETON (THIRSK) DFAS | 223 | Thirsk, N. Yorkshire |
| HARROGATE DFAG | 4 | Harrogate, N. Yorkshire |
| HELMSLEY DFAS | 301 | Helmsley, N. Yorkshire |
| HEXHAM DFAS | 271 | Hexham, Northumberland |
| HOLDERNESS DFAS | 140 | Hornsea, E. Yorkshire |
| HULL & EAST RIDING AFAS | 9 | Willerby, E. Yorkshire |
| LEEDS DFAS | 53 | Leeds, W. Yorkshire |
| NIDD VALLEY DFAS | 124 | Harrogate, N. Yorkshire |
| NORTH YORKSHIRE & SOUTH DURHAM DFAS | 55 | Teesside, Co. Durham |
| SALTAIRE DFAS | 260 | Saltaire, W. Yorkshire |
| SCARBOROUGH & DISTRICT DFAS | 145 | Wykeham, N, Yorkshire |
| SHEFFIELD DFAS | 81 | Sheffield, S. Yorkshire |
| SKIPTON & WHARFEDALE DFAS | 151 | Skipton, N. Yorkshire |
| TYNESIDE DFAS | 255 | Newcastle-upon-Tyne, Tyne & Wear |
| WENSLEYDALE DFAS | 320 | Middleham, N. Yorkshire |
| WEST RIDING DFAS | 291 | Huddersfield, W. Yorkshire |
| YORK DFAS | 46 | York, N. Yorkshire |

**NORTH WEST**

| | | |
|---|---|---|
| BOLTON DFAS | 79 | Bolton, Greater Manchester |
| BOWDON & DISTRICT DFAS | 136 | Bowdon, Greater Manchester |
| CAVENDISH DFAS | 170 | Buxton, Derbyshire |
| CHESTER DFAS | 326 | Chester |
| CLWYDIAN DFAS | 254 | Mold, Clwyd |
| CROSBY DFAS | 19 | Waterloo, Merseyside |
| CUMBRIA DFAS | 73 | Cockermouth, Cumbria |
| ISLE OF MAN DFAS | 292 | Douglas, Isle of Man |
| LIVERPOOL DFAS | 35 | Liverpool, Merseyside |
| LLANDUDNO DFAS | 342 | Llandudno, Gwynedd |
| LUNESDALE DFAS | 333 | Borwick, Lancashire |
| NORTH EAST CHESHIRE DFAS | 48 | Bramhall, Cheshire |
| RIBBLE & CRAVEN DFAS | 122 | Bolton-by-Bowland, Lancashire |
| SAMLESBURY DFAS | 58 | Hoghton, Lancashire |
| SOUTH LAKELAND DFAS | 202 | Kendal, Cumbria |

| | | | |
|---|---|---|---|
| | SOUTHPORT & FORMBY DFAS | 28 | Southport, Merseyside |
| | TARPORLEY & DISTRICT DFAS | 118 | Tarporley, Cheshire |
| | WESTMORLAND DFAS | 261 | Appleby-in-Westmorland, Cumbria |
| | WILMSLOW DFAS | 212 | Wilmslow, Cheshire |
| | WIRRAL DFAS | 26 | Birkenhead, Merseyside |
| SCOTLAND | | | |
| | AYRSHIRE DFAS | 191 | Ayr |
| | BEARSDEN & MILNGAVIE DFAS | 343 | Bearsden, East Dunbartonshire |
| | BORDERS DFAS | 232 | Kelso, Roxburghshire |
| | EDINBURGH DFAS | 163 | Edinburgh, Mid-Lothian |
| | FIFE DFAS | 274 | Cupar, Fife |
| | GRAMPIAN DFAS | 224 | Garthdee, Aberdeenshire |
| | HIGHLAND DFAS | 237 | Croy, Inverness-shire |
| | LOMOND & ARGYLL DFAS | 300 | Helensburgh, West Dunbartonshire |
| | MORAY BANFF & BADENOCH DFAS | 276 | Elgin, Moray |
| | PERTH DFAS | 239 | Dunkeld, Perthshire |
| | SOUTH WEST SCOTLAND DFAS | 238 | Dumfries |
| | STIRLING DFAS | 215 | Stirling |
| | ULSTER DFAS | 296 | Belfast, Co. Antrim |
| SOUTH MERCIA | | | |
| | ABINGDON DFAS | 272 | Abingdon, Oxfordshire |
| | AMERSHAM DFAS | 294 | Amersham, Buckinghamshire |
| | BALLINGER DFAS | 306 | Ballinger, Buckinghamshire |
| | BEACONSFIELD DFAS | 186 | Beaconsfield, Buckinghamshire |
| | BUCKINGHAM DFAS | 234 | Buckingham |
| | CHALFONT FAS | 21 | Chalfont St. Peter, Buckinghamshire |
| | CHILTERN DFAS | 1 | Chalfont St. Peter, Buckinghamshire |
| | COTSWOLD ASG | 18 | Bradwell, Oxfordshire |
| | GERRARDS CROSS DFAS | 5 | Gerrard's Cross, Buckinghamshire |
| | GORING DFAS | 187 | Goring-on-Thames, Oxfordshire |
| | HENLEY DFAS | 82 | Henley-on-Thames, Oxfordshire |
| | MARLOW DFAS | 324 | Marlow, Buckinghamshire |
| | NEWBURY DFAS | 61 | Newbury, Berkshire |
| | THAMES DFAS | 3 | Bourne End, Buckinghamshire |
| | VALE OF AYLESBURY DFAS | 2 | Westcott, Buckinghamshire |
| | WANTAGE DFAS | 176 | Wantage, Oxfordshire |
| | WEST OXON DFAS | 16 | Witney, Oxfordshire |
| | WEST WYCOMBE DFAS | 65 | Lacey Green, Buckinghamshire |
| | WINDSOR & MAIDENHEAD DFAS | 283 | Old Windsor, Berkshire |
| | WINDSOR & MAIDENHEAD EVENING DFAS | 336 | Old Windsor, Berkshire |
| SOUTH WEST | | | |
| | BODMIN DFAS | 280 | Bodmin, Cornwall |
| | DARTMOUTH & KINGSWEAR DFAS | 315 | Dartmouth, Devon |
| | DEVON DFAS | 68 | Exeter, Devon |
| | EXE DFAS | 189 | Topsham, Devon |
| | EXMOOR DFAS | 160 | Brushford, Somerset |
| | FALMOUTH DFAS | 317 | Falmouth, Cornwall |
| | HONITON DFAS | 143 | Honiton, Devon |
| | KINGSBRIDGE ESTUARY DFAS | 265 | Kingsbridge, Devon |
| | LISKEARD DFAS | 318 | Liskeard, Cornwall |
| | NEROCHE DFAS | 49 | Ilminster, Somerset |
| | NORTH DEVON DFAS | 108 | Northam, Devon |
| | NORTH SOMERSET DFAS | 281 | Woolavington, Somerset |
| | SIDMOUTH DFAS | 229 | Sidmouth, Devon |
| | SOUTH DEVON DFAS | 89 | Plymouth, Devon |
| | TAUNTON DFAS | 209 | Taunton, Somerset |
| | TEIGNBRIDGE DFAS | 205 | Newton Abbot, Devon |
| | TIVERTON DFAS | 313 | Tiverton, Devon |
| | TORQUAY DFAS | 293 | Torquay, Devon |
| | TOTNES DFAS | 242 | Totnes, Devon |
| | TRURO DFAS | 121 | Truro, Cornwall |
| | WEST SOMERSET DFAS | 302 | Cheddon Fitzpaine, Somerset |
| SUSSEX | | | |
| | ADUR VALLEY DFAS | 22 | Henfield, West Sussex |
| | ARUN DFAS | 137 | Rustington, West Sussex |
| | ASHDOWN FOREST DFAS | 34 | Nutley, East Sussex |
| | BRIGHTON & HOVE DFAS | 185 | Hove, East Sussex |
| | CHICHESTER DFAS | 92 | Chichester, West Sussex |
| | CITY OF CHICHESTER DFAS | 284 | Chichester, West Sussex |
| | EAST GRINSTEAD DFAS | 174 | East Grinstead, West Sussex |
| | EAST SUSSEX DFAS | 222 | Hove, East Sussex |

| | | |
|---|---|---|
| EASTBOURNE DFAS | 50 | East Dean, East Sussex |
| HASTINGS & ROTHER DFAS | 104 | St Leonards-on-Sea, East Sussex |
| HORSHAM DFAS | 36 | Horsham, West Sussex |
| LAVANT VALLEY DFAS | 171 | Chichester, West Sussex |
| MID SUSSEX DFAS | 109 | Haywards Heath, West Sussex |
| MIDHURST DFAS | 227 | Midhurst, West Sussex |
| NEWICK DFAS | 173 | Plumpton Green, West Sussex |
| OKEWOOD DFAS | 158 | Rudgwick, West Sussex |
| SOUTH DOWNS DFAS | 113 | Fittleworth, West Sussex |
| STEYNING DFAS | 339 | Steyning, West Sussex |
| STORRINGTON DFAS | 218 | West Chiltington, West Sussex |
| TURNERS HILL DFAS | 275 | Turners Hill, West Sussex |
| UCKFIELD DFAS | 286 | Uckfield, East Sussex |
| WALBERTON DFAS | 204 | Yapton, West Sussex |
| WEALDEN DFAS | 257 | Heathfield, West Sussex |
| WEST SUSSEX DFAS | 20 | Fittleworth, West Sussex |

**WESSEX**

| | | |
|---|---|---|
| BATH DFAS | 117 | Bath, Somerset |
| BATH EVENING DFAS | 236 | Bath, Somerset |
| BLACKMORE VALE DFAS | 130 | Stalbridge, Dorset |
| BOURNEMOUTH & EAST DORSET DFAS | 47 | Bournemouth, Dorset |
| BRISTOL DFAS | 147 | Bristol, Somerset |
| DEVIZES DFAS | 341 | Devizes, Wiltshire |
| DORSET COUNTY DFAS | 97 | Dorchester, Dorset |
| KENNET DFAS | 182 | Wroughton, Wiltshire |
| KINGTON LANGLEY DFAS | 263 | Kington Langley, Wiltshire |
| MENDIP DFAS | 119 | Shepton Mallet, Somerset |
| MID SOMERSET DFAS | 249 | Shepton Mallet, Somerset |
| NEW SARUM DFAS | 288 | Salisbury, Wiltshire |
| NORTH WILTSHIRE DFAS | 102 | Melksham, Wiltshire |
| PEWSEY VALE DFAS | 246 | Pewsey, Wiltshire |
| POOLE DFAS | 192 | Poole, Dorset |
| SARUM DFAS | 178 | Salisbury, Wiltshire |
| SHERBORNE DFAS | 233 | Sherborne, Dorset |
| WARMINSTER DFAS | 159 | Frome, Wiltshire |
| WEST DORSET DFAS | 201 | Bridport, Dorset |
| WIMBORNE & BLANDFORD DFAS | 142 | Wimborne, Dorset |
| WIMBORNE DFAS | 270 | Wimborne, Dorset |
| WYLYE VALLEY DFAS | 94 | Wilton, Wiltshire |

**WEST MERCIA**

| | | |
|---|---|---|
| BLOCKLEY DFAS | 168 | Blockley, Gloucestershire |
| BRECKNOCK DFAS | 196 | Brecon, Powys |
| CHELTENHAM DFAS | 267 | Charlton Kings, Gloucestershire |
| CIRENCESTER DFAS | 181 | Cirencester, Gloucestershire |
| EVESHAM DFAS | 273 | Evesham, Worcestershire |
| GLOUCESTERSHIRE DFAS | 112 | Andoversford, Gloucestershire |
| MALVERN HILLS DFAS | 77 | Colwall, Worcestershire |
| MONMOUTHSHIRE DFAS | 328 | Abergavenny, Monmouthshire |
| NORTHLEACH DFAS | 322 | Northleach, Gloucestershire |
| PAINSWICK DFAS | 162 | Painswick, Gloucestershire |
| ROSS-ON-WYE DFAS | 282 | Ross-on-Wye, Herefordshire |
| SEVERN VALLEY DFAS | 123 | Chipping Sodbury, Gloucestershire |
| SOUTH WALES DFAS | 84 | Cardiff, South Glamorgan |
| TEME VALLEY DFAS | 74 | Tenbury Wells, Worcestershire |
| UPPER THAMES DFAS | 190 | Highworth, Wiltshire |
| WEST GLOUCESTERSHIRE DFAS | 245 | Minsterworth, Gloucestershire |
| WEST WALES DFAS | 340 | Clynderwen, Pembrokeshire |
| CITY OF WORCESTER DFAS | 188 | Worcester |

**WEST MIDLANDS**

| | | |
|---|---|---|
| ARDEN DFAS | 189 | Solihull, West Midlands |
| BIRMINGHAM DFAS | 231 | Birmingham, West Midlands |
| NEEDWOOD DFAS | 146 | Barton-under-Needwood, Staffordshire |
| NORTH POWYS DFAS | 76 | Tregynon, Powys |
| NORTH STAFFORDSHIRE DFAS | 180 | Hanley, Staffordshire |
| ROYAL LEAMINGTON SPA DFAS | 264 | Leamington, Warwickshire |
| RUGBY DFAS | 88 | Rugby, Warwickshire |
| SHREWSBURY DFAS | 133 | Shrewsbury, Shropshire |
| SOLIHULL DFAS | 175 | Solihull, West Midlands |
| STAFFORD DFAS | 327 | Stafford, Staffordshire |
| STOURBRIDGE DFAS | 299 | Stourbridge, West Midlands |
| STRATFORD UPON AVON DFAS | 39 | Stratford Upon Avon, Warwickshire |

|  |  |  |  |
|---|---|---|---|
| | SUTTON COLDFIELD DFAS | 217 | Four Oaks, West Midlands |
| | WOLVERHAMPTON DFAS | 179 | Wolverhampton, West Midlands |
| | WREKIN DFAS | 59 | Cosford, Shropshire |
| **WEST SURREY** | | | |
| | ASCOT DFAS | 208 | Ascot, Berkshire |
| | CAMBERLEY DFAS | 150 | Camberley, Surrey |
| | COBBETT'S WEY DFAS | 334 | Farnham, Surrey |
| | CRANLEIGH DFAS | 268 | Cranleigh, Surrey |
| | ENGLEMERE DFAS | 321 | Ascot, Berkshire |
| | FARNHAM DFAS | 144 | Farnham, Surrey |
| | GUILDFORD EVENING DFAS | 120 | Guildford, Surrey |
| | HASLEMERE DFAS | 30 | Haslemere, Surrey |
| | MAYFORD DFAS | 258 | Woking, Surrey |
| | RUNNYMEDE DFAS | 23 | Egham, Surrey |
| | SHALFORD DFAS | 56 | Shalford, Surrey |
| | SURREY HEATH DFAS | 278 | Bagshot, Surrey |
| | WALTON & HERSHAM DFAS | 331 | Hersham, Surry |
| | WEST SURREY DFAS | 17 | Shalford, Surrey |
| | WEY VALLEY, THE DFAS | 220 | Shalford, Surrey |
| | WEYBRIDGE DFAS | 311 | Whiteley, Surrey |
| | WINDLEBROOK DFAS | 332 | Bisley, Surrey |
| | WOKING DFAS | 206 | Bisley, Surrey |
| **NEW ZEALAND** | | | |
| | AUCKLAND DFAS | 802 | Auckland, New Zealand |
| | CANTERBURY (NZ) DFAS | 801 | Christchurch, New Zealand |
| | DFAS of WELLINGTON | 803 | Wellington, New Zealand |
| **AUSTRALIA** | | | |
| | ADELAIDE | 931 | South Australia |
| | ARMIDALE | 906 | New South Wales |
| | BOWRAL & DISTRICT | 907 | New South Wales |
| | BRISBANE | 914 | Queensland |
| | BRISBANE RIVER | 935 | Queensland |
| | BYRON BAY | 936 | New South Wales |
| | CAIRNS | 929 | Queensland |
| | CAMDEN | 941 | New South Wales |
| | CANBERRA | 904 | ACT |
| | CENTRAL VICTORIA | 943 | Victoria |
| | DUBBO & DISTRICT | 934 | New South Wales |
| | GEELONG | 922 | Victoria |
| | GOLD COAST | 937 | Queensland |
| | HOBART | 944 | Tasmania |
| | KU-RING-GAI | 924 | New South Wales |
| | MELBOURNE | 905 | Victoria |
| | MORNINGTON PENINSULA | 940 | Victoria |
| | MUDGEE | 938 | New South Wales |
| | NARRABRI & NORTHWEST DISTRICT | 926 | New South Wales |
| | NEWCASTLE | 908 | New South Wales |
| | ORANGE & DISTRICTS | 930 | New South Wales |
| | POKOLBIN | 933 | New South Wales |
| | RIVERINA | 923 | New South Wales |
| | ROCKHAMPTON | 927 | Queensland |
| | SCONE | 917 | New South Wales |
| | SHOALHAVEN | 916 | New South Wales |
| | SUNSHINE COAST | 910 | Queensland |
| | SYDNEY | 902 | New South Wales |
| | TOOWOOMBA | 912 | Queensland |
| | YARRA | 915 | Victoria |

FRIENDS OF THE ART GALLERY OF WESTERN AUSTRALIA          Perth
(Affiliated to ADFAS)

SOCIETIES WHICH HAVE CLOSED
BANBURY
CINQUE PORTS
GODALMING
PENZANCE
SPITHEAD
WHITBY AND DISTRICT
WHITEKNIGHTS
COPENHAGEN
RHEINDAHLEN

# NADFAS Patrons

| | |
|---|---|
| HRH The Duchess of Kent | 1977-1987 |
| The Marchioness of Salisbury | 1989-1994 |
| HRH The Duchess of Gloucester | 1995- |

# NADFAS Presidents

| | |
|---|---|
| Sir Trenchard Cox CBE | 1968-1995* |
| Dr (later Sir) Timothy Clifford | 1996-2006 |
| Christopher Lloyd CVO | 2007- |

# Chief Executives

| | |
|---|---|
| Jeremy Warren | 1999-2001 |
| Dr Thomas Cocke | 2001-2006 |
| David Bell | 2006- |

# Past National Chairmen

Top row (left to right)

| | |
|---|---|
| 1968-1969 | Patricia Fay* |
| 1969-1970 | Lesley (Lally) Robinson* |
| 1970-1972 | Sheila Marshall* |
| 1972-1974 | Ann Parkinson (later The Lady Parkinson) |
| 1974-1976 | Kathleen Wareham* |
| 1976-1978 | Jay Atkinson* |

Second row (left to right)

| | |
|---|---|
| 1978-1980 | Pamela Cowen |
| 1980-1982 | June Fenwick* |
| 1982-1984 | Sheila Chapman |
| 1984-1986 | Judith Waples |
| 1986-1988 | Penelope Chitty |
| 1988-1990 | Shirley Hewett |

Third row (left to right)

| | |
|---|---|
| 1990-1992 | Jennifer Stephenson |
| 1992-1994 | Nancy Hodgson |
| 1994-1996 | Lady (Anthea) Johnston |
| 1996-1998 | Judith Thomas |
| 1998-2000 | Pamela Cohn |
| 2000-2002 | Jean Read |

Bottom row (left to right)

| | |
|---|---|
| 2002-2004 | Sheila Jones |
| 2004-2006 | Nesta Waine |
| 2006- | Susan Sellers |

* deceased

# NADFAS Vice Presidents

| Appointed | Vice President | Retired |
|---|---|---|
| 1968 | Sir John Pope-Hennessy | 1994* |
| | Helen Lowenthal OBE | 1993* |
| | Sir Oliver Millar | 2007* |
| 1975 | Norman Brommelle | 1989* |
| | Sir Roy Strong | 1996 |
| 1980 | Sir Hugh Casson | 1999* |
| 1983 | The Most Rev & Rt Hon Dr Robert Runcie, Archbishop of Canterbury | 1994* |
| 1984 | AVB (Nick) Norman | 1989 |
| 1985 | Lesley (Lally) Robinson | 1995* |
| 1987 | Lady (Anne) White | 1997 |
| 1990 | Dr Timothy Clifford | 1996 |
| | Prof. Michael Kauffmann | 1995 |
| | Sheila Marshall | 2000* |
| | Viscount Norwich | 2000 |
| 1992 | Christopher Chavasse | 1997 |
| 1995 | Dr Alan Borg | 2000 |
| | The Most Rev & Rt Hon Dr George Carey, Archbishop of Canterbury | 2002 |
| | Dame Elizabeth Esteve-Coll | 2000 |
| | Michaela Jenkerson-Kenshole | 2000 |
| 1997 | Pamela Cowen | 2006 |
| | Lady Victoria Leatham | 2006 |
| 1998 | Sir Richard Foster | 2001* |
| | Giles Waterfield | 2006 |
| | Dr Simon Thurley | |
| 2000 | Dr Christopher Brown | 2006 |
| | Dr Ian McKenzie-Smith | 2006 |
| | The Lady (Ann) Parkinson | 2006 |
| | Dr Duncan Robinson | 2006 |
| 2003 | The Rt Rev & Rt Hon Richard Chartres, Bishop of London | |
| 2006 | Desmond Shawe-Taylor | |